W0113906

BRUSSELS

BRUGES, ANTWERP AND GHENT

BRUSSELS

BRUGES, ANTWERP AND GHENT

CONTENTS

DISCOVER 6

EXPERIENCE 54

NEED TO KNOW 186

Left: Brussels-themed street art
Previous page: Ghent at night
Front cover: Scenic Rozenhoedkaai, Bruges

DISCOVER

Bruges, a picturesque medieval city

WELCOME TO
BRUSSELS, BRUGES, ANTWERP AND GHENT

Stately squares and swan-lined canals. Brilliant beer and melt-in-your-mouth chocolate. Colourful comic-book murals and Flemish Primitive masterpieces. Jam-packed with attractions, Belgium's four big cities make for a magical getaway. Whatever your dream trip to Brussels, Bruges, Antwerp and Ghent includes, this DK travel guide is the perfect companion.

1

2

3

1 Bustling pavement cafés in Antwerp.

2 Steen Brugge, a classic craft beer of Belgium.

3 Artwork on display at Sint-Janshospitaal, Bruges.

4 Travelling down a scenic waterway in Bruges.

4

Brussels, Bruges, Antwerp and Ghent: Belgium's four great cities have been cultural centres for centuries. While the region's mighty medieval past is still prominent in its architecture, this city quartet is also surprisingly cool and cosmopolitan. Most famous of the four, Brussels is the home of the European Union – and comic hero Tintin. It's a grand city, hosting top museums, great street art, a thriving craft-beer scene and countless, and far-too-tempting, chocolatiers.

Within easy reach of the capital are the country's trio of big-hitting cities: picture-perfect Bruges, fashionable Antwerp and foodie Ghent. With their easily walkable city centres and plethora of attractions, all three make for popular weekend getaways. Bruges remains the jewel in the area's crown, with its swoon-worthy canals and enchanting architecture.

Antwerp also packs a punch; historic bars and mega-museums are the name of the game in this port city. Ghent, meanwhile, has become a centre for veggie cuisine, with top-notch plant-based restaurants clustered in the city centre. There's plenty to see beyond the cities, too: World War I battlefields lie nearby and sandy retreats beckon on the North Sea coast.

With so much to see, a visit to Brussels and the surrounding region requires some careful planning. We've broken the area down into easily navigable chapters, with detailed itineraries, expert local knowledge and comprehensive maps to help plan the perfect trip. Whether you're visiting for a weekend or longer, this DK travel guide will ensure that you see the best of the cities on offer. Enjoy the book, and enjoy Brussels, Bruges, Antwerp and Ghent.

REASONS TO LOVE
BRUSSELS, BRUGES, ANTWERP AND GHENT

World-class galleries, exuberant beer bars, romantic views and awe-inspiring architecture. There are countless reasons to love Brussels, Bruges, Antwerp and Ghent. Here are some of our favourites.

1 TOP SHOPPING

Swish design stores in fashion capital Antwerp, vintage shops in Ghent and the famous Galeries Royales St-Hubert (*p82*) in Brussels: shopping in this region is not to be missed.

BRUGES'S WATERWAYS 2

A boat trip is a brilliant way to discover the medieval heart of Belgium's most beautiful city. Take a trip via the ultra-scenic Rozenhoedkaai for the very best views of Bruges.

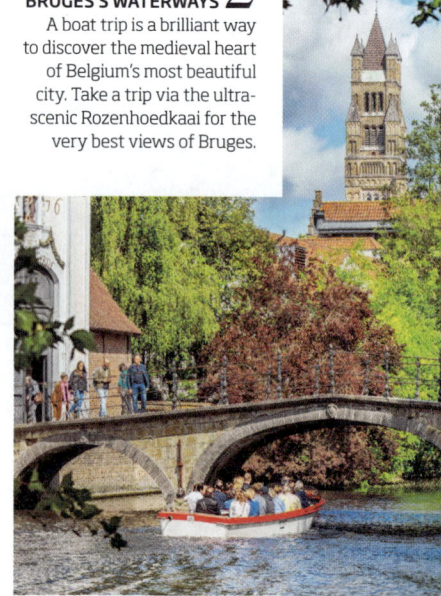

3 GREAT BEER

Belgium has long been famous for its beer and the country's breweries continue to churn out the good stuff. You'll find the best selection in Brussels, but each city has its share.

ARCHITECTURAL ICONS *4*

These cities are open-air museums of architecture. Don't miss Antwerp's Art Nouveau-style Centraal Station or Brussels' beloved Atomium *(p105)* and stunning Horta Museum *(p102)*.

ASTONISHING ART *5*

From the world's most-stolen artwork, *The Adoration of the Mystic Lamb (p158)* in Ghent, to the Flemish Primitive masterpieces in Bruges, these four cities overflow with great art.

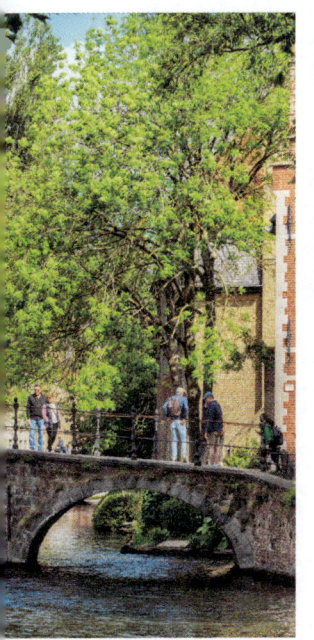

FANTASTIC FRIES *6*

Invented by Belgium, this satisfying snack can be found everywhere. Grab them to go from a street kiosk or settle in at a hip café to taste them with all the gourmet toppings.

CALM CORNERS 7

Created to house religious lay-women, the region's beautifully preserved *begijnhofs* are replete with gorgeous gardens and quiet chapels. Wander in for a retreat from city life.

CYCLING THE CITIES 8

With plenty of pedestrian zones, bikes for hire and an excellent network of cycling paths across the country, it's easy to explore all four cities on two wheels.

9 THE SWEET STUFF

As the world's chocolate capital, Belgium is home to hundreds of chocolate shops. Beautiful boxes of these masterfully crafted treats make for the perfect souvenir.

10 MARVELLOUS MUSEUMS

Belgium hosts museums in abundance. Brussels' uber-cool Design Museum *(p105)*, Ghent's innovative STAM *(p167)* and Antwerp's Red Star Line Museum *(p147)* are highlights.

MILITARY HISTORY 11

History buffs are spoiled for choice in this region. Stand on the site of Napoleon's final defeat in Waterloo *(p178)* or take a tour of the famous World War I battlefields *(p43)*.

COMIC-BOOK ART IN BRUSSELS 12

Fans of the Ninth Art will love being in the land of Tintin and the Smurfs. The Comics Art Museum *(p66)* is a must-visit, but you'll also see murals all around the capital's streets.

EXPLORE
BRUSSELS, BRUGES, ANTWERP AND GHENT

This guide divides the region into five colour-coded sightseeing areas, as shown on the map below. Find out more about each area on the following pages. For day trips around the region, see p170.

Terneuzen

Watervliet

Boekhoute

De Hoorn

Bassevelde

Bruges

BRUGES
p116

Maldegem

Zelzate

Eeklo

Oosteeklo

Beernem

Zomergem

Evergem

Merendree

Wingene

Ruiselede

Nevele

Ghent

GHENT
p152

Ghent

**WEST-
VLAANDEREN**

Merelbeke

Tielt

Deinze

De Pinte

**OOST-
VLAANDEREN**

Dentergem

Oosterzele

Gavere

Kruisem

Zottegem

Oudenaarde

Brakel

Ronse

HAINA UT

LOCATOR MAP

North Sea

NETHERLANDS

GREAT
BRITAIN

GERMANY

Bruges ● Antwerp
Ghent ● ● Brussels

BELGIUM

FRANCE

LUX.

0 kilometres 10

0 miles 10

N

NETHERLANDS

Oosterschelde

Kloosterzande

Kapellen

Terneuzen

Merksem

Hulst

Axel

Sint-Gillis-Waas

Antwerp

ANTWERP
p136

Moerbeke

Sint-Niklaas

Wachtebeke

Kontich

Sinaai

Temse

ANTWERPEN

Rupel

Lokeren

Bornem

Zele

Willebroek

BELGIUM

Mechelen

Wetteren

Lebbeke

Londerzeel

Dender

Zemst

Lede

Moorsel

Merchtem

Aalst

VLAAMS-BRABANT

Herzele

Ternat

BRUSSELS

Brussels

CENTRAL BRUSSELS
p56

Ninove

OUTER BRUSSELS
p96

Geraardsbergen

Gaasbeek

Vollezele

Halle

GETTING TO KNOW
BRUSSELS, BRUGES, ANTWERP AND GHENT

Brussels is an independent enclave within Flanders, the Dutch-speaking region occupying the northern half of Belgium. The city forms a triangle with Antwerp to the north and Ghent to the northwest, while towards the North Sea coast lies canal-lined Bruges.

PAGE 56

CENTRAL BRUSSELS

The city centre of Brussels is divided into two areas: the Upper Town and Lower Town. Most tourists head for the Lower Town, which hosts medieval treasures such as the epic Grand Place. Today, such timeless riches are bolstered by superior shopping and socializing, whether in the trendy Antoine Dansaert or foodie Sainte-Catherine areas. Overlooking the Lower Town, the traditionally aristocratic Upper Town is home to stately museums and expansive parks. In among all the sights, you'll find contemporary craft breweries and, of course, plenty of irresistible chocolate shops.

Best for
Major museums, buzzing bars and acclaimed restaurants

Home to
Grand Place, Comics Art Museum, Cathédrale Sts-Michel-et-Gudule, Palais Royal, Royal Museums of Fine Arts

Experience
Spotting Belgium's famous cartoon characters along the Comic Strip Route

PAGE 96

OUTER BRUSSELS

Ranging from affluent Uccle to multicultural Schaerbeek, the city's diverse outlying communes are well worth the pilgrimage beyond the ring road. The closest and chicest, Ixelles is loved for its luxury shopping and Art Nouveau architecture, an attraction it shares with St-Gilles, where you'll find the Horta Museum. Northwest of the centre, little Koekelberg hosts a huge draw in the form of the Basilique Nationale du Sacré-Coeur. Further north, leafy Laeken offers the celebrated Atomium, arty Design Museum Brussels and the grand royal greenhouses.

Best for
Iconic architecture and green spaces

Home to
Parc and Palais du Cinquantenaire, Horta Museum, Domaine de Laeken

Experience
Gazing at astonishing Art Nouveau treasures in Ixelles

PAGE 116

BRUGES

Enclosed by an oval-shaped moat and packed with medieval masterpieces, the entire historic centre of Bruges is a UNESCO World Heritage Site. Nicknamed the "Venice of the North", this pocket-sized city is crisscrossed by canals and pivots around two squares – the Markt and the Burg. The surrounding streets share the bulk of tourist-friendly cafés, scenic corners and centuries-old sights. Beyond the buzz, peaceful Sint-Anna Quarter, with its churches and convents, and lovely Minnewater Lake, which is steeped in local legend, offer serenity.

Best for
Romantic canalside strolls and Flemish Masters

Home to
Groeningemuseum, Gruuthusemuseum

Experience
Climbing the Belfort's 366 steps for epic views of the city

→

PAGE 136

ANTWERP

Rising on the right bank of the Scheldt river, Belgium's slick second city is an international hub for avant-garde fashion and diamond trading. Not far from its extravagant Centraal Station, the city's historic centre is dominated by a Gothic cathedral and the guildhouses of the Grote Markt. Many of Antwerp's museums and cool cafés are concentrated in this cobbled quarter, while the port area to the north promises modern architecture and the Zuid district to the south hosts a number of trendy restaurants. Among it all, students linger late at techno clubs and fashionistas frequent design stores.

Best for
A variety of architecture and great shopping

Home to
Koninklijk Museum voor Schone Kunsten

Experience
Boutique and vintage shopping in the fashionable Sint-Andries Quarter

GHENT

PAGE 152

Bruges's lesser-known cousin, Ghent is a thriving university town. Its largely pedestrianized centre is strong on stunning quaysides and historic buildings, with a trio of iconic towers including Sint-Baafskathedraal, the setting for Jan van Eyck's altarpiece *The Adoration of the Mystic Lamb*. Just north lies the tiny Patershol district, home to a labyrinth of cute shops and cosy bars, while beyond the university to the south, the Arts Quarter offers a culture fix with its renowned museums. Besides a handful of Michelin-starred places to eat, Ghent is also Europe's self-styled vegetarian food capital.

Best for
Vegetarian dining and quaint streets

Home to
Het Gravensteen, Sint-Baafskathedraal

Experience
Soaking up Ghent's medieval splendour while relaxing at the Graslei and Korenlei quays

DAYS OUT

PAGE 170

Brilliant day trips radiate from this quartet of great cities in every direction. Just outside Brussels, bluebell forests and swathes of green await; as does the town of Leuven, famed for its staggering town hall and bustling market square full of cafés. Key military sites are also dotted around the region. Waterloo, just over the border from Brussels in the French-speaking Wallonia, and Ypres, not far from Ghent, are unmissable sights. Mechelen, meanwhile, is a medieval powerhouse set halfway between Brussels and Antwerp. It promises important World War II sites, as well as a superb brewery.

Best for
Military history

Home to
Leuven, Waterloo

Experience
Climbing the 226 steps to Waterloo's Butte du Lion, an iconic war monument

→

1 Artwork on display at Brussels' Royal Museums of Fine Arts.

2 Galeries Royales St Hubert, in Brussels.

3 Delicious Belgian chocolates.

4 Canal scenery in Bruges.

Exploring compact Belgium is a breeze. Whether you want to stroll the cities or cycle to beaches and battlefields, these itineraries will help you make the most of your visit.

5 DAYS
in Brussels and Bruges

Day 1

Begin your first day in Brussels. The magnificent Grand Place (p60) is a logical starting point – spot the famous Manneken Pis statue (p78) just around the corner. For lunch, grab some oysters and steaming fish soup from beloved fish shack La Mer du Nord (noordzeemerdunord.be). Then, treat yourself to some chocolate from Neuhaus, located in the Galeries Royales St Hubert (p82). Spend the rest of the day in the Comics Art Museum (p66), before dining on Flemish classics at In't Spinnekopke (spinnekopke.be) and bedding down at The Dominican (p85).

Day 2

This morning is all about art: scope out Magritte and the Old Masters at the vast Royal Museums of Fine Arts (p74). The pretty Place du Grand Sablon (p91) nearby is full of appealing spots for lunch when you're ready. Strolling west, you'll soon spy the hulking Palais de Justice (p89). Peek inside before whizzing down the glass lift to the Quartier Marolles (p78); here you can do a self-guided tour of local comic murals and browse the flea market on Place du Jeu de Balle. Linger in Les Marolles for dinner: Le Wine Bar des Marolles (www.lewinebardesmarolles.be) promises delicious food in a cosy setting.

Day 3

Take a break from the busy centre today and make a beeline for the House of European History (historia.europa.eu). This museum charts the rise (and trials) of the EU. Nearby is famed fries kiosk Maison Antoine (maisonantoine.be) – an ideal spot

for a quick lunch. Once satiated, jump on the metro at Schuman station and make your way up to leafy Laeken. Here you'll find the iconic Atomium (p105) and cute Mini-Europe models. It's your last night in the capital, so splash out on North Sea lobster at Michelin-starred Comme Chez Soi (www.commechezsoi.be).

Day 4

Take an early train to Bruges and begin your trip here with bracing views from the Belfort (p124). Back at ground level, stroll southeast to see the Gothic Stadhuis (p124) and highly decorative Heilig Bloed Basiliek (p123). Hungry yet? Fuel up on mussels at the nearby Breydel de Coninc (restaurant-breydel.be) before setting off to bag more must-see attractions. Cross the Djiver canal for the unbeatably scenic Rozenhoedkaai quayside, then continue by the water to the Groeningemuseum (p120) for its horde of Flemish Primitive art. After a busy day, settle in for Flemish classics at atmospheric townhouse De Stove (www.restaurantdestove.be) – be sure to book ahead. Finally, it's time to put your feet up at Casa Romantico (p127).

Day 5

On your final day, embark on a scenic canal ride, gliding from Jan van Eyckplein to the Begijnhof (p130). Spend the rest of the day strolling around scenic Minnewater lake (p130), stopping for a beer tour at brewery De Halve Maan (www.halvemaan.be) en route back into town. If you fancy another drink, the ancient Café Vlissinghe (cafe vlissinghe.be) is calling your name. End with a homely dinner at 'T Gezelleke (p131).

1

2

3

4

←
1 Antwerp's epic Centraal Station.
2 The medieval Het Steen fortress.
3 Historical treasure trove, Museum Plantin-Moretus.
4 Locals enjoying the sunshine in one of the city's leafy squares.

2 DAYS
in Antwerp

Day 1

Morning Antwerp is best reached by train from Brussels – not only because it's practical but because you can admire the city's Centraal Station, one of the world's most beautiful railway hubs. After taking it in, head down the Meir to the historic centre. Here you can't miss the Grote Markt *(p142)*, which hosts a fountain depicting the myth of the city's founding, and the towering Onze-Lieve-Vrouwekathedraal *(p142)*. The latter contains Rubens' epic triptych *The Descent from the Cross*. Lunch outside at cheap but cheerful seafood joint Fish A'Go Go *(p143)*.

Afternoon Back across the Grote Markt, the bling-tastic DIVA Diamond Museum *(p145)* lifts the lid on Antwerp's rise to fame as a world diamond hub, with interactive exhibits and lavish jewels on display. A 20-minute walk north, past the waterfront Het Steen fortress, brings you to buzzing former docks. Here, the iconic MAS *(p142)* investigates the city's maritime history – it also offers gorgeous rooftop views. The nearby Red Star Line Museum *(p147)* is worth a visit, too.

Evening Celebrated for the city's best *stoofvlees* (Flemish beer stew), De Arme Duivel *(armeduivel.be)* is a convivial spot for dinner, in the prime location of shopping street Schuttershofstraat. Head back to the cathedral area for a nightcap: top picks are brown bar Café de Kat *(Wolstraat 22)*, with its neon sign and eccentric clientele, and the atmospheric De Muze *(jazzcafedemuze.be)*, hosting jazz gigs most nights. HotelO is a lovely place to stay *(Handschoenmarkt 3)*.

Day 2

Morning Kick off the day at the world's only UNESCO-listed museum, Museum Plantin-Moretus *(p144)*. Making your way through its creaking rooms, you'll discover the old home of 16th-century bookbinder Christophe Plantin, whose publishing house Officina Plantiniana became the largest of its kind in the Low Countries. The world's two oldest printing presses can be found here, alongside the second-oldest printed Bible. Afterwards, join the crowds on the adjoining Vrijdagmarkt square for lunch.

Afternoon Start your afternoon with some shopping, seeking out the hand-shaped *speculoos* (traditional spiced biscuits) at Philip's Biscuits *(www.philips biscuits.online)* – they make for the perfect souvenir. Antwerp Six designer Dries van Noten's HQ is nearby, too (though you'll need deep pockets to shop here). Next, head down Nationalestraat – possibly stopping at stylish museum MoMu *(p144)* – towards the posh Zuid district. On its main square, fine arts museum KMSK *(p140)* has a rich collection of Old Masters. Ready for a drink? Unwind with a spritz at one of the trendy bars on tucked-away Marnixplaats.

Evening Finish your trip to this fashionable city with dinner at van Noten's favourite eatery: the exclusive Sir Anthony van Dijck *(www.siranthonyvandijck.be)*. Set down a magical medieval alley, it features décor by guru to the stars Axel Vervoordt. A five-minute walk away, hip Dogma Cocktails *(dogmacocktails.be)* promises strong drinks to toast the end of your trip.

→

1 Walking the historic streets of Ghent.

2 *Genever* cocktails.

3 Visitors at the Museum voor Schone Kunsten (MSK).

4 A scenic boat ride.

24 HOURS

in Ghent

Morning A short train from Brussels, Ghent makes for the perfect getaway from the big city. Get your bearings on Sint-Michielsbrug, from where you'll spy the medieval Graslei and Korenlei quaysides, lined with guildhouses that conjure up Ghent's medieval past. Your eye will also be drawn towards the city's famous Gothic towers: first Sint-Niklaaskerk *(p160)*, and then the Belfort, topped with a giant copper dragon. Grab a coffee and sourdough cinnamon roll from the tucked-away café Koffeine *(Lange Kruisstraat 6)* before exploring the third building dominating the skyline: Sint-Baafskathedraal *(p158)*. Inside this lofty tower is van Eyck's oft-stolen *The Adoration of the Mystic Lamb*, shining after restoration. Depending on your energy levels, you could take a 20-minute tram ride south to fine art spot the Museum voor Schone Kunsten (MSK) *(p167)* to watch restorers working on some of the altarpiece's panels. Otherwise, head north via the vivid murals of Ghent's official graffiti street, Werregarenstraat, to the Patershol *(p162)*, where Roots *(rootsgent.be)* offers affordable, vegetable-led multi-course lunches.

Afternoon Come afternoon, explore the shops and cafés of the tiny, labyrinthine Patershol district, an area that feels completely out of time. Dip into the Huis Van Alijn museum *(p163)* to discover Flemish life in days gone by through a range of intriguing objects. If you're visiting at the weekend, stop by the former Carmelite monastery, the Caermersklooster *(kunsthal.gent)*, which is now an engaging contemporary arts hub (pay what you like for entry). A four-minute walk away, the hulking, 12th-century Het Gravensteen *(p156)* has gruesome exhibits that are sure to entertain the kids, alongside sweeping views from its ramparts. If there's time left in your afternoon, hop on one of Gent Watertoerist's vessels for a guided boat trip; if you take the 50-minute version, you'll pass Geraard de Duivelsteen, a Romanesque castle that belonged to a diabolical knight. Time it right and you should arrive back on Graslei just in time for sunset, when the guildhouses' spires are bathed in an orange glow, and locals cluster on the waterside, beers in hand.

Evening For dinner, head to Ghent's only two-Michelin-star restaurant, Vrijmoed *(vrijmoed.be)*. Ghent is vegetarian heaven, and this smart establishment has a dedicated meat-free tasting menu combining high-end and everyday ingredients to killer effect. Want a taste of the local nightlife afterwards? Head to beloved staple Het Waterhuis Aan De Bierkant *(Groentenmarkt 9)*, which offers an extensive beer selection on the river. If you really want to party, the nearby Vrijdagsmarkt and adjoining Sint-Jacobs area are the place to go – Café Charlatan *(charlatan.be)* is great for dancing. Want something more refined? Upscale hotel 1898 The Post *(p167)* has a cocktail bar with libations that nod to the local juniper-flavoured spirit, *genever*. It's also a cool place to stay the night.

1

2

3

7 DAYS
cycling the region

Day 1

There's no better way to explore this low-lying area than on two wheels – and Brussels is the perfect place to start. Pick up a bike at Pro Velo *(provelo.org)*; the friendly staff at this hire shop can also help you finesse your itinerary. Once equipped, it's time to explore the capital on a self-guided route from Bike Brussels *(bike.brussels)*. You can choose the tempting "Fries Tour", which takes in city-centre hits, or unwind on the "Royal Route", which passes the famous Atomium *(p105)* and Domaine de Laeken *(p104)*.

Day 2

It's around a half hour's train ride (bike supplement €4) to bike-friendly Ghent, where the low-traffic pedestrian zone is ideal for exploring. After brunch at the cycling-themed Bar Bidon *(barbidon.be)*, in the heart of the city, spend your day zipping between must-see sights such as Het Gravensteen *(p156)* and

Sint-Baafskathedraal *(p158)*. The region just beyond Ghent is prime cycling territory, too; the Chateau Route *(visit.gent. be/en/see-do/chateau-route)* is a highlight.

Day 3

On your third day, head to the mythic cycle town of Oudenaarde, which marks the finish line of the famous Tour of Flanders (Ronde van Vlaanderen; p45). You can reach it via the easy 30-km (18-mile) route east of Ghent's Citadelpark; it follows the river Scheldt most of the way to Oudenaarde. Once here, you'll want to visit the Centrum Ronde van Vlaanderen *(crvv. be)*, which is packed with exhibits on the history of the bike race; you can fill up on beer and spaghetti in the lively attached brasserie. Up for a climb? From town, three loops offer access to notorious stages of the Tour *(cyclinginflanders.cc/routes)*. At day's end, overnight at the bike-friendly Leopold Hotel *(leopoldhoteloudenaarde. com)* or get the train back to Ghent.

1 The coastline of Ostend.

2 Local food served up in Ypres.

3 Centrum Ronde van Vlaanderen.

4 Cycling around Bruges.

5 The leafy route to Damme.

Day 4

After a leisurely morning in Ghent, make your way to Bruges. Head south out of the city along the river Leie, switching onto the tree-lined Coupure bike path. This lovely 45-km (28-mile) ride hugs the ancient canal almost the entire way, taking you through peaceful farmland and sleepy towns. You'll then pedal into Bruges via the Gentpoort, one of the city's four medieval gates. In Bruges, take a wander around the historic centre before dining on Flemish fare in the bustling Langestraat quarter. Your base for the night is the gorgeous Hotel Jan Brito (*janbrito.com*).

Day 5

The country's most glorious bike route, the Damse Vaart, leads out of Bruges along a poplar-lined canal to the picture-perfect village of Damme, 5 km (3 miles) away. Here you can browse the array of independent bookshops, climb the tower of Onze-Lieve-Vrouw-Hemelvaartkerk, and lunch on the large terrace of De Damse Poort (*damsepoort.be*). It's an easy ride back to Bruges for dinner and drinks.

Day 6

Today it's time to explore Belgium's coast, freewheeling along the blissfully flat Kustroute, which is dotted with artworks made for the Beaufort Triennial. The port of Ostend, a quick train ride from Bruges, makes a handy base for activities. From here, ride west to see the horseback fishermen of Oostduinkerke and Surrealist Paul Delvaux's studio (*delvauxmuseum. com*). The coastal tram will then take you back to Ostend for a slap-up steak at Bistro Mathilda (*bistromathilda.be*).

Day 7

Devote your last day to World War I history. Zip along the coast to the Westfront Nieuwpoort museum (*westfrontnieuwpoort. be*), charting the town's role in halting the Germans' advance. Following the old Frontzate railway line, you'll soon arrive at the IJzertoren monument. Continue along the IJzer river for another 18 km (11 miles) and you'll find the Yorkshire Trench. From here, the sobering Peace Route loop takes in the area's key battle sights. End your trip with a farewell meal in Ypres (*p183*).

BRUSSELIZATION

From the 1950s to the 1970s, the local authorities' laissez-faire approach to city planning led to a concrete-fuelled free-for-all in Brussels. Initially linked to prepping the city for the 1958 Brussels World's Fair, this notorious period saw buildings torn down with little care for their historic importance. In their place came new boulevards and a flurry of high-rise office buildings. Today "brusselization" is a byword for slapdash urban redevelopment.

AMAZING ARCHITECTURE

The splendour of Belgium's medieval heyday is on full display in these four cities. But it's not all about Baroque and Brabantine Gothic: architecture fans can also marvel at an array of ornate Art Nouveau mansions and cool contemporary buildings.

Art Nouveau Architecture

Developed in the 19th century as a reaction to the traditional buildings of the past, this ornate style was born in Brussels. You'll spot examples all over the city, but for the very best, seek out the work of pioneering Belgian architect Victor Horta. The dazzling Horta Museum *(p102)* provides the perfect overview of his style. And if you're in the mood for more, invest in an Art Nouveau pass from the tourist office *(www.visit.brussels)*.

TOP 3 **MODERN MARVELS**

Villa Empain
An Art Deco residence-turned-art-space made by the Swiss-Belgian architect Michel Polak *(www.villaempain.com)*.

The Atomium
This futuristic icon *(p105)* was a product of the 1958 World's Fair.

Huis van Roosmalen
Striking 1980s building on Antwerp's waterfront *(Goedehoopstraat 1)*.

Examples of stylish Art Nouveau townhouses in Brussels

Contemporary Creations

These four cities aren't just dominated by historic buildings. Starchitects continue to weave their magic across the skylines, with Antwerp in particular promising a host of contemporary treasures. The eye-popping law courts by British-Italian architect Richard Rogers and the gravity-defying port authority building *(p147)* by Zaha Hadid are city icons. Another highlight in the region is De Krook *(www.gent.bibliotheek. be)*, an award-winning modern library in Ghent.

Ghent's futuristic library, De Krook, located by the waterfront

Baroque Beauties

For the best of Baroque, head to Antwerp. The city counts five churches crafted in this dizzyingly theatrical style. Sint-Jacobskerk *(p146)* contains over 1,000 kinds of marble, while nearby Sint-Carolus Borromeuskerk *(p145)* ups the ante with a jaw-dropping façade.

→

Sint-Jacobskerk's incredibly ornate nave, Antwerp

Gothic Giants

Many of Belgium's medieval masterpieces are Brabantine Gothic, a Low Countries variant on the style with soft stone and intricate carving. The finest is arguably Brussels' Hôtel de Ville *(p64)*, but Ghent is also packed with Gothic gems. Don't miss its trio of towers: the Belfort *(p124)*, Sint-Baafskathedraal *(p158)* and Sint-Niklaaskerk *(p160)*.

→

The mammoth Gothic Sint-Niklaaskerk, in Ghent

Sweet Treats

Chocolatiers galore, iconic waffles and candy delights: these cities are heaven for sweet-tooths. For the main event, hit up historic chocolatier and inventor of praline, Neuhaus *(p82)*. You'll find the beloved company's stores in all four cities. When it comes to waffles, choose between the airy Brussels waffle and the firmer Liège waffle (you won't have to walk far to find either). As for candy, don't miss *cuberdon*, Ghent's cone-shaped and raspberry-flavoured delicacy – try it at the Friday market on Groentenmarkt square.

→

A beloved regional treat, loaded waffles on display in a store

Did You Know?

It's estimated that there are a staggering 2,000 chocolate shops in Belgium.

FLAVOURFUL FOOD

Belgium's fame as the home of chocolate tends to eclipse the rich diversity of the local larder. Yet venture beyond the cocoa and you'll discover Michelin-starred dining, exciting veggie cuisine, salty fries and – for those who've still got room for dessert – delicious waffles.

Foodie Fun

Not content with simply trying the food? Sign up for a fun-filled cooking class. The friendly team at Waffle Workshop *(www.waffle workshop.com)* can teach you how to make the perfect Belgium waffle in Bruges or Brussels. Or, if you're looking to make your own chocolate, seek out new-wave chocolate star Laurent Gerbaud *(www. chocolatsgerbaud.com)*, who leads chocolate-making classes at his Brussels HQ.

→

Making waffles at the child-friendly Waffle Workshop

NEUHAUS AND THE BELGIAN PRALINE

By the time Jean Neuhaus II took over his grandfather's chocolate shop in Brussels, Belgium had access to the cocoa beans of its colony Congo, allowing the industry to boom. In 1912, Neuhaus would cement its rise by inventing the revolutionary praline: a cold chocolate shell filled with flavoured nougats and creams. It didn't stop there though: Louise Agostini, his wife, then invented the *ballotin*, a gift box still used by chocolatiers today.

Belgian Favourites

You can't go far in Belgium before stumbling on a steaming bowl of *moules-frites*, a dish combining the country's sumptuous seafood with its famous culinary invention: fries. The latter are a meal unto themselves here, with *friteries* or *frituurs* (fry shacks) popping up on all corners. Another hearty classic is *stoofvlees*, a beer-rich beef stew found in most brasseries.

← A crispy serving of Belgium's famous fries from a fry shack in Brussels

Stellar Dining

Perhaps surprisingly, Belgium hosts more Michelin-starred restaurants per capita than France. The country's high-end scene is far from stuffy, however. Antwerp's The Jane (*www.thejaneantwerp.com*), for example, creates a rock-and-roll fine-dining feel with its edgy décor. Vegetarian food is also having its time in the spotlight, with Brussels luminary Humus x Hortense (*www.humushortense.be*) the first 100 per cent plant-based restaurant in the country to get a star for its forage-focused tasting menus and zero-waste cocktails.

↑ Humus x Hortense, the first 100 per cent plant-based restaurant in Brussels

Beyond the Beer

Belgium's wine industry is booming. Head to Antwerp bar Belgian Wines *(www.belgianwines.com)* to explore the home-grown scene, which is strong on whites and sparkling wines. Following 2011 pioneer Titulus *(www.titulus.be)*, the capital also now has a robust natural wine bar scene, with many outfits clustered in the trendy St-Gilles neighbourhood. Locally made, juniper-flavoured spirit *genever* is also worth exploring – you'll find it in most good bars.

← Locals enjoying a glass of wine at a pavement bar in Antwerp

RAISE A GLASS

Beer runs through Belgium's veins, with over 1,500 types produced each year, ranging from world-beating Trappist concoctions (brewed by the eponymous monks) to cutting-edge craft beers. If you're not a hops fan, take refuge in the country's many *genever* or natural wine bars instead.

New Brewers

Belgium's traditional beer scene has been rocked in the past decade by the rise of experimental craft outfits. Brussels' Brasserie de La Senne *(www.brasseriedelasenne.be)* kicked off a movement for more hoppy beers in 2010, followed by nearby En Stoemelings *(www.enstoemelings.be)*, which revisited classics like the *tripel* (a strong golden beer). The vibey Brussels Beer Project *(www.beerproject.be)* is another cool kid on the scene – be sure to visit its summer terrace in Anderlecht (p114).

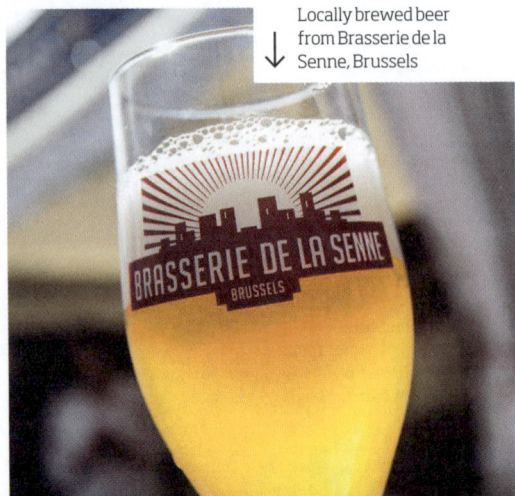

Locally brewed beer from Brasserie de la Senne, Brussels

DRINK

In de Verzekering tegen de Grote Dorst
Just outside Brussels, this unassuming spot has been voted the world's best beer bar seven times.

🅰E3 🏠Frans Baetens-straat 45, Lennik
🌐dorst.be 🕐Mon–Sat

Kulminator
To enter this quirky bar, ring the bell and say you'd like to taste (not drink) the beer.

🅰E2 🏠Vleminckveld 32, Antwerp ☎(03) 232 45 38 🕐Sun–Mon

↑ Quaint Café Vlissinghe, the oldest pub in the city of Bruges

Historic Pubs

Belgium's old-school pubs are delightful time-capsules, with some dating back to the country's medieval heyday. Brussels' Au Bon Vieux Temps *(Sint-Nikolaasgang 8/4)*, which features wooden décor and stained-glass windows, and Bruges's Café Vlissinghe *(p135)*, founded in 1515, are both incredibly atmospheric examples. Unpretentious brown bars, named for their cigarette-stained walls, are also popular – Antwerp's Café de Kat *(Wolstraat 22)* represents the tradition at its best.

 INSIDER TIP
Pace Yourself

Be warned: Belgian beers are strong. The common marketing terms *dubbel, tripel* (named after the beer) and *quadrupel* refer to ABV, which ranges from around 6% for a *dubbel* to 12% for a *quad*.

On the Beer Trail

A brewery visit is a must for hop heads. Start with the capital's only active Lambic brewery, Cantillon, which is home to the beer-oriented Musée Gueuze *(p115)*, too. At Mechelen's Brouwerij Het Anker *(www.hetanker.be)*, admire impressive copper brew-kettles before sampling the unique Gouden Carolus beer. Meanwhile in Antwerp, scope out De Koninck (www. dekoninck.be), which offers tours on the history of the *bolleke*, a malty amber beer.

↑ Local beer being poured at Cantillon, a historic brewery in Brussels

Public Art

Comic-strip murals abound in Brussels, with familiar faces like Tintin, the Smurfs and Lucky Luke popping up on buildings around the capital – spot them all on the Comic Strip Route *(p69)*. More art awaits underground, too, with 90 artworks gracing the city's metro stations. Don't miss Paul van Hoeydonck's flying mannequins at Comte de Flandre, the Tintin mural at Stockel and Surrealist Paul Delvaux's tram-themed painting at Bourse. Outside the capital, Ghent hosts a legal graffiti street, the kaleidoscopic Werregarenstraat, plus various other murals around the city.

→

The Tintin mural at Brussels' Stockel underground station

ART AND DESIGN

Belgium's art and design scene is about as diverse as it gets: Old Masters share the spotlight with contemporary creatives, while classic comic murals sit side by side with modern street art. Here's what to seek out across these four creative cities.

TOP 3 MODERN MUSEUMS

SMAK
Ghent's Municipal Museum of Contemporary Art hosts an edgy art collection *(p166)*.

MHKA
A converted grain silo, the Museum of Contemporary Art Antwerp showcases pieces from the 1970s onwards *(p146)*.

MIMA
This canalside venue honours culture 2.0 (think subcultures and street art) in Brussels *(www. mimamuseum.eu)*.

Iconic Masterpieces

Known for its luminous, hyper-realistic style (achieved through the pioneering use of oil paint), Flemish Primitive art *(p75)* flourished in the 15th and 16th centuries. The genre's standout work, Jan van Eyck's *The Adoration of the Mystic Lamb* (p158), lies in Ghent, but Bruges is ground zero for the style with its world-class Groeningemuseum *(p120)*. Antwerp isn't shy of Old Masters either, with larger-than-life religious works by Peter Paul Rubens bedecking the cathedral *(p142)*.

→

Rubens' *Elevation of the Cross* in Onze-Lieve Vrouwekathedraal, Antwerp

COMIC-STRIP ART

The *bande-dessinée* (comic strip) was born in Belgium in the 1920s, with the rise of youth-oriented magazines and newspaper supplements. Hergé's *The Adventures of Tintin* (1929) was the first big hit, and comics boomed post-World War II, when editors facing paper shortages switched daily sketches for weekly colour spreads. Fast-forward beyond the Smurfs, and comics are now a huge tourist business, with the capital boasting a dedicated museum *(p66)* and famous Comic Strip Route *(p69)*.

← The exterior of Antwerp's popular fashion museum, MoMu

In Vogue

Antwerp landed on the fashion map in the 1980s with the Antwerp Six, a group of avant-garde designers. Today, its fashion school continues to produce stars and shares its quarters with the fashion museum MoMu *(p144)*. Those with deep pockets can also shop the work of these iconic designers; both Ann Demeulemeester *(anndemeulemeester.com)* and Dries Van Noten *(www.driesvannoten.com)* have flagships in the city.

↑ Designer clothes for sale in Dries Van Noten's luxurious flagship store in Antwerp

TAPESTRY AND LACE

Antwerp may be a contemporary fashion capital, but this region has a long history of design. For over six centuries, Belgian tapestry and lace have been highly prized luxury crafts, and today, the country remains home to the very best studios in the world.

TAPESTRY

Originating in Flanders in the 12th century, tapestry has since been handmade in the centres of Tournai, Brussels, Arras (now in France), Mechelen and Oudenaarde. Prized by the nobility, tapestries were portable and could be moved with the court as rulers travelled their estates. As trade grew, techniques were refined; real gold and silver were threaded into the fine wool, again increasing the value. Blending Italian idealism with Flemish realism, Bernard van Orley (1492–1542) revolutionized tapestry designs, as seen in his work *The Battle of Pavia 1525*, the first of a series. Flemish weavers were eventually lured across Europe, where their skill led to the success of the famous Gobelins factory in Paris, which finally stole Flanders' crown in the late 1700s.

↑ *The Battle of Pavia 1525* by Bernard van Orley

LACE

The lace trade rose to the fore during the early Renaissance, with the material becoming fashionable on collars and cuffs, as a status symbol of the nobility. Emperor Charles V decreed that lacemaking should be a compulsory skill for girls in convents and béguinages *(p87)* throughout Flanders, and trade reached a peak in the 18th century. Victorian lace then heralded a revival of the craft after its

↑ A variety of Belgian lace pieces on display in a local shop

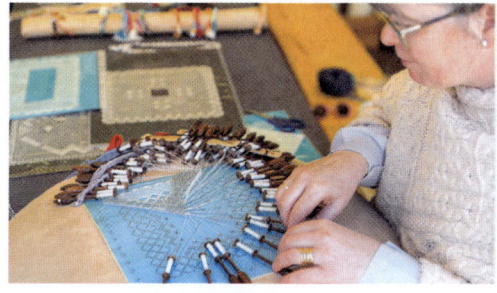

↑ Lace being made using traditional Belgian techniques

SHOP

Belgian Treasures
Ghent boutique selling splendid wall tapestries.

Ⓐ D2 Ⓜ Mageleinstraat 5, Ghent Ⓦ belgian treasures.be

'T Apostelientje
This spot offers a large collection of antique and contemporary lace.

Ⓐ B2 Ⓜ Balstraat 11, Bruges Ⓦ apostelientje.be

Manufacture Belge de Dentelles
Historic lace workshop and shop dating back to 1810.

Ⓐ E3 Ⓜ Galerie de la Reine 6/8, Brussels Ⓦ grsh.be

decline in the austere Neo-Classical period. Although men no longer wore it, the growth of the status of lace as a ladies' accessory and its use in soft furnishing led to its renewed popularity.

THE CRAFTS TODAY

Despite the rise in machine-made lace from other countries, the quality of Belgian lace remains as fine as it was in the Renaissance. Lacemakers, who are traditionally female, are dwindling in numbers but many still work in Bruges and Brussels, creating intricate works by hand and running lacemaking workshops in places like Bruges's popular Kantcentrum *(p128)*.

Weavers also still operate today, using medieval techniques to produce contemporary tapestry, woven in Mechelen and Tournai to modern designs.

Did You Know?

Tapestry weavers numbered over 50,000 in Flanders from 1450 to 1550.

Green Spaces

Brussels promises green spaces galore. Take a walk through the vast Forêt de Soignes *(p113)* for a break from the busy city. Or, spend the day around Domaine de Laeken *(p104)*, which is packed with family-friendly attractions: spot scale models of famous icons in Mini-Europe and explore the lush plants in the royal greenhouses.

Families at Mini-Europe, a popular theme park in Brussels

FAMILY ADVENTURES

Family-friendly Belgium is tailor-made for travelling with kids, and comics and chocolate are just the tip of the iceberg. Expect picturesque castles, prehistoric forests and fun-packed attractions, with reduced family rates and free entry often sweetening the deal.

Fun Festivals

Belgium loves a good festival, with folkloric celebrations featuring puppets and stilt-walkers sure to delight the kids. One of the most famous is Brussels' Ommegang, a vast procession held in summer. It's also worth making the trip from Bruges to the coast for the Sand Sculpture Festival *(zandsculpturenfestival. com)*, which promises giant re-creations of fairytale characters.

Stilt-walkers performing at the Ommegang parade in the center of Brussels

INSIDER TIP
Free Entry

Some of the region's best museums are free for under-18s, including the Royal Museums of Fine Arts *(p74)* and Musée des Instruments de Musique *(p91)*.

Cycling the Cities

Flat terrain and an extensive cycling network make Belgium a paradise for cyclists. All four cities offer bike hire and kid-friendly routes, with Bruges and Antwerp far less hectic than the capital. Seriously scenic routes abound, with the poplar-lined canal path that takes cyclists from Bruges to nearby Damme one of the best.

→

A family cycling through the centre of bike-friendly Bruges

Rainy-day Activities

Belgium is no stranger to rain, but indoor activities offer ample compensation. Combine a museum visit with a chocolate hit at sweet-toothed attractions like Choco-Story Brugge *(choco-story-brugge.be)* or Chocolate Nation *(chocolatenation.be)* in Antwerp. Alternatively, head underground to visit the ruins of Coudenberg palace *(p89)* in Brussels or venture into the Antwerp sewers at De Ruien *(p142)*.

←

Choco-Story Brugge, a fun place to learn about the history of chocolate

Go Back in Time

Plenty of attractions bring the country's medieval past to life. Top of the list is the grisly Het Gravensteen *(p156)*; pick up the audio guide by Belgian comedian Wouter Deprez while you're there; his unusually droll take on the castle's bloody history is sure to raise some smiles. Also in Ghent, the uber-interactive STAM *(p167)* is always a hit with the kids.

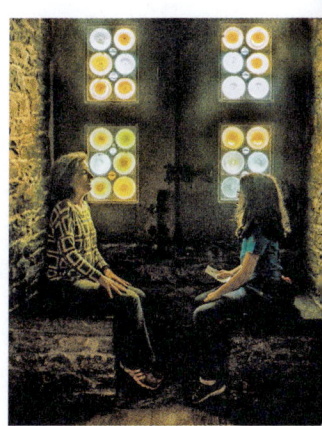

→

Exploring Ghent's hulking medieval castle, Het Gravensteen

Belgian Classics

Belgium is heaven for opera and classical music fans, with the top venues occupying glorious heritage buildings. In Brussels, the spectacular Théâtre Royal de la Monnaie *(p83)* houses the national opera while BOZAR *(www.bozar.be)* has a music hall designed by Horta. Other staples are Concertgebouw *(p125)* in Bruges, which hosts an Early Music festival, and Antwerp's Queen Elisabeth Hall *(www.koninginelisabethzaal.be)*, where Ghent's famed Collegium Vocale perform.

→

The gilded interior of the Théâtre Royal de la Monnaie, Brussels

AFTER DARK

Brussels, Bruges, Antwerp and Ghent have plenty to offer night owls: make a pilgrimage to iconic techno clubs, let loose in happening LGBTQ+ venues or sway to jazz in historic, much-loved bars. These cities don't sleep when the sun sets.

Jazz musicians performing in a bar in Brussels ↑

Live Music

Belgium invented the saxophone, so it's no wonder the capital has a booming jazz scene; hit up mythic spots like L'Archiduc *(archiduc.net)* or the Jazz Station *(jazzstation.be)*. Alternatively, Les Ateliers Claus *(lesateliersclaus.com)* is the capital's best showcase of underground music, while Viernulvier *(viernulvier.gent)* always hosts hip performers.

HIDDEN GEM
Start the Party

The perfect pre-party spot, Kiosk Radio *(kioskradio.com)* broadcasts 24/7 from a wooden kiosk in historic Parc de Bruxelles. Visit any time to find DJs playing for a chilled-out crowd.

TOP 4 LGBTQ+ SPACES

Le Belgica
🌐 lebelgica.be
A Brussels institution.

Le Fontainas
🌐 lefontainas.be
Queer-friendly café
with a terrace and DJs.

Café Blond
🌐 cafeblond.be
Queer safe space and
bar in Ghent.

The Crazy Circle
🌐 thecrazycircle.com
Lesbian bar hosting
slams, karaoke and gigs.

Club Nights

In the days of New Beat (a Belgian-born electronic music genre popular in the late 1980s), Belgium drew clubbers from all over Europe. The scene isn't quite as epic today, but the capital still has a crop of super-cool venues. Fuse *(fuse.be)* is the number-one techno spot while Recyclart *(recyclart.be)* is a fun arts hangout. Outside Brussels, Club Vaag *(clubvaag.be)* in Antwerp and Café Charlatan *(charlatan.be)* in Ghent are the places to go.

← Clubbing in Fuse, a popular
nightclub in Brussels

Let's Dance

The country's dance scene exploded in the 1980s, with a "Flemish Wave" of radical dancers. At the forefront was Anne Teresa De Keersmaeker's company ROSAS, who still perform locally. Antwerp-born Sidi Larbi Cherkaoui and his company are the current superstars; catch them at De Singel *(desingel.be)*.

→ Sidi Larbi Cherkaoui's
popular dance
company, Eastman

Flemish Begijnhofs

These walled religious complexes *(p87)* sprang up across the Low Countries in the 13th century when many single women moved to cities to find work. There are 13 in Flanders, all of which are UNESCO World Heritage-listed. Visits Bruges' *(p130)* in the spring to see a carpet of daffodils in its green courtyard. Or, wander around the quiet corners of Klein Begijnhof *(p166)*, Ghent's well-preserved complex.

→

The peaceful Klein Begijnhof in Ghent

HISTORY BUFFS

Packed with fascinating museums and unmissable historic sights, Belgium is a favourite among history fans. Here you can discover the country's medieval might, grapple with its colonial past or take a moment of remembrance in its vast cemeteries.

COLONIZING CONGO

With the support of several countries in Europe, Belgian King Leopold II seized the area of Congo as his personal possession in 1885. Up until 1908, he mined Congo for its resources, adding to his own fortunes. His desires came at a tragic cost, however, with the Congolese forced into labour and brutally punished for not fulfilling quotas. As these abuses became more widely known, the king was forced to pass the land to Belgium; it became a colony until 1960.

World-Class Museums

Great museums can be found in all four of these cities. In Antwerp, the UNESCO-listed Museum Plantin-Moretus *(p144)* holds the world's two oldest printing presses; just north, the affecting Red Star Line Museum *(p147)* recounts the story of émigrés like Albert Einstein who left the city for Canada and the US. Brussels also hosts an array of intriguing museums. Visit the Africa Museum *(p115)* to see how the museum is dealing with its colonial-era collections today.

→

Historical photographs at the Red Star Line Museum, Antwerp

Getting to Know Napoleon

Corsica-born Napoleon Bonaparte rose to power after the French Revolution, becoming emperor in 1804 and showcasing his military genius during the Napoleonic Wars (1803-1815). He faced a final, unsuccessful confrontation with the Allies at Waterloo *(p178)* in 1815. Today the Belgian town hosts the fascinating museum complex Mémorial 1815, which immerses visitors in the battle, as well as the Butte du Lion, which marks the spot where the Prince of Orange was wounded.

← The Butte du Lion at Waterloo, the site of Napoleon's defeat

Military History

Flanders became a major battleground during World War I. To reckon with the horrors of this history, head to the city of Ypres *(p183)*. Here you can visit the informative "In Flanders Fields" Museum and catch the famous Last Post ceremony at the Menin Gate. From the city, it's a short journey to the World War I battlefields and museums of the Ypres Salient (a major part of the Western Front); famous Commonwealth war cemeteries like Tyne Cot *(p185)* are also nearby. More military sites can be found in the surrounding Westhoek region, including Poperinge and Nieuwpoort, both of which can be explored by bike.

Did You Know?

Tyne Cot is the largest cemetery for Commonwealth forces in the world, for any war.

↑ The entrance to Tyne Cot, a war cemetery near Ypres

Beside the Seaside

Belgium's north coast is easily reachable from Bruges. Here, you'll find the world's longest tram line (the Kusttram), which runs for 67 km (42 miles) across the whole of the country's North Sea coastline. Onboard, you'll pass the pick of the area's beaches: upmarket resort Knokke-Heist and picturesque De Haan, which is lined with *belle-époque* mansions. Head towards the Dutch border for vast wetland Zwin Natuur Park or travel just beyond the arty port of Ostend to visit a forbidding section of World War II fortification, the Atlantikwall.

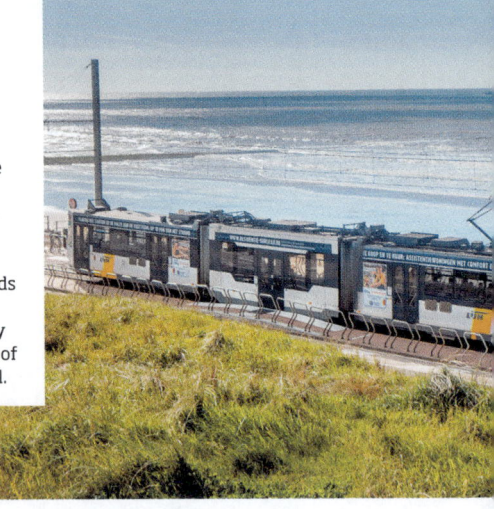

→

Belgium's Coast Tram, linking the country's north coast towns

THE GREAT OUTDOORS

Whether taking a boat trip in Ghent and Bruges or venturing beyond the cities into vast forests and wildlife reserves, travellers will find this region rich with outdoor adventures. Further boons include the superb cycling network and breezy North Sea coast.

TOP 4 RESPONSIBLE TRAVEL

Keep to the path
Stay on designated trails and cycle paths to protect delicate ecological environments.

Protect local species
Refrain from picking flowers or taking rocks and sand home.

Leave no trace
Avoid polluting the local environment by depositing rubbish properly.

Stay hydrated
Brussels has about 100 water fountains to top up your reusable water bottle.

Canal Cruising

This region is crisscrossed by dreamy waterways. In Ghent, take a 40-minute tour down the canals with Gent-Watertoerist *(gent-watertoerist.be)*, passing grand Sint-Baafskathedraal *(p158)* along the way. If you'd rather row your own boat, hire a kayak *(en.kajakskorenlei.be)* here instead. In Bruges, half-hour canal tours (March to November) glide past scenic city corners.

→

Canal boats passing Bruges's beautiful Rozenhoedkaai

On your Bike

Cycling is a joy in Belgium. The country hosts a superb network of cycling paths across its gentle landscape, making self-guided tours a breeze. The tourism board has also created nine iconic circuits for cyclists to follow (flandersbybike.com). Tick off Brussels, Bruges, Antwerp and Ghent on the lovely Art City Route, which ends in the coastal city of Ostend. Or cover the greatest hits of the region on the lengthy Flanders Route. This 800-km (500-mile) loop roams through unique polders, lush heathland, leafy forests and iconic cities.

RONDE VAN VLAANDEREN

Dating from 1919, the country's most famous bike race, the Tour of Flanders, falls on the first Sunday in April. The starting point usually rotates between Antwerp and Bruges, but the best place to watch the action is at the end of the race, in the cycling-fanatic town of Oudenaarde. Nearby, the public areas close to the legendary cobbled climbs of Oude Kwaremont and Paterberg are ideal spots for maximum spectating drama.

Cycling through one of the region's forests

Walking through the snow-covered Grenspark Kalmthoutse Heide

Wonderful Walks

Prime walking territory isn't hard to track down around the region's cities. South of Brussels, the Hallerbos forest is magical in spring, when its burst of bluebells carpets the forest floor. Even closer to the capital, the primeval Fôret de Soignes (p113) was a hunting ground of the Habsburgs and has UNESCO World Heritage status thanks to its giant sequoias. Outside Antwerp, fens and forests lure hikers to the gorgeous Grenspark Kalmthoutse Heide (grensparkkalmthoutseheide.com).

A YEAR IN
BRUSSELS, BRUGES, ANTWERP AND GHENT

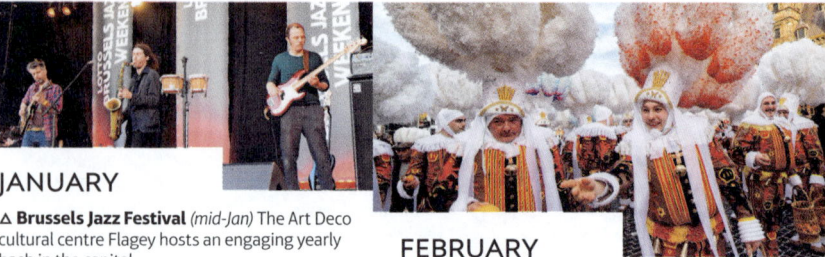

JANUARY

△ **Brussels Jazz Festival** (*mid-Jan*) The Art Deco cultural centre Flagey hosts an engaging yearly bash in the capital.

PhotoBrussels Festival (*late Jan–late Feb*) A month-long celebration of photography at galleries across the city.

FEBRUARY

△ **Carnival Season** (*mid-Feb*) Towns in the region host some of Europe's oldest street festivals.

Anima (*late Feb–early Mar*) This long-running event in Brussels celebrates the world of animated film.

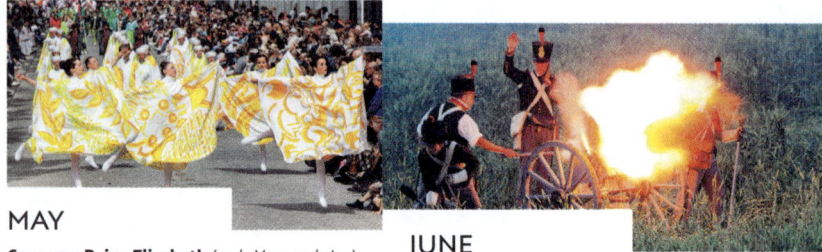

MAY

Concours Reine Elisabeth (*early May–early Jun*) This renowned classical music competition takes place in Brussels.

△ **Heilig Bloedprocessie** (*Ascension Day*) A relic apparently containing Christ's blood is borne through Bruges, followed by street parades.

JUNE

△ **Battle of Waterloo Re-enactment** (*mid-Jun*) Hundreds of volunteers re-enact the famous fight against Napoleon on the historic battlefield.

Ommegang (*late Jun*) Medieval pageant, featuring jousting and stilt-walkers, takes over the Grand Place in Brussels.

SEPTEMBER

△ **Belgian Beer Weekend** (*1st weekend in Sep*) Fifty-plus Belgian breweries descend on the capital's Grand Place.

Open Monumentdag (*2nd Sun in Sep*) Huge Flanders-wide festival with historic sites open for free.

OCTOBER

Brussels Marathon (*early Oct*) This notoriously hilly race takes participants past numerous sights around the capital.

△ **Film Fest Gent** (*mid-Oct*) Belgium's largest cinema festival takes place in Ghent and has an unusual focus on soundtracks.

MARCH

△ **BANAD** (*mid-late Mar*) Brussels shines the spotlight on its Art Nouveau and Art Deco heritage at this event, with visitors granted access to otherwise shuttered buildings.

APRIL

Ronde van Vlaanderen (*first Sun in Apr*) Famously tough cycling race from Antwerp or Bruges to the city of Oudenaarde.

△ **Serres Royales de Laeken** (*mid-Apr–early May*) Brussels' 19th-century greenhouses open for three weeks every spring.

JULY

Ghent Festivities (*mid-Jul*) Annual music and theatre festival drawing over a million visitors.

△ **Tomorrowland** (*mid–late Jul*) This world-famous electronic dance music festival takes place in Boom, near Antwerp.

AUGUST

MA Festival (*early–mid Aug*) Bruges pays homage to Early Music with historically informed performances across the city.

△ **Brussels Flower Carpet** (*mid-Aug*) This showstopping biennial event sees Brussels' Grand Place covered in bright begonias.

NOVEMBER

△ **Six Days of Ghent** (*3rd weekend in Nov*) This world-famous track-cycling race is held in Ghent's Kuipke velodrome.

River Jazz Festival (*late Nov–early Dec*) Concerts animate three iconic venues in Brussels, including the Jazz Station.

DECEMBER

△ **Christmas Markets** (*early Dec–early Jan*) Cities across the region host seasonal ice rinks, warming winter bars and fairground attractions, with endless stalls for Christmas shopping.

Castle Winter Wonderland (*early Dec–early Jan*) Ghent's iconic Het Gravensteen gets cosy with a pop-up winter bar and other festivities.

A BRIEF
HISTORY

Having been passed between various rulers, Belgium's four famous cities rose to prominence in the medieval period. During this time, all four reaped the rewards of powerful trade opportunities, and later Belgium's colonial exploits.

The Region's Beginnings

While human habitation in northern Belgium remained scarce until around 1750 BCE, there is some early evidence of occupation. Food remains, dating to between 8410 and 7930 BCE, have been found at a sand dune near the village of Verrebroek, just outside Antwerp; they indicate repeated human occupation during the Mesolithic era. Evidence of the Linear Pottery Culture, the first settled Neolithic farming civilization in the area of modern Brussels, has also been discovered; the civilization likely lived around 5000 BCE. There is also evidence of

1 A historical map of Belgium.

2 A home dating from the Neolithic period.

3 *The Roman Invasion of Gaul*, 1894, by the Belgian artist Karel De Kesel.

4 Historical illustration of Bruges, founded in 1128.

Timeline of events

c 5000 BCE
Neolithic farmers begin to settle around Brussels.

c 1750 BCE
Celtic settlement in northern Belgium begins to increase.

c 8000 BCE
Mesolithic peoples occupy the Flanders region.

57 BCE
Julius Caesar conquers Gaul, including what is now Belgium.

4th-century CE
Roman influence fades; Antwerp is founded by Franks.

human habitation around Ghent during the Iron Age. From around 1750 BCE, three Celtic peoples dominated prehistoric Belgium: the Urnfield culture, noted for cremating their dead and burying the urns in fields; the Hallstatt culture, who did much to advance metalwork; and the artistic La Tène culture.

Roman and Frankish Period

Despite meeting fierce resistance, Julius Caesar conquered Gaul (a region of western Europe that encompassed Belgium) from 57 BCE, bringing Belgium's peoples under Roman rule. Gallia Belgica, as it was now known, was part of the Roman empire for around 400 years, yet it received little attention or development.

In the 4th century CE, the Western Roman Empire began to crumble and the Franks (a Germanic people) started to exert a greater influence over Europe. The region was taken over by the Merovingian dynasty and then the Carolingian dynasty, known for its ruler, Charlemagne, whose many reforms and military campaigns shaped Europe for centuries. Brussels, Bruges, Ghent and Antwerp's beginnings all date to this era.

THE MENAPII

The Menapii people lived in Flanders when Julius Caesar invaded. Caesar commented that they offered a fierce resistance to occupation, allying with the neighbouring Veneti and Morini tribes to ambush Roman armies. Menapii culture centred on textiles, and the woollen clothing they made was exported as far as Italy, despite their antipathy towards their Roman colonizers.

650
St Peter's and St Bavo's abbeys are founded in Ghent.

768
Famed ruler and "Father of Europe" Charlemagne is born.

979
Descendant of Charlemagne, Duke Charles of Lower Lorraine, founds Brussels.

1128
Bruges receives its city charter.

1

2

Prosperity in Flanders

The late Middle Ages saw control of Flanders (Belgium's northern region) pass between France, Burgundy and the Habsburg Empire. Yet despite this political unrest, the region flourished due to the founding of the Hanseatic League, an international trading alliance. The 12th century saw the area's centres of trade quickly grow into powerful cities, with Bruges, Ghent, Brussels and Antwerp all seeing huge prosperity and cultural development. A thriving wool industry evolved in the 12th century in Bruges, followed by the opening of the Bourse (likely the world's first stock exchange) in the 13th century. Ghent became a powerful city-state in the 1400s and the second-largest European city (after Paris) north of the Alps. Meanwhile, Brussels became the capital of Burgundy.

In the 1500s, Flanders entered its most prosperous era. Flemish trading guilds reached a height of power, while prominent artists, such as Peter Paul Rubens, emerged in the area's cities. Antwerp's port flourished, trading in priceless art, spices and diamonds, and the city soon became the richest in Europe.

THE ZWIN

Bruges's rise to prominence came about in an unlikely twist of fate. A storm battered the Flemish coast in 1134, destroying so much land that it created an inlet, now known as the Zwin. The tidal channel turned the landlocked city into a port, allowing Bruges's wool industry to join the trade networks of Europe. The city grew incredibly wealthy until the Zwin began to silt up in 1500.

Timeline of events

1134
A storm creates the Zwin inlet, turning Bruges into a powerful port.

1336
Ghent's tapestry weavers' guild is established.

1432
Jan van Eyck paints the famous *Adoration of the Mystic Lamb*.

12th century
The Hanseatic League begins to coalesce as a powerful trading alliance.

1285
The world's first stock exchange opens in Bruges.

1456
Lodewyk van Bercken invents the scaif diamond-cutting tool.

The Road to Independence

During the 16th century, Flanders was caught up in the Dutch Revolt, a rebellion against the ruling Spanish government that became known as the Eighty Years' War. The Spanish Sack of Antwerp in 1576 saw the city destroyed and thousands of people murdered. Mass emigration ensued as merchants fled the violence and chaos, and the city's fortunes declined as a result. It was Amsterdam that took up the mantle, becoming a leading cultural centre in the region.

Flanders was later annexed by France in 1795, an occupation that famously ended in 1815 with the defeat of Napoleon at Waterloo. French rule was unpopular, yet their liberal ideas influenced the Belgian drive for independence. The subsequent Dutch rule, led by William I of Orange, was similarly unpopular. His anti-Catholic measures, coupled with high unemployment, poor wages and a bad winter in 1829, provoked mass protests across Belgium; a year later, the Belgian Revolution broke out. Dutch forces quickly pulled out of the region and, at long last, Belgium became independent. On 21 July 1831, nobleman and soldier Leopold I was crowned as the first King of the Belgians.

1 Map of the Zwin. ↑

2 *The Ancient Port of Antwerp* by Sebastien Vrancx (1573-1647).

3 The famous Battle of Waterloo, which saw Napolean defeated in Belgium in 1815.

Did You Know?

The country celebrates 21 July as Belgian National Day every year.

1500
The Zwin inlet begins to silt up, heralding Bruges' decline.

1555
Christophe Plantin opens his influential Antwerp printing press.

1566
The Eighty Years' War begins.

1610
Peter Paul Rubens paints his masterpiece, *The Raising of the Cross.*

1830
The Belgian Revolution breaks out.

The Belgian Empire

Belgium's early years of independence saw it become the second industrialized country in the world, after Great Britain. With increasing prosperity came loftier ambitions, with Leopold I offering support to Belgian merchants and companies extending their influence in Africa. This reached its zenith in the late 19th century, when the Democratic Republic of the Congo was assigned to Leopold II at the Berlin Conference of 1884–5; he ruled it as his personal fiefdom. Horrific atrocities were committed by the Belgian authorities during this period and millions of Congolese died during the occupation.

Two World Wars

The outbreak of World War I refocused Belgian attention on domestic concerns. Although technically neutral, Belgium put up staunch resistance to the German army, who invaded the country in 1914 in the hope of a quick route to France. Due to the country's central position, Belgium (and in particular the region of Flanders) became the setting for many of the war's most horrific battles.

1 Leopold I, the first King of the Belgians.

2 British and Belgian prisoners in World War I.

3 The port of Antwerp.

4 The glass-fronted European Parliament building in Brussels.

Did You Know?

In Flanders Fields, a poem by John McCrae, inspired the use of the poppy as a symbol of remembrance.

Timeline of events

1885
Leopold II is granted huge tracts of land in the Congo region.

1885–1908
Leopold II rules the Congo Free State, overseeing countless atrocities.

1847
Europe's first shopping mall, Galeries Royales St Hubert, opens.

1914
Belgium is invaded by Germany in World War I.

1917
The Battle of Passchendaele, near Ypres, sees close to a million casualties.

World War II again saw a neutral Belgium transformed into a theatre of war. Germany occupied most of the country from 1940 until September 1944, when the Allied forces liberated Brussels. While Antwerp, which was home to a large Jewish population, saw around 25,000 people killed during the war and sustained bombing damage, Ghent and Bruges were both spared by the air raids. Brussels also suffered little damage.

Belgium Today

Belgium saw a period of rapid growth after the war – the so-called "Economic Miracle" – partly thanks to the Allies' wartime use of Antwerp as a major port. Living standards improved nationwide, even as regionalist tensions heightened. Flanders grew significantly richer than south Belgium's French-speaking region of Wallonia, a gap which continues to widen and dominate Belgian politics today. Meanwhile, the 1960s saw Congo finally gain independence from Belgium, and Brussels become the de facto capital of the European Union. Today, Brussels, Bruges, Ghent and Antwerp – as well as the nearby battlefields – are the country's largest tourism draws.

THE EU CAPITAL

Brussels was chosen as the face of the European Union for a number of reasons. Firstly, the city was equidistant between France and Germany. Secondly, as an existing capital, it had the infrastructure to be a political seat. Crucially, though, Belgium was small and politically neutral: Brussels as capital wouldn't be seen as favouring any of the big superpowers.

1940

Nazi Germany occupies Belgium after Leopold III surrenders.

1960

The Democratic Republic of the Congo gains independence.

2003

Belgium becomes the second country in the world to legalize same-sex marriage.

1960

Brussels becomes the de facto capital of the European Union.

2022

Belgium's King Philippe makes a major announcement condemning the atrocities in the Congo under his ancestor Leopold II.

EXPERIENCE

Historic meets modern in Leuven

CENTRAL BRUSSELS

The settlement of Brussels began in 580 CE with the construction of a chapel atop a small island in the River Senne. About 400 years later in 979 CE, the city was officially founded when the Duke of Lower Lorraine decided to house the relics of local St Gudula in the chapel. The relics were later moved to the mighty Cathédrale Sts-Michel-et-Gudule in the city centre. By the 11th-century, Brussels had grown in prominence, its advantageous position on the Senne making it a fixture of the European textile trade. Over the next two centuries, some of the most iconic structures in the city centre were built, including the Grand Place. However, following devastating bombardment in 1695, a result of the Nine Years' War with France, much of the centre was destroyed and consequently rebuilt.

In the 1830s, Belgian independence and the subsequent establishment of Brussels as the country's financial centre sparked a new era for the city. The stately Brussels Stock Exchange and Palace of Justice were constructed, while the explosion of Art Nouveau architecture in the 20th century transformed the city centre. In 1967, Brussels was chosen as the new seat of the European Commission; it has since remained the political capital of Europe.

CENTRAL BRUSSELS

Must Sees
1. Grand Place
2. Comics Art Museum
3. Cathédrale Sts-Michel-et-Gudule
4. Palais Royal
5. Royal Museums of Fine Arts

Experience More
6. Quartier Marolles
7. Musée du Costume et la Dentelle
8. Manneken Pis
9. Notre-Dame de la Chapelle
10. Halles St-Géry
11. Galerie Bortier
12. Chapelle de la Madeleine
13. Bruxella 1238
14. Église St-Nicolas
15. La Bourse
16. Rue des Bouchers
17. Galeries Royales St-Hubert
18. Théâtre Marionettes de Toone
19. Théâtre Royal de la Monnaie
20. Rue Neuve
21. Place de Brouckère
22. Hôtel Métropole
23. Théâtre Royal Flamand
24. Maison de la Bellone
25. Église St-Jacques-sur-Coudenberg
26. Place Royale
27. Palais des Beaux-Arts (BOZAR)
28. Église Ste-Catherine
29. Église St-Jean-Baptiste-au-Béguinage
30. Hôtel Ravenstein
31. Palais d'Egmont
32. BELvue Museum and the Coudenberg
33. Palais de Justice
34. Palais de Charles de Lorraine
35. Place du Petit Sablon
36. Notre-Dame du Sablon
37. Place du Grand Sablon
38. Musée des Instruments de Musique

Eat
1. Wolf
2. Nüetnigenough
3. Friterie Tabora

Drink
4. La Porte Noire
5. Plumette
6. The Green Man

Stay
7. The Dominican
8. Aparthotel Adagio
9. Hotel Agora

Shop
10. Elisabeth
11. Neuhaus
12. Leonidas

Did You Know?

The distinctive spire of the Hôtel de Ville, built by Jan van Ruysbroeck in 1449, is slightly crooked.

①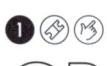

GRAND PLACE

📍D5 🏛Grand Place 🚌🚋3, 4, 32 Ⓜ Gare Centrale 🕐Daily 🚫Public hols, election days 🌐visitbrussels.be

A UNESCO World Heritage Site, this stately square is lined with incredible buildings and forms the geographical, historical and commercial heart of the city. Often the first port of call for most visitors to Brussels, the Grand Place also hosts a flurry of events throughout the year, including musical concerts, Christmas festivities and beautiful light shows.

Even centuries after its creation, this square remains Brussels's civic centre and offers one of the finest surviving examples of Belgium's ornate 17th-century architecture. Open-air markets took place on or near this site as early as the 11th century. By the end of the 15th century, Brussels' town hall, the Hôtel de Ville, was built, and city traders added individual guildhouses in a medley of styles. The square has been the site of some tragic incidents as well. Protestant leaders Jan van Essen and Hendrik Vos were burned here by the Inquisition in 1523, and in 1695, cannon fire by the French destroyed all but the façades of the town hall and a few guildhouses. Trade guilds later rebuilt their halls to styles approved by the Town Council, producing the harmonious unity of Flemish Baroque buildings here today.

 PICTURE PERFECT
Assumption Day Flower Carpet

Every even-numbered year on the 15 August, the Grand Place is decorated with nearly a million begonias. For the best view, book a room in one of the hotels on the square.

↑ The historic Grand Place, lined with Flemish Baroque buildings

1️⃣ The massive biennial Flower Carpet, a bucket-list must, is laid out ahead of Assumption Day.

2️⃣ Flemish-Baroque buildings on the square include Le Renard, Le Cornet and Le Roi d'Espagne – the guildhouses of the haberdashers, boaters and bakers respectively.

3️⃣ A gold statue of Charles de Lorraine, the former governor of Brussels, tops L'Arbre d'Or, the brewers' guildhouse.

EAST AND SOUTH SIDES

This stretch of the Grand Place features the iconic Maison du Roi. Built in 1536 and redesigned in 1873, it was used by the ruling Spanish monarchs. It is now home to the Musée de la Ville de Bruxelles, which includes 16th-century paintings and many tiny outfits of Manneken Pis (p78).

Neighbouring Le Pigeon was the residence of French novelist Victor Hugo in 1852, during the period of his exile.

On the east side is La Maison des Ducs de Brabant, a group of six guildhouses designed by the Controller of Public Works in the likeness of an Italian Baroque palazzo.

Locator Map

↑ Neo-Gothic La Maison du Roi, with its many balconies and spires

① **NORTHEAST CORNER**

② **LA MAISON DU ROI**

WEST AND NORTH SIDES

The highlight of this section is undoubtedly the Hôtel de Ville (p68), which occupies the entire west side of the square. Nearby is a monument to Everard 'T Serclaes (a citizen who helped drive the Flemings from the city); it is said that touching the bronze arm of his statue brings luck.

This section also features Le Renard, which was built in 1699 as the guildhouse of the

haberdashers – façade details show St Nicolas, patron saint of merchants, and cherubs playing with haberdashery ribbons. Next door, Le Cornet displays Italianate Flemish style and a notable gable. Le Roi d'Espagne, built by a powerful guild of bakers, houses the Grand Place's finest bar, with a view of the square.

⑤ **EVERARD 'T SERCLAES**

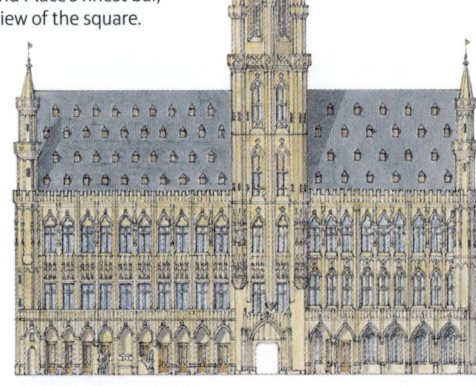

⑥ **HÔTEL DE VILLE**

→ Gold details on the façade of La Maison des Ducs de Brabant

③ LE PIGEON

④ LA MAISON DES DUCS DE BRABANT

→ Sculptures on Le Renard's façade, including that of the goddess Themis

⑦ LE RENARD, LE CORNET AND LE ROI D'ESPAGNE

↑ Enjoying a meal at the charming brasserie in Le Roi d'Espagne

Hôtel de Ville

The idea of having a town hall to reflect Brussels' growth as a major European trading centre had been under consideration since the end of the 13th century. It was not until 1401 that the first foundation stone was laid and the building was finally completed in 1455, emerging as the finest civic building in the country, a status it still enjoys.

Jacques van Thienen was commissioned to design the left wing and belfry of the building, which features ornate columns, sculptures, turrets and arcades. The tower and spire, begun in 1449 by Jan van Ruysbroeck, helped seal its reputation. In 1995, the 1455 statue of the city's patron saint, Michael, was restored and it now resides inside the tower; a copy of the statue sits on top of the tower. Tours are available of the interior, which contains 18th-century tapestries and works of art.

> INSIDER TIP
> **Take a Tour**
>
> Guided tours of the Hôtel de Ville fill up quickly, so it's best to book ahead online *(www.brussels.be/city-hall)*. Tours include ceremonial offices, the mayor's offices, portrait galleries and more.

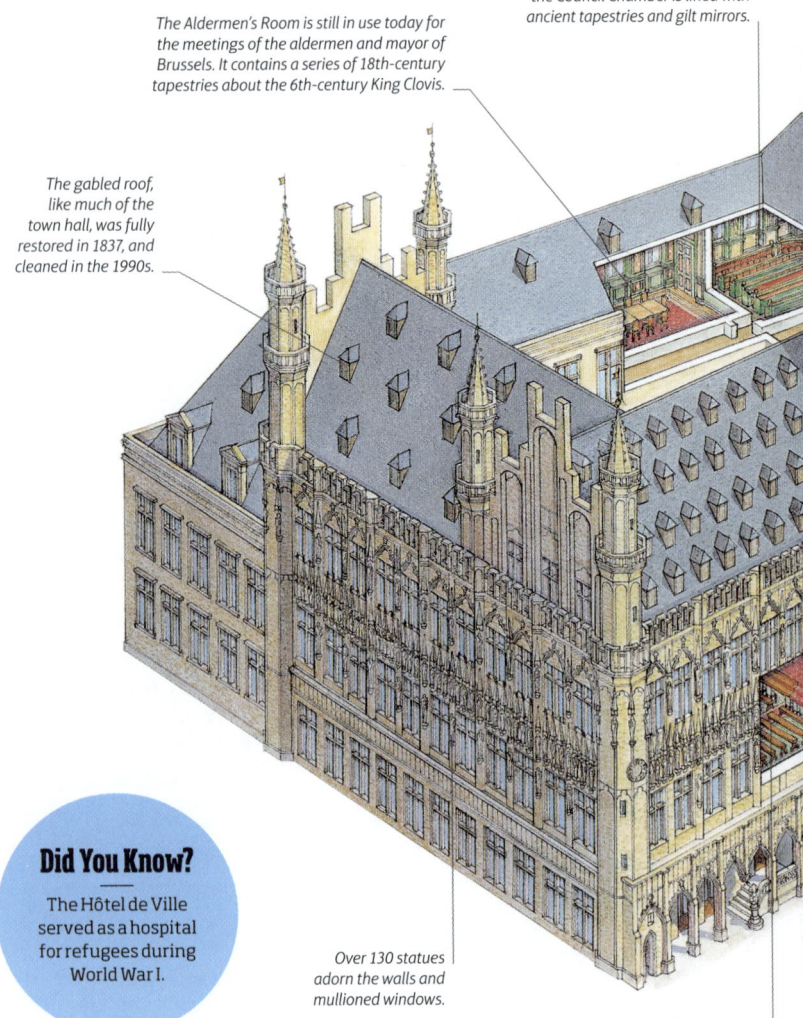

The most splendid of all the public rooms, the Conference Room in the Council Chamber is lined with ancient tapestries and gilt mirrors.

The Aldermen's Room is still in use today for the meetings of the aldermen and mayor of Brussels. It contains a series of 18th-century tapestries about the 6th-century King Clovis.

The gabled roof, like much of the town hall, was fully restored in 1837, and cleaned in the 1990s.

Did You Know?

The Hôtel de Ville served as a hospital for refugees during World War I.

Over 130 statues adorn the walls and mullioned windows.

Banquet room

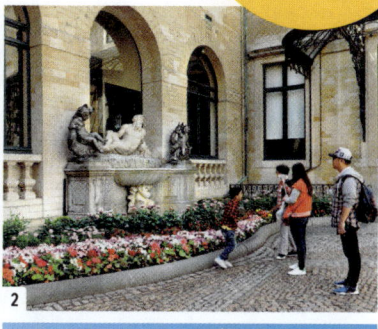

The belfry was built by architect Jan van Ruysbroeck. A statue of St Michael tops the 96-m (315-ft) spire.

1 Marble statues of the dukes and duchesses of Brabant grace the façade of the Hôtel de Ville.

2 Various marble fountains can be found in the town hall's inner courtyard. A highlight is one created by Flemish sculptor Pierre-Denis Plumier, which features a personification of the River Scheldt.

3 A marvel of Gothic architecture, the Hôtel de Ville is a popular attraction.

The Neo-Gothic Wedding Room dominates this civil marriage office, with its many ornate carved timbers, including ancient ebony and mahogany.

↑ Illustration of the Hôtel de Ville

The Hôtel de Ville was finally completed in 1455, emerging as the finest civic building in the country, a status it still enjoys.

2 🎨 Ⓜ 🖥 🛍

COMICS ART MUSEUM

📍E3 🏠20 Rue des Sables 🚌🚋3, 4, 32, 92, 94 🚇Botanique, de Brouckère, Rogier 🕙10am–6pm Tue–Sun 🌐comicscenter.net

A unique and much-loved institution, the Comics Art Museum pays tribute to the Belgian passion for comic strips, or *bandes dessinées*, and to numerous world-famous comic-strip artists from Belgium and abroad.

The beautiful building that houses the Comics Art Museum was constructed between 1903 and 1906 to the design of Belgian Art Nouveau architect Victor Horta. Originally built as a fabric warehouse, and known as the Waucquez Building, it was one in a series of department stores and warehouses in the city designed by Horta. Saved from demolition by the French Cultural Commission of Brussels, in 1989 the building reopened as a museum dedicated to the comic strip, Belgium's so-called Ninth Art *(p72)*. Carefully restored, the building has many classic features of Art Nouveau design, including the use of curves on structural iron pillars. In the impressive entrance hall is a display of Horta's architectural drawings

SHOP

Slumberland

Opened alongside the Comics Art Museum in 1989, this popular bookshop sells all comic-strip classics, including the likes of Tintin, Spike & Suzy and titles by Marvel. More recently, it has acquired a huge manga collection as well.

🏠20 Rue des Sables
🌐slumberlandbd world.com

→ Exhibitions on comic-strip characters in the Comics Art Museum, and *(inset)* its exterior

↑ The elegant interior of the Comics Art Museum

for the building, and on the right, the Brasserie Horta serves traditional Belgian dishes in a charming glass and marble Art Nouveau setting.

Celebrating Comic-Strip Art

One of the museum's most popular permanent exhibitions is on memorable comic-strip characters, from Tintin to the Smurfs, both of whose creators were Belgian. Other displays detail the stages of putting together a comic strip, from examples of initial ideas and pencil sketches through to final publication. The museum also holds exhibitions featuring the work of famous cartoonists and studios, and houses some 8,000 original plates as well as a valuable archive of photographs and artifacts.

THE CHANGING FACE OF HERGÉ'S TINTIN

Arguably the most famous Belgian comic character, Tintin made his debut in a children's paper in 1929. He began life as a simple black line drawing, featuring his characteristic quiff, but no mouth. By 1930, Tintin's creator, Hergé, began to produce the character in book form and gave him both a mouth and a more complex character, suggested by a greater range of facial expressions. By the 1940s, Tintin was appearing in colour, alongside such new characters as Captain Haddock, the Thompsons and Professor Calculus.

BELGIAN COMIC-STRIP ART

Belgium's love of the Ninth Art began in 1908, when the US comic strip *Little Nemo* was published here to huge popular acclaim. Yet it wasn't until after World War II that the country gained its own reputation for producing comic strips. After the war, local artists found that there was a demand for home-grown comic heroes. This explosion was led by the famous Belgian creation, Tintin, who is as recognizable across Europe as Mickey Mouse.

HERGÉ AND TINTIN

Tintin's creator, Hergé was born Georges Remi in Brussels in 1907. He began using his pen name (a phonetic spelling of his initials in reverse) in 1924. At just 15, his drawings were published in the *Boy Scout Journal*. He became the protégé of a Catholic priest, Abbot Norbert Wallez, who managed the journal *Le XXe Siècle*; under him, Hergé managed the children's supplement, *Le petit Vingtième*. Eager to invent an original comic strip, he came up with the character of Tintin the reporter, who first appeared in the story *Tintin au Pays des Soviets* on 10 January 1929. Over the next decade, the character grew in popularity with the publishing of book-length stories.

POST-WAR BOOM

Belgium's oldest comic strip journal *Spirou* was launched in April 1938 and, alongside the weekly *Journal de Tintin*, begun in 1946, became a hothouse for the artistic talent that was to flourish after the war. Artists such as Morris, Jijé, Peyo and Roba worked on the journal. Morris (1923–2001) introduced the cowboy parody Lucky Luke in *Spirou* in 1947. Marc Sleen, another celebrated Belgian cartoonist, created the popular character Nibbs (or Nero in Flemish). During the 1960s, the idea of the comic strip being the Ninth Art (after the seventh and eighth, film and television) expanded to include adult themes in the form of the comic-strip graphic novel.

 A cartoon of the Smurfs, on display at the Comics Art Museum

TOP 4 BELGIAN COMIC CHARACTERS

Tintin
Intrepid reporter who roams the world with his faithful dog, Snowy.

Papa Smurf
Leader of the Smurfs, blue-hued little people in Phrygian caps.

Philip Mortimer
Urbane British physicist embroiled in adventures abroad, created by Edgar P. Jacobs.

Nero
Loveable layabout, created by Marc Sleen, whose exploits are a vehicle for satire.

COMIC-STRIP ART TODAY

Comic-strips are still published in Belgium in all their forms and remains one of the country's major exports. A new generation of artists, such as Schueten and Marvano, have fed the growing demand for comic books, with both French and Flemish publishers issuing more than 22 million comic books each year for sale in over 30 countries.

STREET ART

The sides of buildings around Brussels' city centre are filled with large comic-strip murals. This outdoor exhibition is known as the Comic Strip Route and is organized by the Comics Art Museum *(p66)*. A free walking map is available from tourist offices, the Comics Art Museum and on *www.visit.brussels*.

Since many of Belgium's comic books date back a century, some contain outdated characters and tropes. Some street art murals have consequently become a source of controversy; for example, a mural in Marolles depicts African American dancer Josephine Baker with a leopard on a lead, which many have denounced as a racist work.

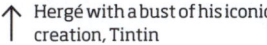

↑ Hergé with a bust of his iconic creation, Tintin

PEYO AND THE SMURFS

Best known for the Smurfs, Peyo (1928–92) was also involved with the *Spirou* journal, which published his poetic medieval series *Johan et Pirlouit* in 1952. The Smurfs first appeared as characters here – tiny blue people whose foibles soon eclipsed any interest in the strip's supposed main characters. Peyo eventually created a strip solely about them, infused with satirical social commentary.

3 ⟨⟩ ⟨⟩

CATHÉDRALE STS-MICHEL-ET-GUDULE

📍E4 🚪Parvis Ste-Gudule 🚌🚋92, 93 Ⓜ Gare Centrale, Parc
🕐8am–6pm daily 🌐cathedralisbruxellensis.be

One of the finest surviving examples of Brabantine Gothic architecture, the Cathédrale Sts-Michel-et-Gudule is a cultural and architectural icon of Brussels. This colossal cathedral is the national church of Belgium, although it was only granted cathedral status in 1962.

There has been a church on the site of this Gothic cathedral since at least the 11th century. Work began on the cathedral in 1225 under Henry I, Duke of Brabant, and continued over a period of three centuries. It was finally completed with the construction of two massive front towers at the beginning of the 16th century. The cathedral is made of a sandy limestone, brought from local quarries. It was fully restored and cleaned in the 1990s, a task that revealed all its splendour. Of particular interest inside the cathedral are the Grenzig organ, the magnificent stained-glass window depicting Christ awaiting saved souls, and the Baroque pulpit depicting Adam and Eve's expulsion from Paradise.

The twin towers rise above the city. Unusually, they were designed as a pair in the 1400s; Brabantine architecture typically has only one.

Facing the altar is the Last Judgement Window, *combining Renaissance and Baroque styles.*

Remains of the first 11th-century church, discovered during renovation work, can be seen in the crypt.

ST GUDULA

The joint patron saint of Brussels along with St Michael, St Gudula (Gudule in French) was born in the 7th century CE in Brabant, in what is now Belgium. Not much is known about her beyond the fact that she lived in the East Flanders village of Moorsel and was famed for her charitable work with the poor, to the extent that she was canonized after her death. A nuns' chapter in her name was subsequently founded in Brussels in 1047.

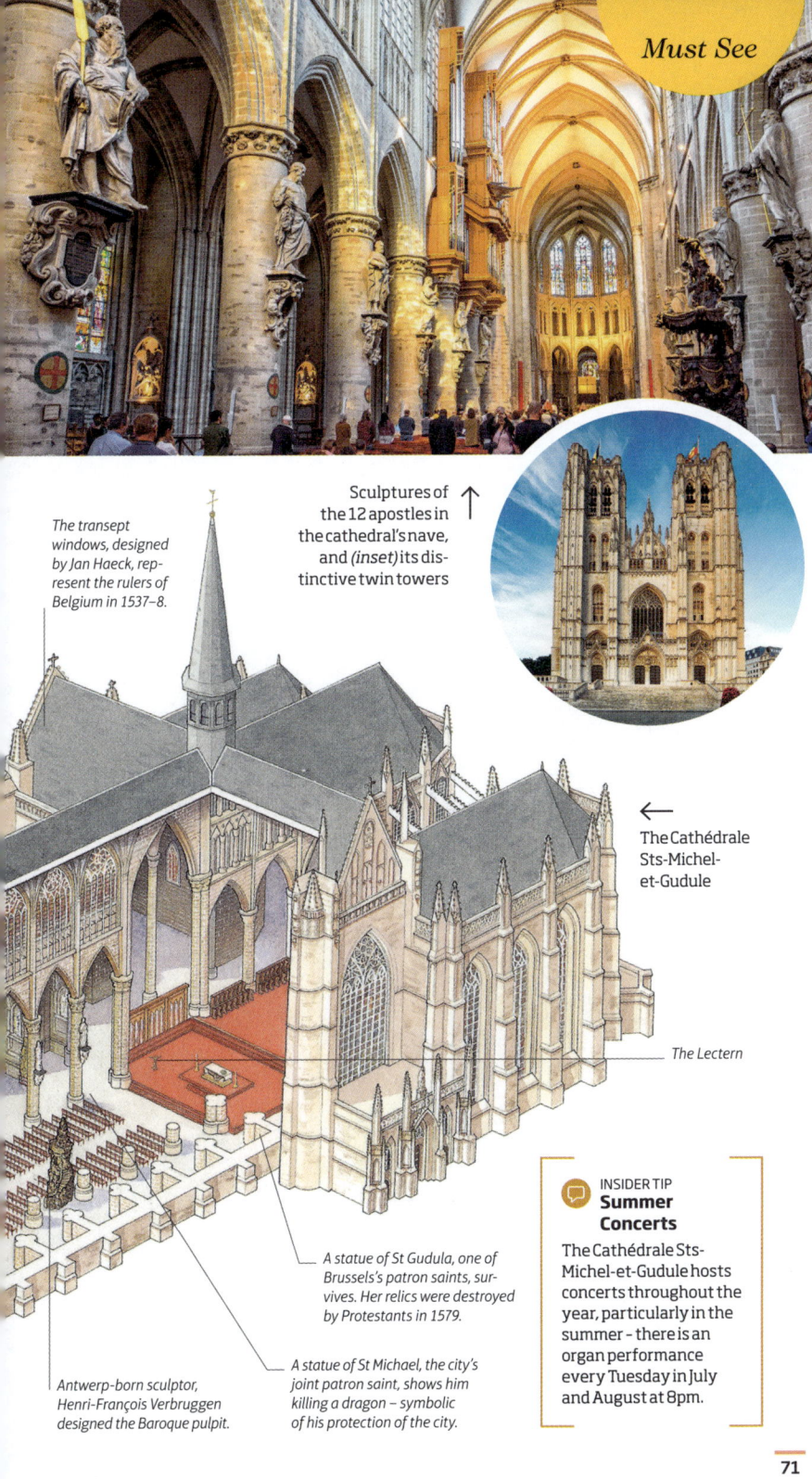

The transept windows, designed by Jan Haeck, represent the rulers of Belgium in 1537–8.

Sculptures of the 12 apostles in the cathedral's nave, and *(inset)* its distinctive twin towers ↑

← The Cathédrale Sts-Michel-et-Gudule

The Lectern

A statue of St Gudula, one of Brussels's patron saints, survives. Her relics were destroyed by Protestants in 1579.

A statue of St Michael, the city's joint patron saint, shows him killing a dragon – symbolic of his protection of the city.

Antwerp-born sculptor, Henri-François Verbruggen designed the Baroque pulpit.

INSIDER TIP
Summer Concerts

The Cathédrale Sts-Michel-et-Gudule hosts concerts throughout the year, particularly in the summer – there is an organ performance every Tuesday in July and August at 8pm.

PALAIS ROYAL

📍F6 🏛Pl des Palais 🚌92, 93 Ⓜ Trone, Parc, Porte de Namur 🕐Late Jul–early Sep: Tue–Sun 🌐monarchie.be

An official (but not active) home of the Belgian monarchy, the Palais Royal is suitably grand: huge chandeliers hang from its opulent ceilings and royal portraits hang on the walls of its carefully furnished rooms. Since 1965, it has opened its doors nearly every summer to the public for free.

The Palais Royal is among the most important palaces around the Parc de Bruxelles and an official residence of the Belgian monarchy. Construction of the modern palace began in the 1820s on the site of the old Coudenberg Palace (p89) and continued under Léopold II (r 1865–1909), when much of the exterior was completed. Throughout the 20th century, the palace underwent interior improvements and restoration of its older sections. It is open only from late July to early September, but this is a fine opportunity to tour Belgium's lavish state reception rooms.

The grand throne room features huge pilastered columns, 11 large candelabras and 28 chandeliers.

The Pilasters Room houses a Franz Winterhalter portrait of the first Belgian king, Léopold I, dating from 1846.

↑ Elegant 18th-century furnishings in the Small White Room

INSIDER TIP
Virtual Tours

You can now explore the grounds and sumptuous interior of the Palais Royal on a virtual tour, by heading to *virtualtour.monarchie.be*. Learn the history of the palace and its rooms.

EXPERIENCE Central Brussels

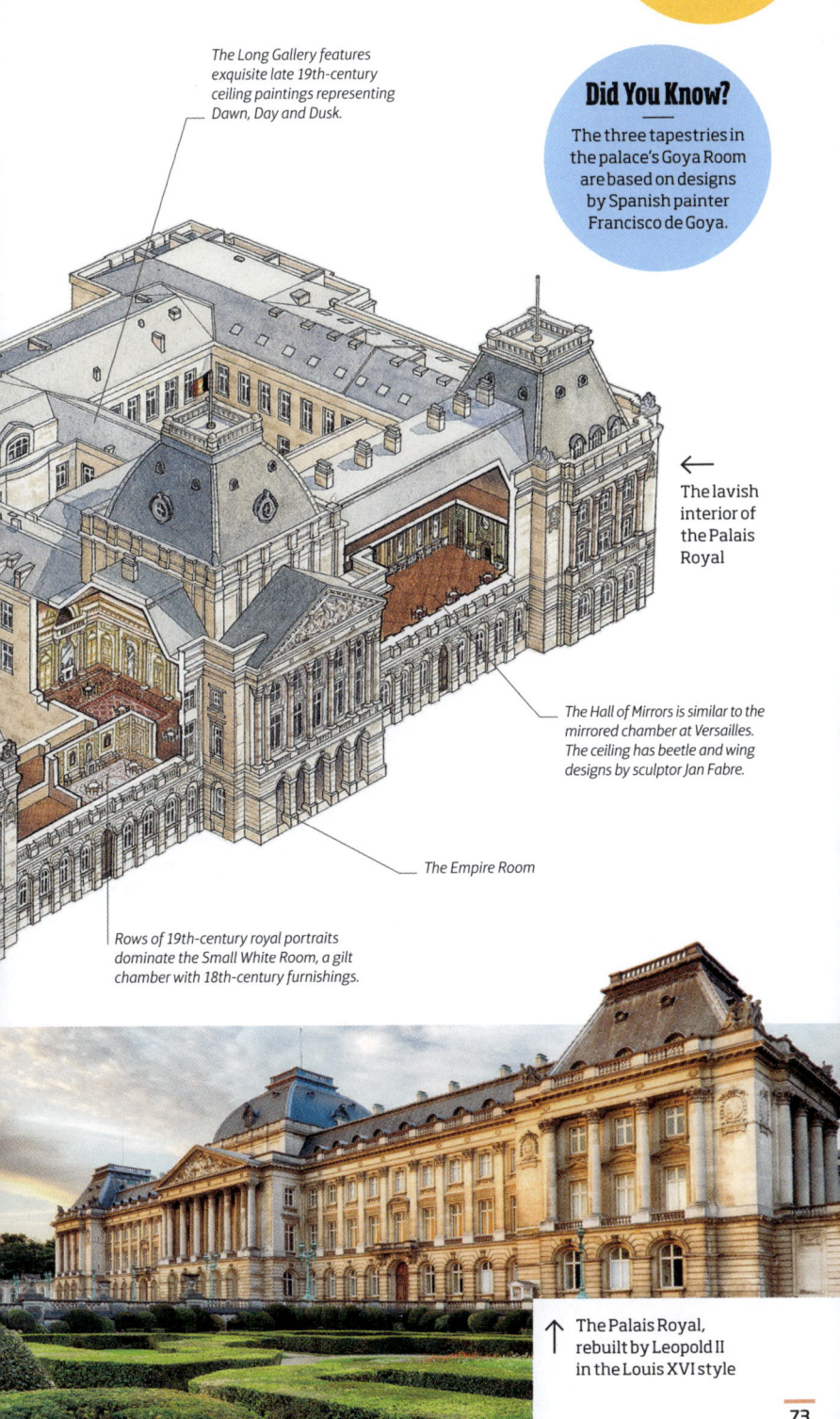

The Long Gallery features exquisite late 19th-century ceiling paintings representing Dawn, Day and Dusk.

Did You Know?

The three tapestries in the palace's Goya Room are based on designs by Spanish painter Francisco de Goya.

← The lavish interior of the Palais Royal

The Hall of Mirrors is similar to the mirrored chamber at Versailles. The ceiling has beetle and wing designs by sculptor Jan Fabre.

The Empire Room

Rows of 19th-century royal portraits dominate the Small White Room, a gilt chamber with 18th-century furnishings.

↑ The Palais Royal, rebuilt by Leopold II in the Louis XVI style

⑤ 🔖 🎨 🍴 ☕ 🛍

ROYAL MUSEUMS OF FINE ARTS

📍 E7 🏛 Musée Old Masters: Rue de la Régence 3; Musée Magritte and Musée Fin-de-Siècle: Pl Royale 1 🚌🚊 92, 93 Ⓜ Gare Centrale, Parc 🕐 10am–5pm Tue–Sun 🚫 Public hols 🌐 fine-arts-museum.be; musee-magritte-museum.be

The most prestigious art museums in Brussels make up the Musées Royaux des Beaux-Arts de Belgique. Across their vast collections, these museums contain over 2,000 paintings and sculptures, charting the history of Belgian and international art.

The museums that make up the Musées Royaux des Beaux-Arts de Belgique are: the Musée Old Masters (on Rue de la Régence), the Musée Magritte (just a short walk away), the Musée Wiertz and the Musée Meunier (both located some distance from the main site). The Musée Fin-de-Siècle and the Musée Modern (both on the same site as the Musée Old Masters) are also part of the collection, but they are temporarily closed.

↑ The Musée Magritte building, an iconic Neo-Classical landmark restored in 1984

Must-visit Museums

Of the six museums, three stand out: the Musée Old Masters, the Musée Magritte and the Musée Fin-de-Siècle. Housed in a Neo-Classical building (along with the Musée Modern), the Musée Old Masters is the largest of the three. Its collection dates back to the Napoleonic era, when several valuable works were left behind by the French Republican army. The collection grew and the present gallery opened in 1887. It's most well known for its collection of 15th- to 18th-century Flemish art.

The Musée Fin-de-Siècle, meanwhile, focuses on the late 19th and early 20th century, a period in which Brussels became a powerhouse for the Art Nouveau movement. The city's key role in the 20th-century Surrealism movement is celebrated in the Musée Magritte, with its superb works by the Belgian master.

FLEMISH ART

Between the 15th and 17th centuries, Flemish painters were at the forefront of the art world. Artists at the beginning of this period, known as the Flemish Primitives, were the first to popularize the use of oil paint; pre-eminent among them was Jan van Eyck. The 16th century was dominated by Brueghel the Elder, who pioneered the use of pastoral landscapes as the subjects of large paintings. In the 1600s, the focus moved to Antwerp and the Flemish Baroque style, spearheaded by Peter Paul Rubens, began to emerge.

← The main gallery of the Musée Old Masters, and *(inset)* its façade

Musée Old Masters

The hulking Musée Old Masters is divided into two different eras of art: the 15th–16th centuries and 17th–18th centuries.

In the first few rooms are works by the renowned school of Flemish Primitives (*p75*). As is the case with most art from the Middle Ages, the paintings are chiefly religious in nature and depict biblical scenes and details from the lives of saints. Many of the works show deeds of horrific torture, martyrdom and violence, attended by the perplexing nonchalance of the elegantly attired bystanders. A typical example is the diptych *The Justice of Emperor Otto III* (c 1460) by Dirk Bouts, which includes a gory beheading (a famous miscarriage of justice in the 12th century) and an execution by burning at the stake. Also on display are works such as *Lamentation* (c 1441) by Rogier van der Weyden, the city painter to Brussels during the mid-15th century, and *The Martyrdom of St Sebastian* (c 1475) by Bruges artist Hans Memling (c 1433–94).

Another unique aspect of the section is the extensive collection of paintings by the Brueghels, father and son. Both were renowned for their scenes of peasant life. On display are *The Fall of Icarus* (1558) by Brueghel the Elder and *The Struggle between Carnival and Lent* (c 1559) by his son, Pieter.

In the following rooms are works from the 17th and 18th centuries. A highlight of this section is the world-famous collection of paintings by Baroque artist Pieter Paul Rubens (1557–1640), which provides a fine overview of his art. As well as key examples of his religious works, there are some excellent portraits, such as *Hélène Fourment* (c 1614–73), his young wife.

TOP 3 MUSEUMS HIGHLIGHTS

The Census at Bethlehem, Pieter Brueghel the Elder (Musée Old Masters)
Shows Bethlehem as a Flemish village.

Head of a Young Peasant in a Peaked Cap, Vincent van Gogh (Musée Fin-de-Siècle)
Intense portrait of a young farm labourer.

The Temptation of St Anthony, Salvador Dalí (Musée Magritte)
Surrealist depiction of St Anthony in the desert.

Other works of note in this section are the paintings by Old Masters such as van Dyck's elegant *Portrait of a Genoese Lady with Her Daughter* from the 1620s and the charming *Three Children with Goatcart* (c 1620) by Frans Hals. Representatives of the later Flemish schools include Jacob Jordaens and his depiction of myths such as *Pan and Syrinx* (c 1645) and *Satyr and Peasant*. Baroque and Flemish pieces of art are all well represented throughout the museum.

Further notable paintings include works such as *Vase of Flowers* (1704) by Dutch artist Rachel Ruysch, who specialized in still-life paintings of beautiful flowers and fruits.

Musée Magritte

Visitors can enter the Musée Magritte and from there, the Musée Fin-de-Siècle, via the escalator behind the Musée Old Masters' restaurant. These two museums of modern art are housed in a unique setting: eight levels of the building are underground, but a lightwell allows many of the works to be seen by natural daylight filtering in from the bustling Place du Musée.

The museum's collection of Magritte's work began in 1953, following an extraordinary public fascination with the talented Belgian Surrealist artist.

Born the son of a wealthy manufacturer in Lessines, Magritte entered the Brussels Academie des Beaux-Arts in 1916. A former poster and advertisement designer, he created visually striking work, frequently displaying a juxtaposition of familiar objects in unusual, sometimes unsettling, combinations and contexts. Many of the artist's best-known paintings are shown here in a striking collection of more than 200 works, including the famous *L'Empire des Lumières* (1954) and *La Voleuse* (1927).

Of particular note are the paintings that date from Magritte's self-titled "Cavernous" period of 1927–30. At this time, while living in Paris, Magritte painted roughly a canvas a day. He then moved back to Brussels, where he

← *Hercules Resting* by Laurent Delvaux, Musée Old Masters

Artworks on display at the Musée Fin-de-Siècle ↑

lived for the rest of his life. Paintings on display from this later period include the eerie *Domain of Arnheim* (1962) and the melancholic *Saveur des Larmes* (1948).

Level 2 is a contemporary multimedia area, showing films dedicated to the artist and others who inspired his work. From here, stairs lead further underground to the Musée Fin-de-Siècle (temporarily closed).

Musée Fin-de-Siècle

The Musée Fin-de-Siècle showcases European and international art from the end of the 19th century and the beginning of the 20th century. This part of the museum has become a cultural institution thanks to the exhibits from the 31 different European art academies which, in 1868, created the Société Libre des Beaux-Arts. The Société introduced Modernism and the avant-garde to Belgium.

The rediscovery of the Primitives, Impressionism, Symbolism and Art Nouveau are all represented by such artists as Khnopff, Seurat, Spilliaert, Gauguin, van de Velde, Mucha, Horta, Ensor and de Vlaminick.

There is an excellent collection of Symbolist art, such as the poetic *Des Caresses* by Fernand Khnopff (1858–1921). Léon Spilliaert (1881–1946) is included via his 1909 Symbolist landscape, *The Dike*.

Many of the artists, such as Nice-born Henri Evenepoel (1872–99), who brought his distinctive post-Impressionist style to *The Orange Market in Blidah* (1898), deserve a close inspection. There are paintings by proto-Expressionist James Ensor (1860–1949), including his 1892 work *Singular Masks*.

Pointillism is represented in *La Seine à la Grand Jatte* (1888) by Georges Seurat (1859–91), who developed the technique, followed by Henry van de Velde's *Village Events VII*. Belgian van de Velde (1863–1957) went on to become one of the founders of Art Nouveau in Belgium.

A highlight of the museum is the extraordinarily rich Gillion Crowet Collection of Art Nouveau, which includes Alphonse Mucha's elegant *La Nature* (1899) and Fernand Khnopff's *Acrasia The Faerie Queen* (1892).

RENÉ MAGRITTE

Born in Lessines, Belgium in 1898, Magritte lost his mother to suicide at the age of 13. He began studying art in the early 20th century and eventually moved to Paris, where he met the Surrealists. Acclaim for his work rose during his life, and by the time of his death in 1967 he was one of Europe's most celebrated artists.

EXPERIENCE MORE

Quartier Marolles

B8 **3, 4, 51, 92, 94, 97** **M** **Louise, Porte de Hal**

Known colloquially as "Les Marolles", this quarter of Brussels is traditionally working class. Situated between the two city walls, the area was home to weavers and crafters. Street names of the district, such as Rue des Brodeurs (Embroiderers' St) and Rue des Charpentiers (Carpenters' St), reflect its artisanal history.

Today, the area is best known for its fine daily flea market, held in the Place du Jeu de Balle. It takes place between 7am and 2pm, with the biggest and best markets on Thursday and Sunday; almost anything from trinkets to pre-war collector's items can be found among the stalls.

Shopping of a different kind is on offer on nearby Rue Haute, an ancient Roman road. A shopping district since the 19th century, it is still popular with art lovers for its specialist stores, and interior and antique shops. The street has a long artistic history, too – the elegant red-brick house at No. 132 was home to Pieter Brueghel the Elder and the sculptor Auguste Rodin had a studio at No. 224.

At the southern end of Rue Haute is Porte de Hal, the stone gateway of the now-demolished outer city walls. Looming over the Marolles is the imposing Palais de Justice *(p89)*, which has hilltop views of the area west of the city, including the 1958 Atomium *(p105)* and the Basilique Nationale du Sacré-Coeur *(p115)*.

Did You Know?

The flea market at Quartier Marolles has been held on its site since 1640.

Musée du Costume et de la Dentelle

D5 **Rue de la Violette 12** **3, 4, 32** **M** **Gare Centrale** **⏰10am-5pm Tue-Sun** **🗓1 May, 1 & 11 Nov, 25 Dec** **W** **fashion andlacemuseum.brussels**

Set inside two 17th-century gabled houses, this museum is dedicated to one of Brussels' most successful exports, Belgian lace *(p36)*. The intricate skill employed by Belgian lacemakers has contributed a vital economic role in the city since the 17th century, and the displays outline the history of this delicate craft. The second floor has a collection of antique lace, carefully stored in drawers, which showcases the schools of lacemaking across France, Flanders and Italy. The museum also has temporary exhibitions of contemporary textiles and fashion.

Manneken Pis

D5 **Rue de l'Etuve & Rue du Chêne** **3, 4, 32** **M** **Gare Centrale**

An unlikely attraction, this tiny statue of a young boy barely 61 cm (2 ft) high relieving himself into a small pool is as much a part of Brussels as the Trevi Fountain is part of Rome or Trafalgar Square's proud lions are of London.

The current statue of Manneken Pis by Jérôme Duquesnoy the Elder has been in place since 1619. However, there is evidence to suggest that a stone fountain depicting the same figure stood there before it, possibly as early as 1451. In its long history, the statuette has been the victim of several thefts. A particularly violent theft in 1965 left the statue broken in two pieces, leaving just the ankles and feet remaining. The missing body of the statue reappeared a year later when it was found in a canal.

In 1698 the governor of the Netherlands, Maximilian Emmanuel, brought a gift to the city in the form of a blue woollen coat for the statue.

←

Shopping at the busy and colourful Quartier Marolles flea market

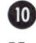

↑ The 15th-century Gothic nave of Notre-Dame de la Chapelle

This is a tradition that continues today, with visiting heads of state donating miniature versions of their national costume. The little boy now has a collection of over 800 outfits, which are housed in the Musée de la Ville de Bruxelles in the Maison du Roi on the Grand Place (p60), where around 100 are on display at any one time. Among the collection are miniature samurai, Santa Claus and Elvis suits.

THE LEGENDS OF MANNEKEN PIS

The are many rumours and fables behind this curious statue. One theory claims that in the 12th century the son of a duke was caught urinating against a tree in the midst of a battle and was thus commemorated in bronze as a symbol of military courage. The inspiration for the statue has been revealed as Cupid.

⑨
Notre-Dame de la Chapelle

📍 D6 🏛 Pl de la Chapelle 1 📞 (02) 513 8940 🚌🚊 3, 4, 32 Ⓜ Anneessens, Centrale 🕐 9am–6:30pm daily (from 10am Sat & Sun)

In 1134, King Godefroid I decided to build a chapel outside the city walls. It quickly became a local shrine, serving the many artisans living nearby. In 1210, its popularity was such that it was made a parish church, but it wasn't until 1250, when a royal donation of five pieces of the True Cross turned the church into a pilgrimage site, that it attracted real fame.

Originally built in Romanesque style, the majority of the church was destroyed by fire in 1405. Rebuilding began in 1421 in a Gothic style typical of 15th-century Brabant architecture, including gables decorated with finials and interior capitals decorated with cabbage leaves at the base. The Bishop of Cambrai consecrated the new church in 1434.

One of the most striking features of the exterior are the monstrously lifelike gargoyles – a representation of evil outside the sacred interior. The Baroque bell tower was added after the 1695 bombardment by the French. Another notable feature is the carved stone memorial to the 16th-century Belgian artist Pieter Brueghel the Elder (p75), who is buried here. The memorial plaque was made by Pieter's son, Jan.

⑩
Halles St-Géry

📍 C4 🏛 Pl St-Géry 23 🚌🚊 3, 4, 32, 51 Ⓜ De Brouckère

In many ways, St-Géry can be considered the birthplace of the city. A chapel to St Géry was built in the 6th century, then in 977 CE a fortress took over the site. A 16th-century church followed and occupied the location until the 18th century. In 1881, a covered meat market was erected here in Neo-Renaissance style. The glass and intricate ironwork was renovated in 1985, and the hall now serves as a local cultural centre hosting an array of exhibitions and events. There is also a lively bar.

Browsing the treasure trove of books at the popular Galérie Bortier

 11

Galerie Bortier

📍 D5 🏠 Rue de la Madeleine 55 🚊Ⓜ Gare Centrale 🕐 9am-6pm Tue-Sat

Galerie Bortier is the only shopping arcade in the city dedicated solely to book and map shops, and it has become the haunt of students, enthusiasts and researchers looking for secondhand French books and antiquarian finds.

The land on which the gallery stands was originally owned by a Monsieur Bortier, whose idea it was to have a covered arcade lined with shops on either side. He put 160,000 francs of his own money into the project, quite a considerable sum in the 1840s. The 65-m- (210-ft-) long Galerie Bortier was built in 1848 and was designed by Jean-Pierre Cluysenaer, the architect of the Galeries Royales St-Hubert nearby (p82). The Galerie Bortier opened along with the then-adjacent Marché de la Madeleine. Once a bustling market, the latter was destroyed by developers in 1958.

A complete restoration of Galerie Bortier was ordered by the Ville de Bruxelles in 1974. The new architects kept strictly to Cluysenaer's plans and installed a replacement glass and wrought-iron roof corresponding to the original 19th-century Parisian style. The Rue de la Madeleine itself also has plenty of shops for bibliophiles and art lovers to browse.

 12

Chapelle de la Madeleine

📍 D5 🏠 Rue de la Madeleine 📞 (02) 502 0568 🚊Ⓜ Gare Centrale 🕐 10am-noon & 2:30-4:30pm daily

This church once stood on the site now occupied by the Gare Centrale, but it was moved, stone by stone, further down the hill to make way for the construction of an Art Deco-style station in the early 1950s.

The 17th-century façade of the church has now been carefully restored. The original 15th-century interior has been replaced by a plain, modest décor, with simple stone pillars and modern stained-glass windows. Off the regular tourist track, the church is used by people as a quiet place for worship and contemplation. Unfortunately, the Baroque chapel which was once attached to it has not survived.

 13

Bruxella 1238

📍 D4 🏠 Rue de la Bourse 📞 (02) 279 4350 🚊🚋 3, 4, 32 Ⓜ De Brouckère 🕐 1st Sun of month: 1:30-5pm

Once home to a church and a 13th-century Franciscan convent, this site became a Butter Market in the early 19th century until the building of the Bourse started in 1867. In 1988, municipal roadworks began alongside the Place de la Bourse. Medieval history must have been far from the minds of the city authorities but, in the course of working on the foundations, important relics were discovered; these included

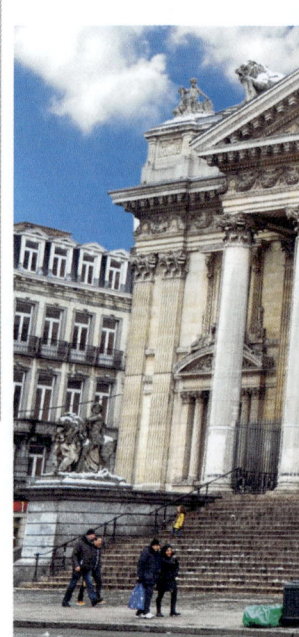

Striking façade of La Bourse, with ornately carved sculptures

13th-century bones, pottery and, most notably, the 1294 grave of Duke John I of Brabant. Today, visitors can see these and other pieces in a small museum constructed on the site.

⓮
Église St-Nicolas

♀ D4 ⌂ Rue au Beurre 1 🚌🚋 3, 4, 32 Ⓜ De Brouckère 🕐 10am–6pm Mon–Fri, 9am–6pm Sat, Sun & public hols 🖥 upbxicentre.be

At the end of the 12th century, a parish church was built on this site but, like much of the Lower Town, it was damaged during the 1695 French Bombardment. A cannon ball lodged itself into an interior pillar and the bell tower finally collapsed in 1714. Numerous restoration projects were planned by the city but none came to fruition until 1956, when the west side of the battered building was given a new, Gothic-style façade. Named after St Nicolas, the patron saint of merchants, the church as it stands today contains choir stalls dating from 1381 which display detailed medallions telling St Nicolas's story. Another interesting feature is the chapel, constructed at an angle, reputedly to avoid the flow of an old stream. Inside the church, works of art by Bernard van Orley and Peter Paul Rubens are also well worth seeing.

⓯
La Bourse

♀ D4 ⌂ Pl de la Bourse 🚌🚋 3, 4, 32 Ⓜ De Brouckère 🕐 9am–11pm daily

Brussels' Stock Exchange, La Bourse, is one of the city's most impressive buildings, dominating the square of the same name.

> **Brussels' Stock Exchange, La Bourse, is one of the city's most impressive buildings, dominating the square of the same name.**

Designed in Neo-Classical style by architect Léon Suys, it was constructed from 1867 to 1873. Among the building's most notable features are the façade's detailed carvings. The renowned French sculptor, Auguste Rodin, is thought to have crafted the groups of carvings representing Africa and Asia, as well as the four caryatids inside. Beneath the colonnade, two beautifully detailed winged figures representing Good and Evil were carved by sculptor Jacques de Haen.

The the interior of the Bourse has now been refurbished. It serves as a mixed cultural and recreational area, complete with informative temporary exhibitions on the history of the building and the city, along with cafés and restaurants. It also serves as a convenient pedestrianized approach to the Grand Place (p60).

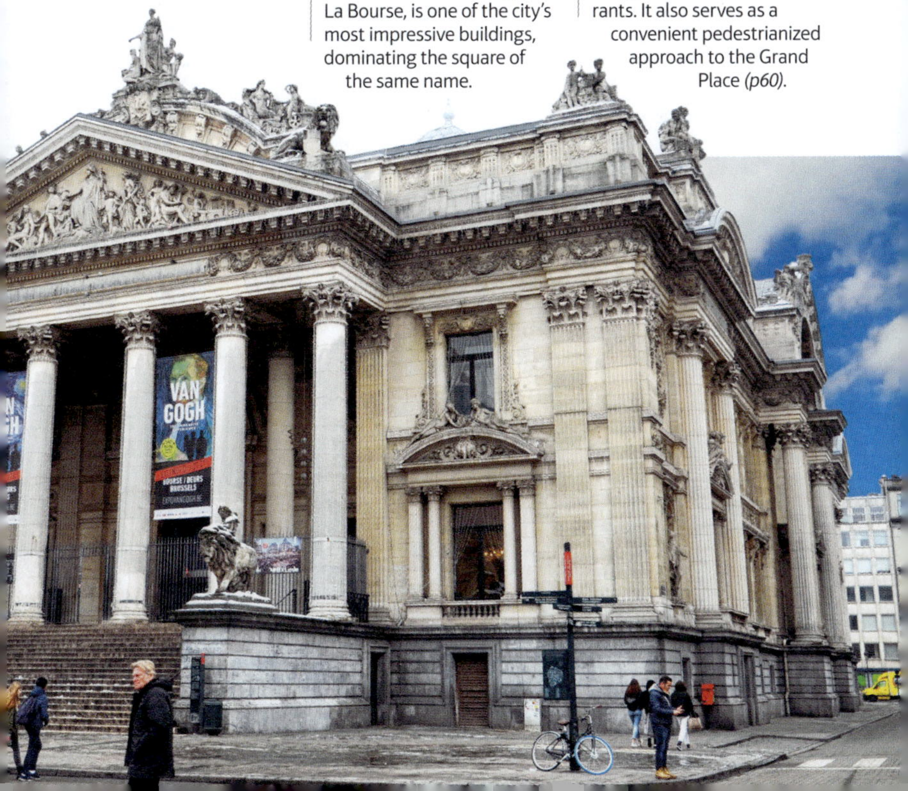

Rue des Bouchers

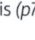 D5 3, 4, 32 De Brouckère, Gare Centrale

Like many streets in this area of the city, Rue des Bouchers retains its medieval name, reminiscent of the time when this meandering, cobble-stoned street was home to the butchers' trade. Aware of its historic importance and heeding the concerns of the public, the city council declared this area the *Ilot Sacré* (sacred islet) in 1960, forbidding any of the architectural façades to be altered or destroyed, and commanding those surviving to be restored. Hence Rue des Bouchers abounds with 17th-century stepped gables and decorated doorways.

Today, this pedestrianized thoroughfare is best known as the "belly of Brussels", a reference to its plethora of cafés and restaurants offering many types of cuisine.

At the end of the street, at the Impasse de la Fidélité, is the Jeanneke Pis, a female version of her "brother", the more famous Manneken Pis *(p78)*.

SHOP

Brussels is famous for its top-tier chocolatiers, and many can be found around Rue des Bouchers and Galeries Royales St-Hubert.

Elisabeth

Shop for truffles, pralines, biscuits and more, hand-picked by the owner from Belgium's best artisans.

D5 Rue au Beurre 43 elisabeth.be

Neuhaus

This store is considered the inventor of the modern-day Belgian praline and the *ballotin* (decorative chocolate gift box).

D5 Rue au Beurre 46 neuhaus chocolates.com

Leonidas

The home of the famed *manon*, a confection of hazelnut, buttercream and chocolate.

D5 Rue au Beurre 34 leonidas.com

Galeries Royales St-Hubert

D4 Rue des Bouchers 3, 4, 32 Gare Centrale

Sixteen years after ascending the throne as the first king of Belgium, Léopold I inaugurated these grand arcades in 1847.

St-Hubert was the first shopping arcade in Europe, and is one of the most elegant. Designed in Neo-Renaissance style by Jean-Pierre Cluysenaer, the vaulted glass roof covers its three sections, Galerie du Roi, Galerie de la Reine and Galerie des Princes, which house luxury shops and cafés.

INSIDER TIP
Lunch Elsewhere

While the food displays along the Rue des Bouchers may look enticing, restaurant standards can be low. Instead, do as the locals do and eat elsewhere in the area.

The galleries were a fashionable meeting place for 19th-century society, including resident literati – Victor Hugo and Alexandre Dumas attended lectures here. The arcades remain a popular venue, with shops, a cinema, theatre, cafés and restaurants.

Théâtre Marionettes de Toone

D4 Impasse Ste-Pétronille, 66 Rue du Marché aux Herbes 3, 4, 32 Gare Centrale Bar: noon-midnight Tue–Sun; shows: 4pm Sat, 8:30pm Thu–Sat Public hols toone.be

A pub by day, this tavern transforms into a puppet theatre at night. During the

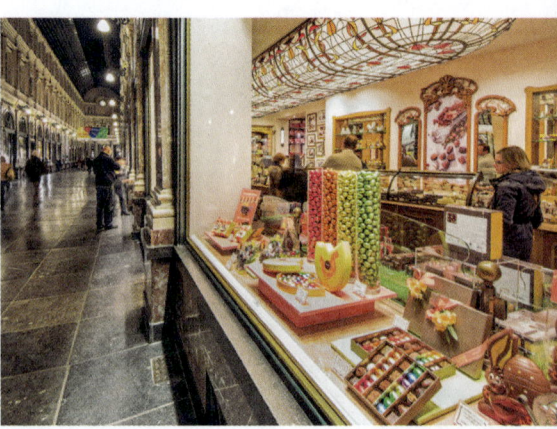

↑ Treats on display at a chocolatier on Galeries Royales St-Hubert

time of the Spanish Netherlands (*p51*), all theatres were heavily censored because of the satirical performances by actors aimed at their Habsburg rulers. This started a trend for puppet shows, the vicious dialogue more easily forgivable from inanimate dolls. In 1830, Antoine Toone opened his own theatre and it has been run by the Toone family ever since; the owner is the eighth generation Toone VIII. The classics are enacted by these wooden marionettes in the local Bruxellois dialect, and occasionally in French, English, German or Dutch.

19 Théâtre Royal de la Monnaie

📍 D4 🏠 Pl de la Monnaie 🚌 3, 4, 32 Ⓜ De Brouckère ⏰ Performance times vary 🌐 lamonnaiedemunt.be

This notable theatre was first built in 1817 on the site of a 15th-century mint but, following a fire in 1855, only the front and pediment of the original Neo-Classical building remain. After the fire, the theatre was redesigned by architect Joseph Poelaert, also

responsible for the imposing Palais de Justice (*p89*).

Before the fire, the original theatre witnessed a major historical event when, on 25 August 1830, a performance of the nationalist "Amour Sacré de la Patrie" (Sacred love of the homeland) in *La Muette de Portici* (The Mute Girl of Portici) began a national rebellion against the then new king, William of the Netherlands, who had been foisted on the Belgians by the Great Powers. Fired by the libertarianism of the revolutions occurring in France, the impassioned audience ran into the street in a rampage that developed into the September Uprising. The theatre remains the centre of Belgian performing arts. Major renovations took place during the 1980s, but the luxurious Louis XIV-style décor was retained.

20 Rue Neuve

📍 D4 🚌 Ⓜ De Brouckère, Rogier

Shoppers in Brussels have been flocking to the busy Rue Neuve since as early as the 19th century for its

↑ Théâtre Royal de la Monnaie's ornate central dome and balconies

reasonably priced goods and well-located stores. It houses international chainstores and shopping malls, such as **City 2**, which has shops, cafés and the media store Fnac all under one roof.

To the east of Rue Neuve is Place des Martyrs, a peaceful square where a monument pays tribute to the 450 citizens killed during the 1830 uprising.

City 2

🏢 🏠 Rue Neuve 123 📞 (02) 211 4060 ⏰ 10am–7pm Mon–Sat (to 7:30pm Fri) 🚫 Public hols

← The stone memorial statue at Place des Martyrs

↑ The plush interior of the bar at the Hôtel Métropole and *(inset)* its façade

21
Place de Brouckère

📍 D3 🚊 3, 4, 32
Ⓜ De Brouckère

In 1872, a design competition was held to encourage the construction of buildings of architectural merit in de Brouckère. Twenty winning applicants were selected and commissioned to give prominence to this Brussels junction. The renowned Parisian contractor Jean-Baptiste Mosnier was responsible for taking the original plans through to completion.

The French influence of Mosnier and his workers is still evident on the square. Many of the buildings were erected in stone, common in France at the end of the 19th century, whereas brickwork was more usual in Brussels. Several façades survive today, including the 1874 Hôtel Continental by Eugene Carpentier.

One of the great hotels of Brussels, the Hôtel Métropole is situated on the south side of the square.

During the 20th century, architectural style was still at a premium in the district. In 1933, a Neo-Classical cinema was erected with an impressive Art Deco interior. During the 1960s, two imposing glass buildings blended the contemporary with the classical. Today, the varied historic architecture of Place de Brouckère enhances one of the city's busiest squares, despite the addition of advertising hoardings.

___

22
Hôtel Métropole

📍 D3 🏠 Pl de Brouckère 31
📞 (02) 217 2300 🚊 3, 4, 32 Ⓜ De Brouckère

The area lying between Place Rogier and Place de Brouckère is known as the hotel district of Brussels, and one of the oldest and grandest hotels in the area is the Métropole.

In 1891, the Wielemans Brewery bought the building and commissioned the architect Alban Chambon to redesign the interior, with money no object. The result was a fine Art Nouveau hotel which opened for business in 1895 and has since accommodated numerous acclaimed visitors, including actress Sarah Bernhardt. In 1911, the hotel was the location of the first science conference Conseil Physique Solvay, attended by the great scientists Marie Curie and Albert Einstein.

The Hôtel Métropole was recently sold and will be closed for refurbishment until 2025, but the grand building can be seen from outside.

___

23
Théâtre Royal Flamand

📍 D2 🏠 Quai au Pierre de Taille 9 🚊 Ⓜ Rogier, Yser
🌐 kvs.be

The former quay area of Brussels, on the banks

STAY

The Dominican
Formerly a monastery, this hotel has tastefully decorated rooms. It houses the Grand Lounge Restaurant.

 D4 🏠 Rue Léopold 9 🌐 thedominican.be

€€€

Aparthotel Adagio
The modern Adagio offers suites with living rooms and kitchens.

 D4 🏠 Blvd Anspach 20 🌐 adagio-city.com

€€€

Hotel Agora
This eco-friendly hotel has cosy rooms; the ones in the attic are lovely.

 D5 🏠 Rue des Eperonniers 3 🌐 hotelagora.be

€€€

of the old River Senne, still survives as a reminder that the city was once a thriving port. In 1882, architect Jean Baes was commissioned to enlarge one of the former water-front warehouses and then turn it into a theatre – but was asked to retain the original 1780 façade. Baes solved this problem by placing the façade directly behind the frontage of the new building. Other inter-esting design features are peculiar to the late 19th century. The four exterior metal terraces and a

staircase leading to the ground were built for audience evacuation in the event of fire. Major renovations have restored the fabric of the original building and added a second building.

 24

Maison de la Bellone

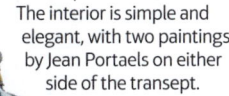 C3 🏠 Rue de Flandre 46 Ⓜ Ste-Catherine 🕐 9am–3pm Mon, 9am–5pm Tue–Fri 🌐 bellone.be

This beautiful 17th-century aristocratic residence, now shielded under a glass roof, was once the headquarters of the Ommegang proces-sion (*p46*). The original façade is notable for its decoration. There is a statue of Bellona (goddess of war), after whom the house is named, above the central arch, and the window ledges have medallions of Roman emperors.

Today, the house, its exhibition centre and once-private theatre are open for dance and cinema shows, and temporary exhibitions of art and furniture.

 25

Église St-Jacques-sur-Coudenberg

📍 E6 🏠 Pl Royale 📞 (02) 511 7836 🚌🚋 92, 93 Ⓜ Trone, Parc 🕐 1–5:45pm Wed–Sat (from 8:30am Sun)

The prettiest building in the Place Royale, St-Jacques-sur-Coudenberg is the latest in a series of churches to have occupied this site. There has been a chapel here since the 12th century, when one was built to serve the Dukes of Brabant. After construction of the Coudenberg Palace in the 12th century, it became the ducal chapel. The chapel suffered over the years: it was ransacked in 1579 during con-flict between Catholics and Protestants, and was so badly damaged in the fire of 1731 that it was demolished. The present church was built in the Neo-Classical style and consecrated in 1787, although it served several years as a Temple of Reason and Law during the French Revolution, returning to the Catholic Church in 1802. The cupola was completed in 1849. The interior is simple and elegant, with two paintings by Jean Portaels on either side of the transept.

→ The magnificent Église St-Jacques-sur-Coudenberg

EAT

Wolf

Dozens of vendors at this food hall showcase cuisines from across the world, including poké bowls, Ethiopian stews, dim sum and tacos.

📍 E4 🏠 Rue du Fossé aux Loups 50 🌐 wolf.be

Nüetnigenough

The menu here includes traditional dishes like Liége meatballs and Fontainebleau dessert.

📍 D5 🏠 Rue du Lombard 25 🌐 nuetnigenough.be

Friterie Tabora

This spot serves piping-hot *frites* topped with a range of sauces, such as traditional mayonnaise and Andalouse sauce.

📍 D4 🏠 Rue de Tabora 2 📞 (03) 479 29 33 10

26

Place Royale

📍 E6 🚌🚊 92, 93 Ⓜ️ Trone, Parc, Porte de Namur

The influence of Charles de Lorraine is still keenly felt in the Place Royale. As Governor of Brussels from 1741 to 1780, he redeveloped the site once occupied by the Coudenberg Palace along Neo-Classical lines reminiscent of Vienna, a city he greatly admired.

When the area was being worked on, the ruins of the palace were demolished and the entire site was rebuilt as two squares. However, in 1995, excavation work uncovered ruins of the 15th-century Aula Magna, the Great Hall of the former palace. This was part of the extension of the palace started under the Dukes of Brabant in the early 13th century and then developed under the rule of the Dukes of Burgundy, in particular Philip the Good. It was in this room that the Habsburg emperor Charles V abdicated in favour of his son, Philip II. The ruins can now be seen as part of the BELvue Museum (p89).

Although crisscrossed by tramlines and traffic, the Place Royale maintains a feeling of dignity with its tall, elegant, cream buildings symmetrically set around a cobbled square. Visitors can tour the area on foot, admiring the exceptional Neo-Classical buildings.

27

Palais des Beaux-Arts (BOZAR)

📍 E6 🏠 Rue Ravenstein 23 🚌🚊 92, 93 Ⓜ️ Gare Centrale, Parc 🕙 10am–6pm Tue–Sun 🚫 Public hols 🌐 bozar.be

The Palais des Beaux-Arts (BOZAR) owes its existence to Henri Le Boeuf, a music-loving financier who gave his name to the main auditorium. In 1922 he commissioned architect Victor Horta (p103) to design a cultural centre that would house concert halls and exhibition areas, be open to all visitors, and embrace the artistic fields of music, art, theatre, cinema, architecture and literature. The centre was the first of its kind in Europe.

The complex has a fine reputation and has played an important

role in the cultural life of Brussels for more than 80 years. It is the focus for the city's music, hosting 250 classical music concerts each year, and is home to the Belgian National Orchestra. The programme also includes about 50 concerts of rock, pop, jazz and world music.

The complex also houses the **CINEMATEK**, set up in 1962, with its fine archive and exhibition of old cameras and lenses. It screens classic films.

CINEMATEK
 Rue Baron Horta 9
Times vary with screenings, check website
cinematek.be

28
Église Ste-Catherine

C3 Place Ste-Catherine 50 (02) 513 3481
Ste-Catherine 9am–8pm Mon–Fri, 9:30am–6pm Sat & Sun

While a church was first built here in the 15th century, the oldest remaining part today is the Baroque tower dating from 1629. Inspired by the Église St-Eustache in Paris, the present church was redesigned in 1854–9 by architect Joseph Poelaert in a variety of styles. Notable features of the interior include a large 14th-century statue

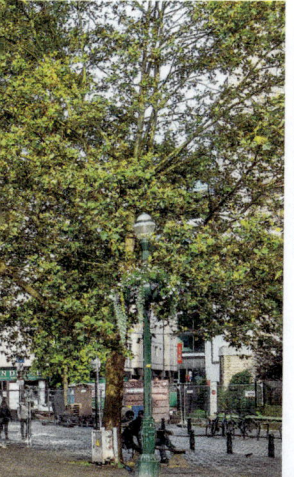

THE BÉGUINE MOVEMENT

The béguine lifestyle swept across western Europe from the 12th century, and Brussels once had a community of over 1,200 béguine women. The religious order is believed to have begun among widows of the Crusaders, who resorted to a pious life of sisterhood on the death of their husbands. The movement dissolved as female emancipation spread during the early 1800s, although 20 convents remain, including those in Bruges (p130) and Ghent (p166).

of the Black Madonna and a stunning portrait of St Catherine – for whom the church was built.

A typically Flemish pulpit was installed at some stage; it may have come from the parish of Mechelen. Two impressive tombs were carved by Gilles-Lambert Godecharle. To the east of the church is the Tour Noire (Black Tower), a surviving remnant of the 12th-century stone city walls.

Although this area has been dedicated to the saint since the 13th century, the square of Place Ste-Catherine was only laid in front of this large church after the basin once here was filled in; it was paved in 1870.

The central square was once the city's main fish market and, though the market is now gone, there are plenty of restaurants in which to indulge in a dish or two of Brussels' famous seafood. The best places to grab a meal flank the square: Quai aux Briques and Quai au Bois à Brûler (Brick Quay and Timber Quay, named after their industrial past) both contain lively parades of fish restaurants. Be warned, however, that prices tend to be quite high.

The façade of the 19th-century Église Ste-Catherine

29
Église St-Jean-Baptiste-au-Béguinage

D3 Pl du Béguinage
Ste-Catherine 10am–5pm Tue–Sat, 2–5pm Sun

This stone-clad church was consecrated in 1676 around the long-standing and largest béguine community in the country, established in 1250. Fields and orchards around the site contained cottages and houses for up to 1,200 béguine women, members of a lay religious order who took up charitable work and enclosed living. In medieval times, the local béguines ran a laundry, hospital and windmill for the people of the city. Still a popular place of worship, the church has also in recent years become a sanctuary for Afghan refugees awaiting regularization.

The architecture is notable for its Flemish Baroque details from the 17th century, especially the onion-shaped turrets and ornamental walls. The nave is also Baroque, decorated with cherubs and scrolls. The confessionals are carved with allegorical figures. A more unusual feature is the aisles, which have been widened to allow more light in. In the apse is a statue of St John the Baptist. The 1757 pulpit is a fine example of Baroque woodcarving, showing St Dominic and a heretic.

Hôtel Ravenstein

E6 **Rue Ravenstein 3** **92, 93** **Gare Centrale, Parc** **Restaurant only**

Over the centuries, the historic Hôtel Ravenstein has been the home of patrician families, soldiers and court officials, and, for the past 100 years, the Royal Society of Engineers. The building was designed at the end of the 15th century for Adolphe and Philip Cleves-Ravenstein; in 1515 it was the birthplace of Anne of Cleves.

Consisting of two parts, joined by gardens and stables, it is the last remaining example of a Burgundian-style manor house. The Hôtel Ravenstein was acquired by the city in 1896 and was primarily used to store artworks. Unfortunately, the building fell into disrepair and renovation took place in 1934. One half is now the Royal Society of Engineers' private headquarters. However, the pretty, original inner courtyard is still intact and can be seen by visitors.

THE SURREALISTS

René Magritte *(p77)* was the key figure of the Belgian Surrealist movement, which had its origins with three others – Camille Goemans, Marcel Lecomte and Paul Nougé. Inspired by a group of French thinkers and artists led by poet André Breton, Surrealism aimed to unite dreams and reality. The Belgian Surrealists gathered at the bar La Fleur en Papier Doré to exchange ideas, and showcased their work in the Hôtel Ravenstein, prioritizing artistic vision over fame.

Palais d'Egmont

E7 **Place du Petit Sablon 8** **92, 93, 94, 97** **Louise, Parc**

The Palais d'Egmont (also known as the Palais d'Arenberg) was originally built in the mid-16th century for Françoise of Luxembourg, mother of Count Egmont, the 16th-century leader of the city's rebels. This palace has twice been rebuilt, in 1750 and again in 1891, following a fire. Today, it belongs to the Belgian Foreign Ministry.

It was here that the nations of Great Britain, Denmark and Ireland signed as members of the EEC in 1972. Though the palace itself is closed to the public, the gardens, whose entrances are on the Rue du Grand Cerf and the Boulevard de Waterloo, are open to visitors. There is also a statue of Peter Pan, a copy of one found in Kensington Gardens in London, where families throng to take pictures. Many of the gardens' buildings are now run down, but the ancient orangery has been restored and now houses a trendy restaurant.

↑ Exhibits on the history of Belgium at the BELvue Museum

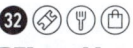

BELvue Museum and the Coudenberg

📍F6 🏠Place des Palais 7 🚌🚋92, 93 Ⓜ️Trone, Parc, Porte de Namur 🕐9:30am-5pm Mon-Fri, 11am-7pm Sat & Sun 📅1 Jan, 21 Jul, 25 Dec 🌐belvue.be

Housed in the former Hôtel Bellevue, this museum holds a wide collection of paintings and other royal memorabilia charting the history of the Belgian monarchy from independence in 1830 to the present day, showcased through around 1,500 unique historical documents, photographs and film extracts. The museum also hosts temporary exhibitions on particular themes, eras or perspectives. The Coudenberg is a separate underground archaeological site and museum that is within the grounds of the BELvue Museum.

← Façade of the late 15th-century Hôtel Ravenstein

Palais de Justice

📍D8 🏠Place Poelaert 1 📞(02) 508 6578 🚌92, 93, 94, 97 Ⓜ️Louise 🕐8am-5pm Mon-Fri; tours on request 📅Public hols

The Palais de Justice rules the Brussels skyline and can be seen from almost any vantage point in the city. Of all the ambitious projects of King Leopold II, this was perhaps the grandest. The palace occupies an area larger than St Peter's Basilica in Rome and was one of the most impressive 19th-century buildings in the world. It was built between 1866 and 1883 by architect Joseph Poelaert, who looked for inspiration in classical temples, but died during the midst of the building's construction in 1879. The Palais de Justice is still home to the city's law courts.

Did You Know?

The Palais de Justice occupies an area larger than St Peter's Basilica in Rome.

Palais de Charles de Lorraine

📍E6 🏠Place du Musée 1 🚌🚋92, 93 Ⓜ️Gare Centrale, Parc 🕐9am-5pm first Sat of the month 🌐kbr.be

Hidden behind this Neo-Classical façade are the few rooms that remain of the palace of Charles de Lorraine, Governor of Brussels during the mid-18th century. Few original features remain, as the palace was ransacked by marauding French troops in 1794. The bas-reliefs at the top of the stairway, symbolizing air, earth, fire and water, reflect Charles de Lorraine's interest in alchemy. Most spectacular of all the original features is the 28-point star set in the floor of the circular drawing room. Each of the points is made of a different Belgian marble taken from Charles de Lorraine's personal mineral collection.

The governor was a keen patron of the arts, and the young Mozart is believed to have performed here, though this is a matter of conjecture. Certainly, Charles de Lorraine would like it to have happened.

The Place du Petit Sablon garden, and *(inset)* a stained-glass window at Notre-Dame du Sablon ↑

35

Place du Petit Sablon

📍E7 🚌🚋92, 93, 94, 97
Ⓜ Gare Centrale, Louise, Parc

These pretty, formal gardens were laid out in 1890 and are a charming spot to stop for a rest. On top of the railings that enclose the gardens are numerous bronze statuettes by Art Nouveau artist Paul Hankar, each one representing a different medieval guild of the city. At the back of the gardens is a fountain built to commemorate Counts Egmont and Hornes, the martyrs who led a Dutch uprising against the tyrannical rule of the Spanish under Philip II, and were beheaded in the Grand Place *(p60)* in 1568. On either side of the fountain are 12 statues of 15th- and 16th-century figures, including Flemish artist Bernard van Orley and the Flemish map-maker Gerhard Mercator.

HIDDEN GEM
Jewish Museum of Belgium

A five-minute walk from Notre-Dame du Sablon, this museum displays religious artifacts that showcase Jewish tradition and teaching. It also highlights prominent members of Belgium's Jewish community.

36

Notre-Dame du Sablon

📍E7 🏛 Pl du Grand Sablon
🚌🚋92, 93, 94, 97 Ⓜ Gare Centrale, Louise, Parc
🕙10am–6pm Mon–Fri, 9am–6pm Sat, 9am–noon & 1:30–6pm Sun 🌐fond samiseglisesablon.be

Along with the Cathédrale Sts-Michel-et-Gudule *(p70)*, this is one of the best remaining examples of Brabantine Gothic architecture in Belgium.

A church was first erected here when the guild of crossbowmen was granted permission to build a chapel to Our Lady on this sandy hill. Legend has it that a young girl in Antwerp had a vision of the Virgin Mary who instructed her to take her statue to Brussels. The girl carried the statue of the Virgin to Brussels down the River Senne by boat and gave it to the crossbowmen's chapel, which became a place of pilgrimage. The statue was destroyed in 1565, but visitors can see two carvings depicting the young girl in a boat. Work to enlarge the church began around 1400 but was not completed until 1550.

The interior of the church features interconnecting side

chapels and a 17th-century pulpit. Of particular interest are the 11 magnificent stained-glass windows, 14 m (45 ft) high, which dominate the inside of the church and filter in light through the windows in colourful hues. Also worth a visit is the chapel of the Tour et Taxis family, whose mansion once stood near the Place du Petit Sablon. In 1517, the family had tapestries commissioned to commemorate the legend that led to the chapel becoming a place of pilgrimage. Some now hang in the Musée Art & Histoire in Parc du Cinquantenaire (p101), but others were stolen by the French Revolutionary army in the 1790s.

 37

Place du Grand Sablon

📍D7 🚊92, 93, 94, 97
Ⓜ Gare Centrale, Louise, Parc

Situated on the slope of the escarpment that divides Brussels in two, the Place du Grand Sablon is like a stepping stone between the upper and lower halves of the city. The name "sablon" derives from the French "sable" (sand) and the square is so-called because this old route down to the city centre once passed through an area of sandy marshes.

Today, the square, more of a triangle in shape, stretches from a 1751 fountain by Jacques Berge at its base uphill to the Gothic church of Notre-Dame du Sablon. The fountain was a gift from the Englishman Lord Bruce, out of gratitude for the hospitality shown to him in Brussels. The square is surrounded by elegant townhouses, some with Art Nouveau façades. This is a chic and busy part of Brussels, featuring up-market antiques dealers, trendy

restaurants and bars: a good place in which to soak up the atmosphere. Wittamer, at No. 6, is a well-known chocolate shop; at No. 12 is Wittamer's pâtisserie, which also has its own tearoom.

Every weekend the area near the church plays host to a lively, if rather expensive, antiques market.

_____

38

Musée des Instruments de Musique

📍E6 🏠 Rue Montagne de la Cour 2 🚊92, 93 Ⓜ Gare Centrale, Parc ⏰9:30am-5pm Tue-Fri, 10am-5pm Sat & Sun 📅1 Jan, 1 May, 1 & 11 Nov, 25 Dec 🌐mim.be

Once a department store, the building known as Old England is a striking showpiece of Art Nouveau architecture designed by architect Paul Saintenoy. The façade is made entirely of glass and wrought iron. There is a domed gazebo on the roof, and a turret to one side. The building is now home to the Musée des Instruments de Musique, known as the "mim", which moved from the Sablon in 2000. The museum's collection began in the 19th century when the state bought 80 ancient instruments from across the globe. It was doubled in 1876 when King Léopold II donated a gift of 97 Indian musical instruments presented to him by a maharajah. A museum displaying all of these artifacts opened in 1877, and by 1924 it featured 3,300 pieces and was recognized as a leader in its field.

Today, the collection contains more than 6,000

 ←

A side-blown trumpet in the Musée des Instruments de Musique

DRINK

La Porte Noire
Subterranean, brick-walled and dimly lit, this is an extremely atmospheric place for a drink – with a menu of 100 beers and 80 whiskies to choose from – and live music.

📍D6 🏠Rue des Alexiens 67 🌐laportenoire.be

Plumette
This is one of Brussels' finest cocktail bars. The menu includes classics (Negroni, Martini, Old Fashioned et al) alongside creative concoctions of absinthe, cachaça and vermouth.

📍D7/8 🏠Rue de l'Epée 26 🌐plumette-bar.com

The Green Man
Set in a 17th-century building, this cosy pub offers a drinks menu featuring some of the best cocktails in town.

📍D5 🏠Rue des Chapeliers 20 🌐thegreenmanbar.be

items and includes many fine examples of wind, string and keyboard instruments from medieval times to the present. Chief attractions include prototype instruments by Adolphe Sax, the Belgian inventor of the saxophone, mini violins favoured by street musicians and a violin maker's studio. A popular feature of the museum is a unique infrared headset system, which cleverly plays the music of each instrument as visitors get nearer.

A SHORT WALK
QUARTIER ROYAL

Distance 1.5 km (1 mile) **Time** 20 minutes
Nearest metro Trone, Porte de Namur

The Quartier Royal has traditionally been home to Brussels' nobility and rulers. Chosen because the air was purer on the hill than it was in the Lower Town, the area once known as Coudenberg Hill was occupied by the 15th-century Coudenberg Palace, home to the Dukes of Brabant and Habsburg rulers and governors. In 1731, the palace was destroyed by a fire and was rebuilt during the 18th and 19th centuries. Its new palaces and much of the park were designed in Neo-Classical style, chosen by Charles de Lorraine. Today, the royal quarter presents a peaceful elegance, with some of Europe's finest 18th-century buildings framing the tree-lined paths and fountains of Parc de Bruxelles.

↑ Stately façade of Église St-Jacques-sur-Coudenberg

*Many fine examples of Victorian and Art Nouveau architecture stand out along the 2-km- (1-mile-) long **Rue Royale**.*

RUE ROYALE

START ▶

0 metres 100
0 yards 100
N ↑

PLACE ROYALE

*In the centre of the **Place Royale** (p86) is a statue of Godefroi of Bouillon, a Brabant nobleman, who fought in the first Crusade and died in 1100.*

*One of Brussels' prettiest churches, **Église St-Jacques-sur-Coudenberg's** (p85) 18th-century façade was modelled exactly on a classical temple.*

***Place des Palais** divides Palais Royal and the park. In French, "Palais" refers to any large stately building, and does not necessarily have royal connotations.*

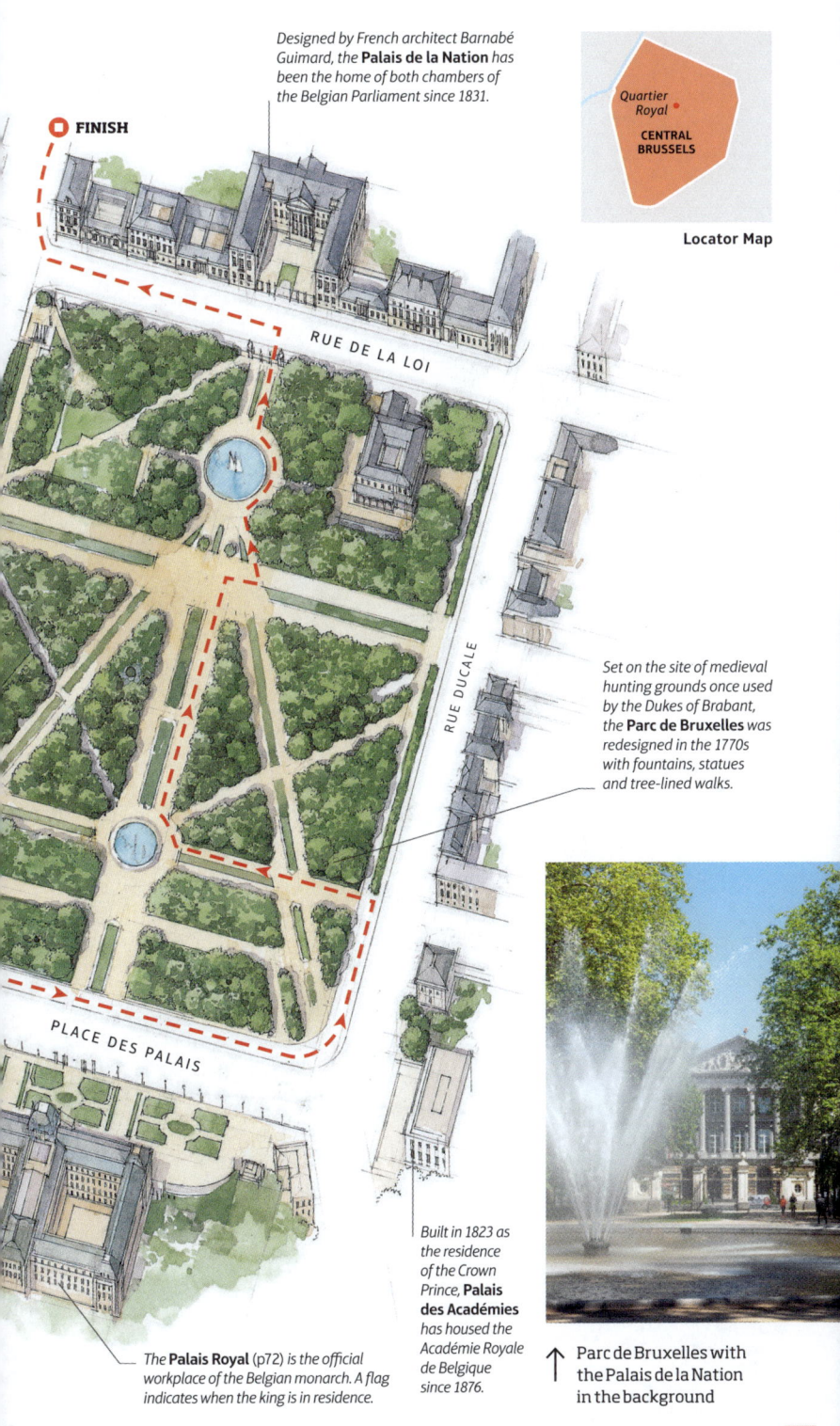

Designed by French architect Barnabé Guimard, the **Palais de la Nation** has been the home of both chambers of the Belgian Parliament since 1831.

FINISH

Quartier Royal

CENTRAL BRUSSELS

Locator Map

RUE DE LA LOI

RUE DUCALE

Set on the site of medieval hunting grounds once used by the Dukes of Brabant, the **Parc de Bruxelles** was redesigned in the 1770s with fountains, statues and tree-lined walks.

PLACE DES PALAIS

Built in 1823 as the residence of the Crown Prince, **Palais des Académies** has housed the Académie Royale de Belgique since 1876.

The **Palais Royal** (p72) is the official workplace of the Belgian monarch. A flag indicates when the king is in residence.

↑ Parc de Bruxelles with the Palais de la Nation in the background

A LONG WALK
AROUND THE HEART OF BRUSSELS

Distance 2 km (1 mile) **Stopping-off points** The area around Pl Ste-Catherine is known for its fish restaurants **Nearest metro** Gare Centrale

It is impossible to tire of the Grand Place, and there is nowhere better to start a walk that traces the history of the city. This route leads first to the island site where Brussels originated, and then follows the watery landscape of the old, walled city before the river and canals disappeared. Along the way, you'll pass numerous shopping galleries, popular restaurants and lovely historic squares.

Stop off around Quai au Bois à Brûler and Quai aux Briques for a fish lunch.

*The **Église St-Jean-Baptiste-au-Béguinage** (p87) stood at the heart of a béguinage in medieval times.*

RUE DU GRAND HOSPICE
GROOTGODSHUISSTRAAT

QUAI AU BOIS À BRÛLER

QUAI AUX BRIQUES

RUE DE LAEKEN

Église St-Jean-Baptiste-au-Béguinage

Ste-Cathérine St- Katelijne Ⓜ

*Leave the square by the Rue Pont de la Carpe and turn left at Rue Dansaert. Then, head to Place Ste-Catherine, with the **Église Ste-Catherine** (p87).*

Église Ste-Catherine

PLACE STE-CATHERINE

Tour Noire

RUE DE L'EVEQUE

*To the right of the church you'll see the **Tour Noire** (Black Tower), a rare remnant of the first ring of city walls built in the 13th century.*

VLAAMSE STEENWEG

R DE LA VIERGE NOIRE ZWARTE LIEVEVROUWSTR

R.DES HALLES HALLENSTR.

BLVD ANSPACH ANSPACHLAAN

RUE GRETRY

*Continue to the **Halles St-Géry** (p79), the old meat market on Place St-Géry. This square was an island until the mid-19th century, and the site of one of Brussels' earliest chapels.*

La Bourse

Halles St-Géry

Falstaff

Maison Dandoy

RUE DES PIERRES STEENSTRAAT

ⓘ

*Facing La Bourse on Rue Henri Maus is **Falstaff**, one of the few genuine Art Nouveau cafés in Brussels.*

*Leave the square on the Rue au Beurre (butter), an appropriate address for the **Maison Dandoy** at No. 31, famous for its traditional, buttery biscuits.*

← Relaxing near Place Ste-Catherine and the Jules Anspach fountain

Locator Map

*Next, make a beeline for the **Place de Brouckère** (p84). Opposite is the **Hôtel Métropole** (p84), one of the city's grandest hotels.*

The Neo-Classical façade of the Théâtre Royal de la Monnaie ↑

RUE DU CIRQUE CIRCUSSTRAAT

RUE VAN DER ELST STRAAT

BLVD. ADOLPHE MAX LAAN

RUE AUX CHOUX KOOLSTRAAT

PLACE DES MARTYRS MARTELAARS PLEIN

PLACE DE BROUCKÈRE

De Brouckère Ⓜ

RUE NEUVE NIEUWSTRAAT

R D'ARGENT ZILVERSTR

R DES BOITEUX KREUPELENSTR

RUE DU MARAIS BROEKSTRAAT

Hôtel Métropole

RUE DU FOSSE

AUX LOUPS WOLVENGRACHT

*Stop to shop at nearby Passage du Nord and Rue Neuve, before ending your walk at the Place de la Monnaie, the site of the fine **Théâtre Royal de la Monnaie** (p83).*

FINISH

BISSCHOPS STRAAT

Théâtre Royal de la Monnaie

| 0 metres | | 200 | N ↑ |
| 0 yards | | 200 | |

RUE DES FRIPIERS KLEERKOPERSSTR

GRETRY STRAAT

RUE DE L'ECUYER SCHILDKNAAPSSTRAAT

RUE LEOPOLD STRAAT

R D'ASSAUT STORMSTR

Théâtre Marionettes de Toone

Galeries Royales St-Hubert

RUE D'ARENBERG ARENBERGSTR

*On the opposite side of the road is the **Église St-Nicolas** (p81), while ahead lies the Neo-Classical façade of the Stock Exchange, **La Bourse** (p81).*

Église St-Nicolas

RUE DES BOUCHERS BEENHOUWER ST.R

START

Maison du Roi Broodhuis ℹ

RUE DE LA MONTAGNE BERGSTRAAT

GRAND PLACE

Hôtel de Ville Stadhuis

*Start with a quick wander around the **Grand Place** (p60) to savour its magnificent gilded architecture.*

Did You Know?

In the 1500s, the Tour Noire was a tavern called "In the Tower".

95

OUTER BRUSSELS

The region surrounding central Brussels was once a series of leafy local villages. St-Gilles was known for its cabbage cultivation, Anderlecht was a beacon of culture and Laeken was a quiet village – at least it was until Prince Albrecht and Duchess Maria Christina (governors of the Habsburg Netherlands) chose it as the site for their royal residence in 1782. Yet it was Belgian independence in the 1830s that changed the area dramatically. As Brussels became capital of a new Belgium, the city witnessed huge expansion, with separate towns and villages absorbed into its urban sprawl. To celebrate 50 years of Belgian independence, King Leopold II further expanded the city's boundaries by overseeing the construction of the Parc du Cinquantenaire in 1880. Around this time, the Horta Museum, home and workshop of Art Nouveau icon Victor Horta, was built in the southern suburb of St-Gilles. More significant developments in the area followed the crowning of the city as European capital, with the glass-fronted buildings of the European Quarter symbolizing the modern Brussels of today.

A   B   C

STROMBEEK-BEVER

④ Design Museum Brussels
⑥ Bruparck   ⑤ The Atomium

③ Domaine de Laeken

LAEKEN
LAKEN

JETTE

○ Musée René Magritte
René Magritte Museum

Schaerbeek 🚉 ○ Train World

GANSHOREN

SCHAERBEEK

② ㉑ Basilique Nationale
du Sacré-Coeur

○ Maison Autrique

BERCHEM-STE-AGATHE
ST-AGATHA-BERCHEM

🚉 Brussel-Noord

KOEKELBERG

CENTRAL
BRUSSEL

ST-JOSSE

ANDERLECHT

🚉 Brussel-Centraal

Anderlecht
⑳

See St-Josse map top right

🚉 Brussel-Zuid

Ixelles ⑮   IXELLES

OUTER BRUSSELS

Must Sees

① Parc and Palais du Cinquantenaire
② Horta Museum
③ Domaine de Laeken

Experience More

④ Design Museum Brussels
⑤ The Atomium
⑥ Bruparck
⑦ Le Botanique
⑧ Quartier Européen
⑨ Parc Léopold
⑩ Square Ambiorix
⑪ Parliament Quarter
⑫ Musée Wiertz
⑬ Institut Royal des Sciences Naturelles
⑭ Musée Charlier
⑮ Ixelles
⑯ St-Gilles
⑰ Avenue Louise
⑱ Forêt de Soignes
⑲ Uccle
⑳ Anderlecht
㉑ Basilique Nationale du Sacré-Coeur
㉒ Africa Museum
㉓ Musée du Tram

⑯ St-Gilles

⑰ Avenue
Louise

② Horta
Museum

Etterbeek 🚉

Hotel Hannon

○ Musée Meunier
Museum

Uccle ⑲

○ Musée van Buuren Museum

Bois de la
Cambre
Terkamerenbos

DIEWEG

C

St-Josse

Jardin Botanique
7 Le Botanique
Kruidtuin

M **Botanique Kruidtuin**
PLACE QUETELET

Brussels-Congrès
PLACE DES BARRICADES

PLACE DE LA LIBERTÉ

M **Madou**
PLACE MADOU PLEIN

Palais de la Nation
Paleis der Naties
14 **Musée Charlier**

M **Parc Park**
Parc de Bruxelles Warande

M **Arts-Loi Kunst-Wet**

Théâtre du Parc Parktheater

Palais Royal

Palais des Académies

M **Trone Troon**
DE MEEUS SQUARE

M **Porte de Namur Naamse Poorte**

MARIE-LOUIZA SQUARE

10 Square Ambiorix

Berlaymont

Maalbeek **M**

Schuman
M **Schuman**
ROND POINT R SCHUMAN PLEIN
8

Quartier Européen

RUE BELLIARD – BELLIARDSTRAAT

Station Brussel-Luxembourg
11 Parliament Quarter

9 Parc Léopold

Jubel Park

Musée Art & Histoire

TUNNEL BELLIARD – BELLIARDTUNNEL

Parc and Palais du Cinquantenaire
1

Museum van het Leger en de Krijgskunde

Konings Musea voor Kunst en Geschiedenis

PORTE DE TERVUREN TERVUURSEPOORT

PLACE WAPPERS PLEIN

PLACE DE JAMBLINNE DE MEUX PLEIN

Meiser 🚊

RUE DE LA CONSOLATION TROOSTSTRAAT

RUE ARTAN ARTANSTRAAT

AVENUE DAILLY DAILLYLAAN

AVENUE CHAZAL – CHAZALLAAN

AVENUE MILCAMPS – MILCAMPSLAAN

Musée Wiertz **12**

13 Institut Royal des Sciences Naturelles

0 metres 500
0 yards 500

N

DIEGEM

EVERE

N2

Brussels International Airport
6 km (4 miles) ✈

N226

R0

WEZEMBEEK OPPEM

Musée du Tram **23**

WOLUWE-ST-PIERRE

Africa Museum **22**

AUDERGHEM

N3

N3

🚊 **Watermael**

TRANSVAAL

Forêt de Soignes Zoniënwoud

WATERMAEL

Forêt de Soignes **18**

OVERIJSE

RD

E411

HOEILAART

0 kilometres 2
0 miles 2

N

PARC AND PALAIS DU CINQUANTENAIRE

EXPERIENCE Outer Brussels

📍K6 🏛Parc du Cinquantenaire 🚌🚊81 Ⓜ️Schuman, Mérode 🕐Park and museums: hours vary, check website 🌐gardens.brussels

Offering a welcome retreat from the buzz of the city, this vast park is a patchwork of pretty formal gardens and shady green spaces. The palace within the park is home to two beloved museums: the Musée Art & Histoire and Musée Royal de l'Armée et d'Histoire Militaire.

The most bombastic of Leopold II's grand projects, the Parc and Palais du Cinquantenaire were built for the Golden Jubilee celebrations of Belgian independence in 1880. The park was laid out on unused town marshes and the palace, at its entrance, comprised a triumphal arch and two large exhibition areas. Before being converted into museums, the large halls on either side of the central archway were venues for trade fairs. Both have also been used for horse races and to store homing pigeons. During World War II, the grounds of the park were converted for vegetable growing to feed the people of Brussels, but today city folk stroll the extensive parkland, with the more diligent visiting a museum or two.

↑ The Central Archway at the entrance, crowned with bronze sculptures

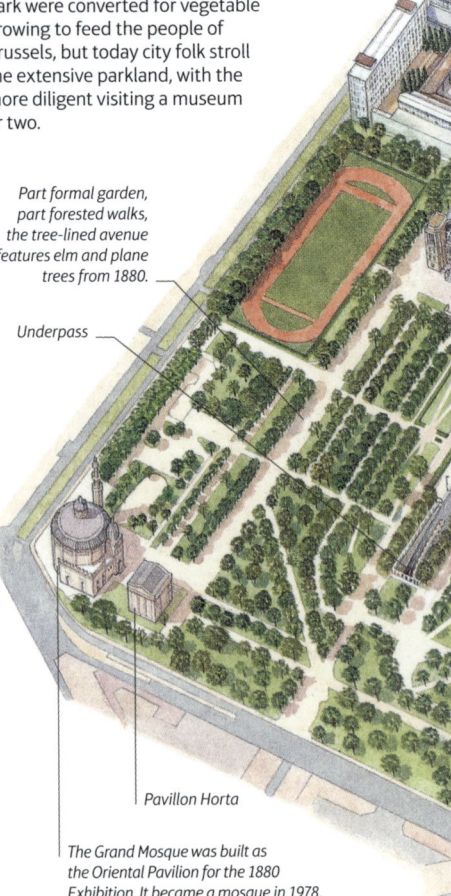

Part formal garden, part forested walks, the tree-lined avenue features elm and plane trees from 1880.

Underpass

Pavillon Horta

The Grand Mosque was built as the Oriental Pavilion for the 1880 Exhibition. It became a mosque in 1978.

Fighter planes on display at the Musée Royal de l'Armée et d'Histoire Militaire

①

Musée Art & Histoire

⌂ Parc du Cinquantenaire 10 ☎ (02) 741 7331 ⏰ 9:30am–5pm Tue–Sun (from 10am Sat, Sun & public hols) ✖ 1 Jan, 1 May, 1 & 11 Nov, 25 Dec

This sprawling museum features four main collections. Highlights of the Antiquities department include Roman mosaics from Apamea (in modern-day Syria), excavated by Belgian archaeologists in the 1930s, and the *Lady of Brussels*, the name given to an Egyptian stone statue almost 5,000 years old. The National Archaeology section covers items discovered in Belgium from the Gallo-Roman period to the Merovingians, while Non-European Civilizations covers Byzantium and Islam, China, Southeast Asia, India and the pre-Columbian Americas.

The final collection, European Decorative Arts, has a fine set of galleries devoted to arts from the Middle Ages to the Baroque period. The collection of objets d'art from the Art Nouveau period is notable, with work by Philippe Wolfers and Charles van der Stappen and Victor Horta.

②

Musée Royal de l'Armée et d'Histoire Militaire

⌂ Parc du Cinquantenaire 3 ⏰ 9am–5pm Tue–Sun ✖ 1 Jan, 1 May, 1 Nov, 25 Dec 🌐 klm-mra.be

Along with a section on aviation, displays in this museum cover the Belgian Army and its history from the late 1700s to today, including weapons, uniforms, decorations and paintings. There is a section covering the 1830 struggle for independence (p51). Two other sections show both World Wars, including the activities of the Resistance.

The Central Archway was based on the Arc de Triomphe in Paris.

In the south wing, Autoworld is one of the best collections of automobiles in the world.

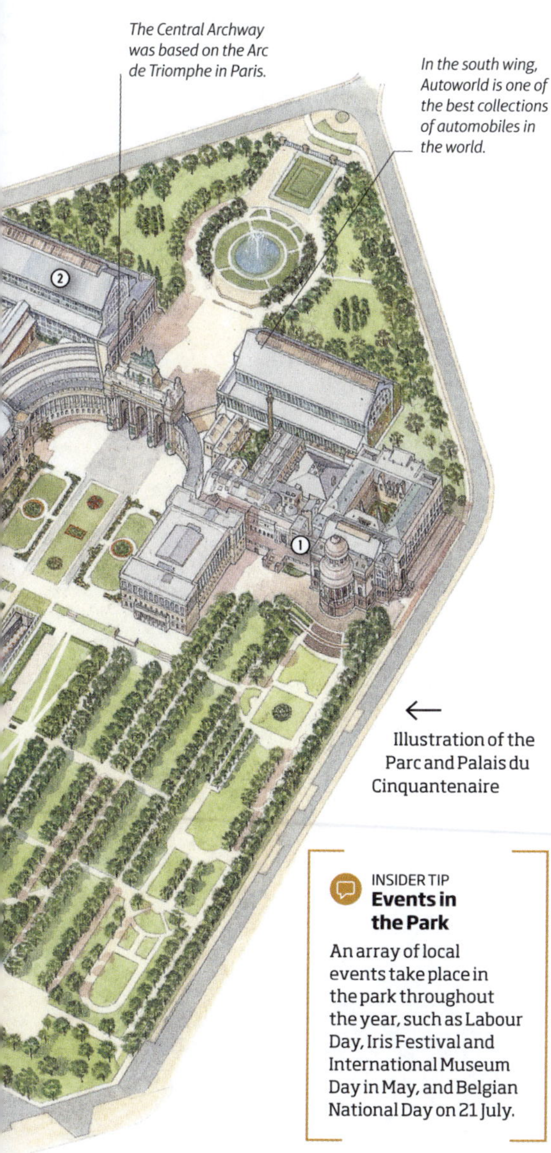

← Illustration of the Parc and Palais du Cinquantenaire

💬 INSIDER TIP
Events in the Park

An array of local events take place in the park throughout the year, such as Labour Day, Iris Festival and International Museum Day in May, and Belgian National Day on 21 July.

EXPERIENCE Outer Brussels

2 🅰️ Ⓜ️

HORTA MUSEUM

🏠 Rue Américaine 25 🚌🚊 51, 81, 92, 93, 94, 97
Ⓜ️ Louise 🕐 2–5:30pm Tue–Fri (from 11am Sat & Sun)
🚫 Public hols 🌐 hortamuseum.be

The beautiful home of Victor Horta, a leading figure of the Art Nouveau movement, is a treat for art and design lovers.

Architect Victor Horta (1861–1947) is considered by many to be the key figure of Art Nouveau style, and his impact on Brussels, architecture is unrivalled by any other designer of his time. A museum dedicated to his unique style is housed in his restored family home, built to his design between 1898 and 1901. His skill lay not only in his grand, overall vision but also in his talent as an interior designer, blending themes and materials into each detail. The airy interior displays trademarks of the architect's style – iron, glass and curves – in every detail, while retaining a functional approach. Sinuous staircases, elegant wall decorations and shimmering stained glass come together to create this masterpiece of Belgian design. Note that photography is banned inside.

↑ The Horta Museum's elegant exterior

← The stairwell's glass ceiling, bringing light into the house

↓ The living room, with its vaulted ceiling and sculpted bannisters

VICTOR HORTA

Born to a shoemaker in Ghent in 1861, Victor Horta initially studied music, before being expelled from the Royal Conservatory and switching to visual art. He eventually moved to Brussels, studied architecture and developed the Art Nouveau style with the building of several beautiful townhouses in the 1890s, starting with Hôtel Tassel (p113).

Sinuous staircases, elegant wall decorations and stained glass come together to create this masterpiece of Belgian design.

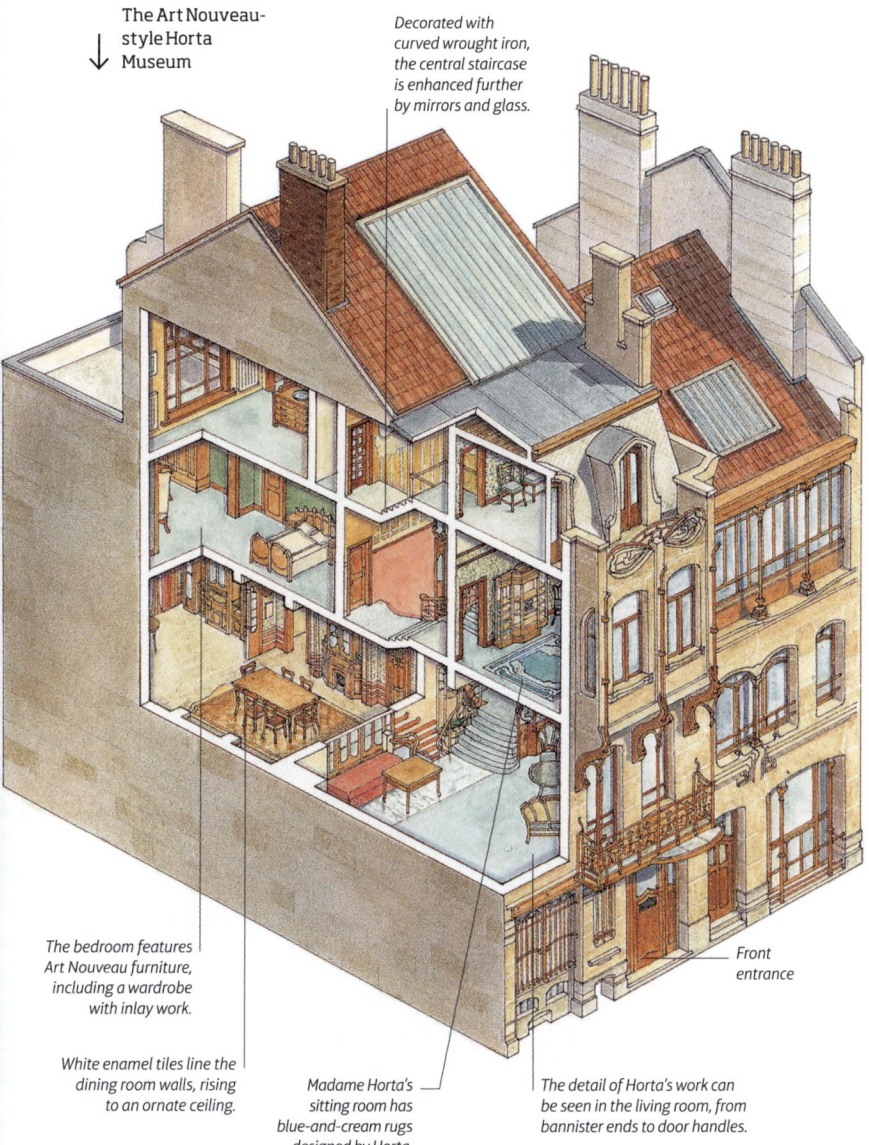

The Art Nouveau-style Horta Museum
↓

Decorated with curved wrought iron, the central staircase is enhanced further by mirrors and glass.

The bedroom features Art Nouveau furniture, including a wardrobe with inlay work.

White enamel tiles line the dining room walls, rising to an ornate ceiling.

Madame Horta's sitting room has blue-and-cream rugs designed by Horta.

The detail of Horta's work can be seen in the living room, from bannister ends to door handles.

Front entrance

DOMAINE DE LAEKEN

🏛 Laeken 🚊 3, 7, 19, 51, 62, 93 Ⓜ Heysel, Bockstael
ℹ Serres Royales: Ave de Prince Royal, open mid-Apr–mid-May, www.monarchie.be; Pavillon Chinois & Tour Japonais: Ave J van Praet 44, temporarily closed until further notice; Église Notre-Dame de Laeken: Parvis Notre-Dame, (02) 479 2362, open 2–5pm Tue–Sun

Leafy glasshouses, cultural pavilions, grassy plains: this lovely park has it all. While much of it is owned by the royal family, there's plenty of space for the public to explore.

In the 11th century, Laeken was known among pilgrims after reported sightings of the Virgin Mary. Since the 19th century, it has been firmly associated with the nation's monarchy. A walk around the sedate and peaceful area reveals impressive buildings constructed in honour of the royal location, not least the sovereign's official residence and its beautifully landscaped parkland.

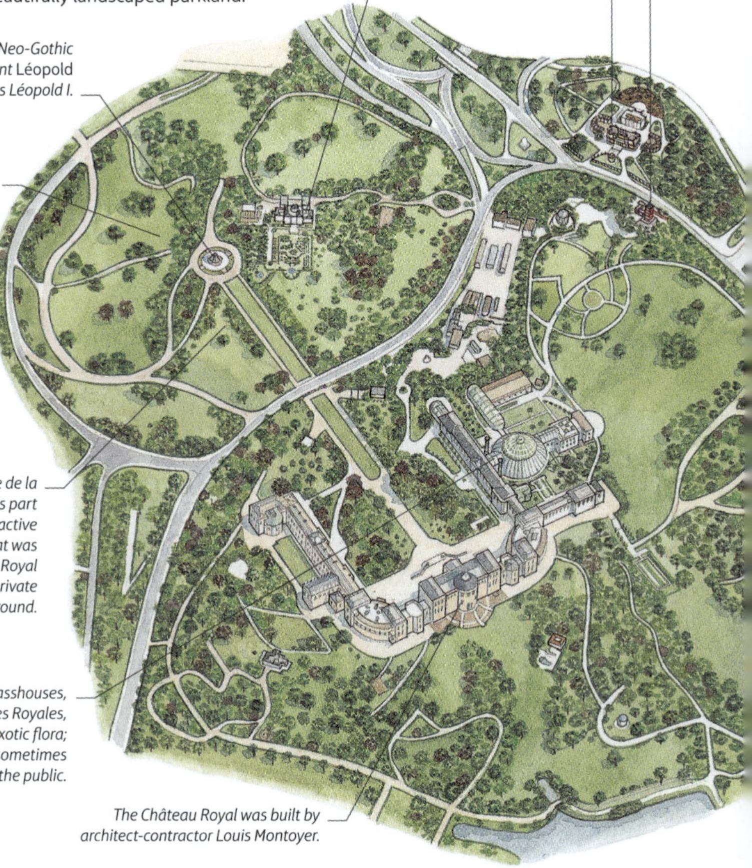

Tour Japonais

Architect Alexandre Marcel designed the elaborate Pavillon Chinois as part of Leopold II's grand vision.

Villa Belvedere is home to King Albert II and Queen Paola.

The Neo-Gothic Monument Léopold honours Léopold I.

Parc Royal

Place de la Dynastie is part of the attractive park that was once the Royal Family's private hunting ground.

The glasshouses, Serres Royales, feature exotic flora; they are sometimes open to the public.

The Château Royal was built by architect-contractor Louis Montoyer.

EXPERIENCE Outer Brussels

The dome of the Serres Royales surrounded by flowering trees

Did You Know?

There's a replica of the Château Royal in the Democratic Republic of the Congo.

The lush woodland in Domaine de Laeken features magnolias and blooming hawthorns.

Illustration of the Domaine de Laeken

EXPERIENCE MORE

④

Design Museum Brussels

⌂ Belgiëplein 1
🕐 11am–7pm daily
ⓦ designmuseum.brussels

The eye-catching Design Museum opened in 2015 next door to the Atomium. It is housed in a beautiful sleek glass building accessed by a colourful set of stairs which open wide like a crocodile's jaws. The museum exhibits fascinating works of design across a range of disciplines from the 20th and 21st centuries. The Plastic Design Collection focuses on the role of plastic from the 1960s until the present, including pieces by Ettore Sottsass and Perry King's iconic Olivetti Valentine typewriter. The Belgisch Design Belge exhibit includes classic Belgian pieces like a famous armchair by designer Alfred Hendrickx. Temporary exhibits focus on more specific themes and individual artists.

The giant structure of the Atomium towering over the city ↓

⑤

The Atomium

⌂ Square de l'Atomium 🚌
🚋 3, 7, 19, 51, 93 Ⓜ Heysel
🕐 10am–6pm daily
ⓦ atomium.be

Built for the 1958 World's Fair, the Atomium is probably the most identifiable symbol of Brussels. At the end of the 1950s, the world moved into a new age of science and space travel, which is reflected in the structure's design of an iron crystal, magnified 165 billion times by Belgian engineer André Waterkeyn. Each of the nine spheres that make up the "atom" are 18 m (60 ft) in diameter, and linked by escalators and stairs. They include exhibition rooms and a smart restaurant at the top of the structure.

 GREAT VIEW
Atomium Panorama

For the finest views over Brussels, ascend to the upper sphere of the Atomium to find the Panorama, a viewing deck with telescopes and a 360-degree view.

Sunset over the glasshouses of Domaine de Laeken

DRINK

Brasserie du Primerose

This friendly bar and restaurant with views of Parc de Laeken and the Planetarium offers refreshing drinks and bistro bites.

📍B1 🏠Ave du Gros Tilleul 41 📞(02) 717 3817

L'Aquarelle

On the western edge of the Parc de Laeken, this is a cosy spot for a beer; burgers, sandwiches and salads are also available.

📍B1 🏠Ave Houba de Strooper 73 🅦barapates.be

À La Morte Subite

Among the oldest café-bars in town, this atmospheric place has played host to Belgian legends such as Jacques Brel.

📍B3 🏠Rue Montagne aux Herbes Potagères 7 🅦alamortsubite.com

 6

Bruparck

📍B1 🏠Blvd du Centenaire 🚋3, 7, 19, 51, 93 Ⓜ️Heysel 🕐Mar–Sep: 9:30am–6pm daily (Jul–Aug: to 8pm); Oct–mid-Jan: 10am–6pm daily 🕐End Jan–Feb 🅦bruparck.com

Although nowhere near as large or as grand as many of the world's theme parks, Bruparck's sights and facilities are a popular family destination. The favourite port of call for most visitors is **Mini-Europe**, where more than 300 miniature reconstructions take you around the landscapes of the European Union. Built at a scale of 1:25, the collection displays buildings of social or cultural importance, such as the Acropolis in Athens, the Brandenburg Gate of Berlin and the Houses of Parliament from London. Even at this scale, the detail is such that it can be second only to visiting the sights themselves.

For film fans, **Kinepolis** is unmissable. Large auditoriums show a wide range of popular films from different countries on 24 screens. The IMAX cinema features surround sound and a semicircular 600 sq m (6,456 sq ft) widescreen.

Mini-Europe
 📞(02) 474 1313 🅦minieurope.com

Kinepolis
📞(02) 474 2600 🅦kinepolis.be

7

Le Botanique

📍F2 🏠Rue Royale 236 🚋92, 93 Ⓜ️Botanique 🕐11am–7pm daily (to 10pm on concert nights) 🅦botanique.be

In 1797, a botanical garden was created in the grounds of the Palais de Lorraine as a source of reference for botany students. The garden closed in 1826 and new gardens were relocated to Meise, 13 km (9 miles) from Brussels, but here at Le Botanique, a grand glass and iron rotunda was designed at the centre of the gardens by the French architect Gineste. This iron glasshouse still stands, as does much of the 19th-century statuary by Constantin Meunier, including depictions of the Four Seasons. The glasshouse is now home to the French Community Cultural Centre and offers concerts and contemporary art exhibitions.

→ The 19th-century glasshouse at the centre of Le Botanique

8

Quartier Européen

◎ J7 🚇 M Maelbeek, Schuman

The area at the top of the Rue de la Loi and around the Schuman roundabout is where the main buildings of the European Union's administration can be found.

The most recognizable of all the EU seats is the cross-shaped Berlaymont building, a gigantic Modernist structure which is sometimes, rather unflatteringly, referred to as the "Berlaymonster". This is the headquarters of the European Commission, whose workers are, in effect, civil servants of the EU. The Council of Ministers, which comprises representatives of member-states' governments, now meets in the sprawling pink granite block across the road from the Berlaymont. This building is known as Justus Lipsius, after a Flemish philosopher.

Further down the road from the Justus Lipsius building is the Résidence Palace, a luxury 1920s housing complex that features a theatre, an Art Deco pool and a roof garden, as well as several floors of private flats. It now houses the International Press Centre.

→
Ornate façade of the Art Nouveau house No. 11 at Square Ambiorix

Only the theatre is open to the public, though EU officials have access to the pool.

This whole area is naturally full of hustle and bustle during the day, but visitors will find it much quieter in the evenings and it can feel almost deserted at weekends. What is pleasant at any time, though, is the proximity of a number of the city's wonderful green spaces, which include Parc du Cinquantenaire *(p100)*, Parc Léopold and the verdant Square Ambiorix.

9

Parc Léopold

◎ J7 🚇 Rue Belliard 🚇 M Maelbeek, Schuman

Parc Léopold is a public park that occupies part of the grounds of an old estate. At the end of the 19th century, scientist and industrialist Ernest Solvay put forward the idea of a science park. Solvay was given the Parc Léopold, the site of a zoo since 1847, and set up five university centres here. Leading figures including Marie Curie and Albert Einstein met here to discuss the latest scientific developments. The park is still home to many science institutes, as well as a haven of peace in the heart of this busy political area. A walk around the pond follows the old path of the Maelbeek River.

10

Square Ambiorix

◎ K5 🚇 M Schuman

Close to the EU district, but totally different in style and spirit, lies the beautiful Square Ambiorix. Together with the Avenue Palmerston and the Square Marie-Louise below, this marshland was transformed in the 1870s into one of the loveliest residential parts of Brussels, with a large central area of gardens, ponds and fountains.

The elegant houses have made this one of the truly sought-after suburbs in Brussels. The most spectacular Art Nouveau example is at No. 11. Known as the Maison St Cyr, after the painter whose home it once was, this wonderfully ornate house, with its curved wrought-iron balustrades and balconies, is a fine architectural feat considering that the man who designed it, Gustave Strauven, was only 22 years old when it was built at the turn of the 20th century.

Did You Know?

The pond in Square Marie-Louise, next to Square Ambiorix, is home to a population of Florida tortoises.

11

Parliament Quarter

📍 H8 🚇Ⓜ Maelbeek, Schuman

The vast, modern, steel-and-glass complex, situated just behind Quartier Léopold train station, is one of three homes of the European Parliament, the elected body of the European Union. Its permanent seat is in Strasbourg, France, where the plenary sessions are held once a month. The administrative centre is in Luxembourg and the committee meetings are held in Brussels.

This gleaming state-of-the-art building has many admirers, not least the parliamentary workers and MEPs themselves. But it is not without its critics: the huge domed structure housing the hemicycle that seats the 700-plus MEPs has been dubbed the *"caprice des dieux"* ("whim of the gods"), which refers both to the shape of the building – similar to a French cheese of the same name – and to its lofty aspirations. Many people also regret that, to make room for the new complex, a large part

Massive oil paintings displayed at the Musée Wiertz ↑

of Quartier Léopold has been lost, though there are still plenty of lively bars and restaurants on Place Luxembourg, in front of the parliament. When the MEPs are absent, the building is often used for meetings of European Union committees.

Parlamentarium, the visitor centre of the European Parliament, offers an interactive and impressively high-tech introduction to this often misunderstood institution. There is a space-age 360-degree digital surround screen, a Tunnel of Voices in which the multitude of EU languages can be heard, and a touch-screen feature that allows visitors to meet the MEPs who shape European laws. The Luna Game scavenger hunt – with a prize at the end – is designed to keep younger children entertained.

As this is an important government building, it is a good idea to carry your photo ID when visiting so as to ensure access. Visitors should also expect airport-style security checks on entry.

Parlamentarium

👥♿ 🏠 Rue Wiertz 60 🕐 1–6pm Mon, 9am–6pm Tue–Fri, 10am–6pm Sat & Sun 🌐 visiting.europarl. europa.eu

---

12

Musée Wiertz

📍 H8 🏠 Rue Vautier 62 🚇Ⓜ Maelbeek, Schuman, Trone 🕐 10am–noon & 12:45–5pm Tue–Fri 🔒 Public hols 🌐 fine-arts-museum.be

Musée Wiertz houses some 160 works, including oil paintings, drawings and sculptures, which form the main body of Antoine Wiertz's (1806–65) artistic work. The collection fills the studio built for Wiertz by the Belgian state, where he lived and worked from 1850 until his death in 1865, when the studio became a museum.

The huge main room contains Wiertz's largest paintings, many depicting

↑ Exterior of the Parlamentarium, in Brussels

> The huge domed structure of the European Union's headquarters, housing the hemicycle that seats the 700-plus MEPs, has been dubbed the *"caprice des dieux"* ("whim of the gods").

biblical and Homeric scenes, some in the style of Rubens. Also on display are sculptures and his death mask. The last of the six rooms contains his more gruesome efforts, notable among which is one entitled *Madness, Hunger and Crime*.

13

Institut Royal des Sciences Naturelles

📍J8 🏠Rue Vautier 29 Ⓜ️Maelbeek, Schuman, Trône 🕐9:30am–5pm Tue–Fri, 10am–6pm Sat, Sun & school hols 🚫1 Jan, 1 May, 25 Dec 🌐natural sciences.be

The Institut Royal des Sciences Naturelles is one of the most important scientific establishments in Belgium. Its Museum of Natural Sciences is best known for its impressive

→ Olorotitan skull on display at the Institut Royal des Sciences Naturelles

collection of iguanadon skeletons dating back 250 million years. The museum also contains interactive and educational displays covering all eras of natural history.

14

Musée Charlier

📍G4 🏠Ave des Arts 16 Ⓜ️Madou, Arts-Loi 🕐Noon–5pm Mon–Thu, 10am–1pm Fri (guided tours in French & Dutch only) 🚫Public hols 🌐charliermuseum.be

This museum was once the home of Henri van Cutsem, a wealthy collector and patron of the arts. In 1890, he asked the architect Victor Horta to redesign his house as an exhibition space for his extensive collections. When Van Cutsem died in 1904, his heir, the sculptor Charlier, cared for the house and the collections. On Charlier's death in 1925, the house and contents were left to the city.

The Musée Charlier opened in 1928. It contains paintings by a number of different artists, including portraits by Antoine Wiertz, landscapes by Hippolyte Boulenger and Guillaume Vogels, and impressionistic still lifes by James Ensor and Anna Boch. The collection also includes sculptures by Charlier and Rik Wouters. Of special note is the collection of tapestries, some from the Paris studios of Aubusson, on the staircases and the first floor; also the extensive displays of Louis XV- and Louis XVI-style furniture on the first floor of the museum.

Kitchen 151
This homely Mediterranean restaurant has a menu featuring the best of Israeli, Moroccan and Middle Eastern cuisine.

📍C3 🏠Chau de Wavre 145 🌐kitchen.onefive one.be

€€€

Positano
Set in a handsome townhouse, this Italian restaurant offers good pizzas, bruschettas and a large rotating menu of delicious mains, such as Lombard escalopes and scampi linguine.

📍C3 🏠Rue de Pascale 20 📞(02) 280 0682

€€€

Atrio
Finnish-Italian fusion is the mission statement of this acclaimed restaurant. Try the smoked reindeer, wild mushroom and lingonberry risotto.

📍E2 🏠Rue Stevin 132 🌐atriorestaurant.com

€€€

Uncle Richard's Ixelles
Top-end hamburgers are the order of the day here, made with high-quality beef (chicken and veggie falafel versions are also available) and served with your choice of toppings, including cheese, lettuce, pickles and other sundries.

📍D3 🏠Pl de Londres 10 📞(02) 466 0366

€€€

15

Ixelles

C3 🏠 **3 km (1.8 miles) from the centre** 🚌🚋 **7, 25, 81, 93, 94** Ⓜ**Porte de Namur**

Although one of Brussels' largest suburbs and a busy transport hub, the heart of Ixelles remains a peaceful oasis of lakes and woodland.

The idyllic **Abbaye de la Cambre** was founded in 1201, achieving fame in 1242, when St Boniface chose the site for his retirement. The abbey then endured a troubled history in the wars of religion during the 16th and 17th centuries. It finally closed as an operational abbey in 1796 and now houses a school of architecture. The pretty Gothic church can be toured and its grounds are great for a walk. South of the abbey, the Bois de la Cambre, created in 1860, remains one of the city's most popular public parks. Its lakes, bridges and lush grass make it a favoured picnic spot.

Nearby, the **Musée d'Ixelles** has a fine collection of posters by 19th- and 20th-century greats, such as Toulouse Lautrec and Magritte, as well as sculptures by Rodin. The former home of one of Belgium's finest sculptors is now **Musée Constantin Meunier**, with 290 sculptures and paintings by the artist, plus his studio preserved in its turn-of-the-century style.

Did You Know?

Renowned British actress Audrey Hepburn was born in Ixelles in 1929.

Abbaye de la Cambre

📍 Ave Emile Duray
🕐 Grounds: 6am–6pm daily
🚫 Public hols

Musée d'Ixelles

🎨 📍 Rue J Van Volsem 71
📞 (02) 515 6421
🚫 Temporarily until 2025

Musée Constantin Meunier

📍 Rue de l'Abbaye 59
🕐 10am–noon & 12:45–5pm
Tue–Fri 🚫 Public hols
🌐 fine-arts-museum.be

16

St-Gilles

C4 🏠 **3.5 km (2 miles) from the centre** 🚌🚋 **3, 4, 51, 81** Ⓜ**Porte de Hal, Parvis St-Gilles**

Named after the patron saint of this district's main church, St-Gilles is traditionally one of Brussels' impoverished areas. However, amid the low-quality functional housing are architectural remnants which make the suburb well worth a visit. Art Nouveau delights can be found in streets such as Avenue Jean Volders and Rue Vanderschrick. The **Hôtel Hannon** (1902) remains one of the city's most spectacular Art Nouveau structures. Restored in 1985, it has a stained-glass window and ornate statuary that take this architectural style to its peak. Art Nouveau details can be seen in the nearby streets, particularly in Rue Felix Delhasse and in the nearby Rue Africaine.

One of the most striking features of St-Gilles is the **Porte de Hal**. Brussels' second set of town walls, built in the 14th century, originally included seven gateways, of which Porte de Hal is the only survivor. Used as a prison from the 16th to 18th centuries, it was restored in 1870. Today, it houses a small museum dedicated to medieval and Renaissance

↓ Abbaye de la Cambre with its terraced gardens, Ixelles

Brussels, and is part of the fascinating Musée Art & Histoire (p101).

Hôtel Hannon

Ave de la Jonction
M Albert

Porte de Hal

Blvd du Midi 3, 4, 51 M Porte de Hal 9:30am–5pm Mon–Thu, 10am–5pm Sat & Sun hallegate museum.be

---

 17

Avenue Louise

C4 81, 92, 93, 94, 97 M Louise

Most visitors to Brussels travelling by car will come across this busy thoroughfare, its various underpasses built in the 1950s and 1960s to link the city centre with its suburbs. In fact, the avenue was constructed in 1864 to join the centre with the suburb of Ixelles. The north end of the avenue retains a chic atmosphere; by the Porte de Namur, fans of designer labels can indulge themselves in Gucci and Versace, as well as investigating the less expensive but no less chic boutiques.

The avenue also has many architectural treasures. The Hôtel Solvay at No. 224 was built by Victor Horta in 1894 for the industrialist Solvay family. Its ornate doorway, columns and balconies are a fine example of Art Nouveau style (p28). The house is a

PICTURE PERFECT
Hôtel Tassel

Also on Avenue Louise, this hotel has an interior designed by Victor Horta (p103). Its mosaic floor is adorned with his characteristic "whip-lash" motif, while a staircase curves stylishly upstairs.

↑ Forêt de Soignes swathed in autumnal colours

private home, but guided tours can be arranged (www.hotelsolvay.be). At No. 346, Hôtel Max Hallet is one of Horta's masterpieces, built in 1903. Continuing south leads to fashionable Ixelles.

18

Forêt de Soignes

E5 11 km (7 miles) from the centre M Hermann Debroux Guided walks: 10am Thu & Sun (not in English); check website for recommended walking routes in English sonianforest.be

The large forested area southeast of Brussels city centre is popular among visitors for walking and cycling. It has a long history: thought to have had prehistoric beginnings,

it was here that the Gallic citizens suffered their defeat by the Romans (p49). However, the forest really gained renown in the 12th century when wild boar roamed the landscape and local dukes enjoyed hunting trips in the woodland.

The density of the landscape has provided tranquillity over the ages. In the 14th and 15th centuries it became a favoured location for monasteries and abbeys. Few have survived, but Abbaye de Rouge-Cloître is a rare example from this era.

In a former 18th-century priory is the **Groenendaal Arboretum**, in which more than 400 forest plants are housed, many extinct elsewhere.

Groenendaal Arboretum

Duboislaan 6 1–5pm Wed–Sun natuurenbos.be

⑲ Uccle

◉C4 **⌂7 km (4 miles) from the centre** 🚋3, 7

This smart residential district, dotted with tree-lined avenues, is home to the **Musée David et Alice van Buuren**. The 1920s residence of Dutch couple David and Alice van Buuren is now a small museum, displaying their eclectic acquisitions. Amid the Dutch Delftware and French Lalique lamps are great finds, such as original sketches by Van Gogh. Visitors will also enjoy the modern landscaped gardens here.

Musée David et Alice van Buuren

⊘ ⌂Ave Léo Errera 41
🕐2–5:30pm Wed-Mon
📅1 Jan, 25 Dec ⓦmuseum vanbuuren.be

⑳ Anderlecht

◉B3 **⌂6 km (3.5 miles) from the centre** 🚋81 Ⓜ Bizet, Clemenceau, St-Guidon

Considered to be Brussels' first genuine suburb

(archaeological digs have uncovered remnants of Roman housing), Anderlecht is now best known as an industrial area, and for its meat market and successful football club, named for the area. Fans of street art should look out for the bright, cartoon-like murals on Rue Porcelaine, inspired by Joan Miró.

Although only a few pockets of the suburb are now residential, during the 15th century this was a popular place to live and some houses remain from that era. **Maison d'Erasme**, built in 1468, is now named after the great scholar and religious reformer, Erasmus (1466–1536), who lived here for five months in 1521, one of the most well-regarded thinkers of his generation. The house was restored in the 1930s, and is now a museum dedicated to him. It displays a collection of 16th-century furniture and portraits of Erasmus by Holbein and van der Weyden.

Nearby is the huge edifice of **Église Sts-Pierre-et-Guidon**. This 14th-century Gothic church, completed with the addition of a tower in 1517, is notable for its sheer size and exterior gables, typical of Brabantine architecture. The life of St Guidon, patron saint of peasants, is depicted on interior wall murals.

Illustrating a more recent history, the **Musée Gueuze** is a family brewery that has opened its doors to the public to witness the production of *gueuze*, a type of Belgian beer.

Maison d'Erasme

⊘ ⌂Rue du Chapitre 31
🕐10am–6pm Tue-Sun
📅1 Jan, 25 Dec ⓦeras mushouse.museum

→ The stunning façade of the Basilique Nationale du Sacré-Coeur in Koekelberg, and *(inset)* its interior

Église Sts-Pierre-et-Guidon

📍 Pl de la Vaillance
🕐 2–5pm Mon–Fri

Musée Gueuze

♿ 📍 Rue Gheude 56
🕐 10am–5pm Mon, Tue, Thu & Fri (to 4pm Sat)
🚫 Public hols 🌐 cantillon.be

㉑

Basilique Nationale du Sacré-Coeur

📍 B2 📍 Parvis de la Basilique 1, Koekelberg
🚎 19 Ⓜ Simonis
🕐 Summer: 9am–5pm daily; winter: 10am–4pm daily (by appt) 🌐 basilica koekelberg.be

Although a small and popular suburb among Brussels' residents, there is little for the visitor to see in Koekelberg other than the striking Basilique Nationale du Sacré-Coeur, but this does make the journey worthwhile for those interested in Art Deco architecture.

King Léopold II was keen to build a church in the city which could accommodate

vast congregations to reflect the burgeoning population of early 20th-century Brussels. He commissioned the church in 1904, but the building was not finished until 1970. Originally designed by Pierre Langerock, the final construction, which uses sandstone and terracotta, was a less expensive adaptation by Albert van Huffel. Very much a 20th-century church, in contrast to the many medieval religious buildings in the city centre, it is dedicated to those who died for Belgium, in particular the thousands of Belgian soldiers who were killed in battles fought on their own soil during the two World Wars.

The most dominating feature of the church is the vast green copper dome, rising 90 m (295 ft) above ground. For those who do not manage to visit the church itself, it is this central dome that is visible from many points in the city, including the Palais de Justice.

㉒

Africa Museum

📍 F3 📍 Leuvensesteenweg 13, Tervuren
🚎 44 🕐 10am–5pm Tue–Fri, 10am–6pm Sat & Sun
🌐 africamuseum.be

Presented with the vast River Congo basin by the European Powers in 1885, King Leopold II of Belgium became one of the world's richest men through the ruthless exploitation of its people and resources. To celebrate his colonial "achievements", the king built himself a large museum here in Brussels and this has now evolved into the Africa Museum, whose various displays now attempt to be honest about this dire episode in Belgian history. The museum has an extensive collection of all things Congolese, from ceremonial

↑ Statues on display in the fascinating Africa Museum

dresses and masks, dugout canoes, pagan idols and weapons through to stuffed wildlife.

㉓

Musée du Tram

📍 D3 📍 Ave de Tervuren 364b 🚎 39, 44, 94
🕐 Hours vary, check website 🌐 trammuseum. brussels

This museum traces the history of public transport in Belgium, with marvellous displays of heritage machinery. Horse-drawn trams are available to transport visitors round the site, which features fully working early versions of the electric tram, local buses and plenty of interactive exhibits ideal for families.

💬 INSIDER TIP
Thursday Market

Every Thursday a market pops up near Woluwe Park, opposite the Musée du Tram. There's always a lively atmosphere, with pop-up bars and food trucks – try the tasty *flammekueche* (flatbreads).

BRUGES

Bruges received its city charter in 1128; a few decades later its oldest surviving building was constructed, the Heilig Bloed Basiliek (Basilica of the Holy Blood), which opened in 1157. Perhaps the most significant moment in the city's history, however, was the formation of the Zwin inlet. Following the destructive storm of 1134, the coastline just north of Bruges was obliterated, turning the city into a port. This opened Bruges up to trade (particularly in textiles) and propelled the city to prominence – the Hanseatic League of merchant guilds nominated Bruges as one of its most important outposts. The city grew increasingly wealthy and in the 13th century the world's first stock exchange, the Bourse, opened. Bruges's prosperity made it a sanctuary for the arts, too, with painters such as Jan van Eyck and Hans Memling turning the city into a hub of culture in the 15th century.

Yet the city's significance dwindled as quickly as it had risen when the Zwin inlet silted up, cutting Bruges off from maritime trade. The rise of the city's high-quality lace industry in the 16th century provided a lifeline for Bruges's international stature, but its real salvation came in the late 18th century, when its wealth of well-preserved buildings and artworks made it one of the world's first tourist destinations, drawing aristocratic visitors from Britain and France. The city remains a significant tourism hub for Belgium today.

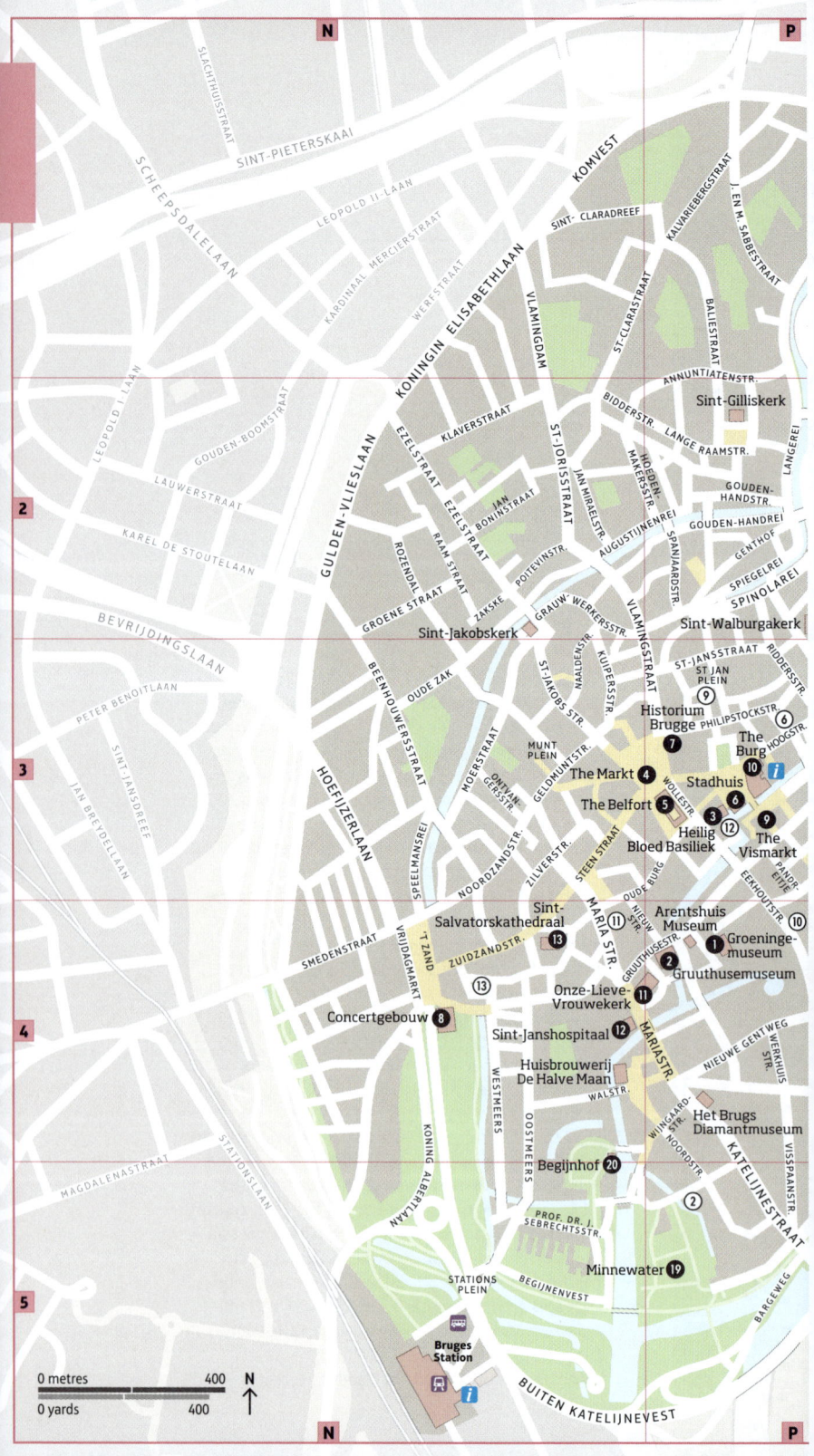

N

P

SLACHTHUISSTRAAT

SINT-PIETERSKAAI

SCHEEPSDALELAAN

LEOPOLD II-LAAN

KARDINAAL MERCIERSTRAAT

WERFSTRAAT

SINT- CLARADREEF

KOMVEST

KALVARIEBERGSTRAAT

J. EN M. SABBESTRAAT

VLAMINGDAM

BALIESTRAAT

ANNUNTIATENSTR.

Sint-Gilliskerk

LEOPOLD I LAAN

GOUDEN-BOOMSTRAAT

LAUWERSTRAAT

KONINGIN ELISABETHLAAN

GULDEN-VLIESLAAN

KLAVERSTRAAT

EZELSTRAAT

ST-JORISSTRAAT

JAN BONINSTRAAT

RAAM STRAAT

ST-CLARASTRAAT

BIDDERSTR.

LANGE RAAMSTR.

HOEDEN-MAKERSSTR.

JAN MIRAELSTR.

AUGUSTIJNENREI

SPANJAARDSTR.

VLAMINGSTRAAT

GOUDEN-HANDSTR.

GOUDEN-HANDREI

GENTHOF

LANGEREI

RIDDERSSTR.

2

KAREL DE STOUTELAAN

ROZENDAL

GROENE STRAAT

ZAKSKE

POITEVINSTR.

GRAUW WERKERSSTRAAT

NAALDENSTR.

KUIPERSSTR.

ST-JANSSTRAAT

SPIEGELREI

SPINOLAREI

Sint-Walburgakerk

BEVRIJDJNGSLAAN

Sint-Jakobskerk

ST JAN PLEIN

⑨

PHILIPSTOCKSTR.

⑥

HOOGSTR.

PETER BENOITLAAN

JAN BREYDELLAAN

BEENHOUWERSSTRAAT

OUDE ZAK

ST-JAKOBS STR.

MUNT PLEIN

ONTVAN-GERSSTR.

GELDMUNTSTR.

Historium Brugge **⑦**

The Burg **⑩**

i

3

HOEFIZERLAAN

MOERSTRAAT

SPEELMANSREI

NOORDZANDSTR.

ZILVERSTR.

The Markt **④**

The Belfort **⑤**

WOLLESTR.

STEEN STRAAT

Stadhuis

③ **⑥**

Heilig Bloed Basiliek

⑫

The Vismarkt **⑨**

PANDR-EITJE

EEKHOUTSTR.

⑩

SMEDENSTRAAT

'T ZAND

VRIJDAGMARKT

ZUIDZANDSTR.

Sint-Salvatorskathedraal **⑬**

MARIA STR.

OUDE BURG

NIEUW STR.

GRUUTHUISESTR.

⑪

②

Arentshuis Museum

① Groeninge-museum

Gruuthusemuseum

4

⑬

Concertgebouw **⑧**

Onze-Lieve-Vrouwekerk **⑪**

Sint-Janshospitaal **⑫**

MARIASTR.

NIEUWE GENTWEG

WERKHUIS STR.

Huisbrouwerij De Halve Maan

WESTMEERS

WALSTR.

WIJNGAARD

NOORDSTR.

Het Brugs Diamantmuseum

KATELIJNESTRAAT

VISSPAANSTR.

OOSTMEERS

Begijnhof **⑳**

②

MAGDALENASTRAAT

STATIONSLAAN

KONING ALBERTLAAN

PROF. DR. J. SEBRECHTSSTR.

BEGIJNENVEST

Minnewater **⑲**

BARGEWEG

5

STATIONS PLEIN

Bruges Station

i

BUITEN KATELIJNEVEST

0 metres   400
0 yards   400

N

↑

N

P

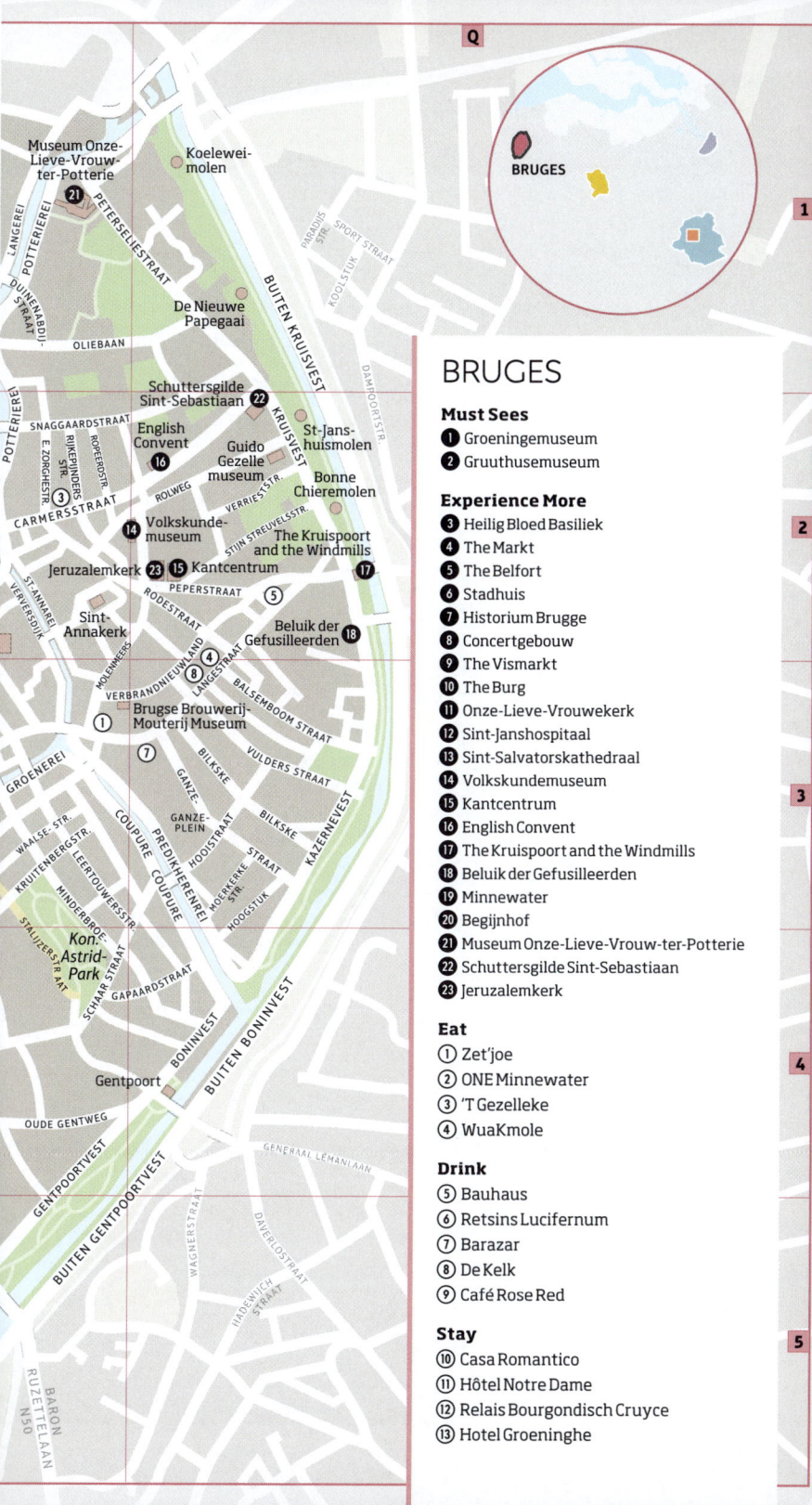

BRUGES

Must Sees
1. Groeningemuseum
2. Gruuthusemuseum

Experience More
3. Heilig Bloed Basiliek
4. The Markt
5. The Belfort
6. Stadhuis
7. Historium Brugge
8. Concertgebouw
9. The Vismarkt
10. The Burg
11. Onze-Lieve-Vrouwekerk
12. Sint-Janshospitaal
13. Sint-Salvatorskathedraal
14. Volkskundemuseum
15. Kantcentrum
16. English Convent
17. The Kruispoort and the Windmills
18. Beluik der Gefusilleerden
19. Minnewater
20. Begijnhof
21. Museum Onze-Lieve-Vrouw-ter-Potterie
22. Schuttersgilde Sint-Sebastiaan
23. Jeruzalemkerk

Eat
1. Zet'joe
2. ONE Minnewater
3. 'T Gezelleke
4. WuaKmole

Drink
5. Bauhaus
6. Retsins Lucifernum
7. Barazar
8. De Kelk
9. Café Rose Red

Stay
10. Casa Romantico
11. Hôtel Notre Dame
12. Relais Bourgondisch Cruyce
13. Hotel Groeninghe

*The Virgin and Child
with Canon van der Paele*
by Jan van Eyck ↑

GROENINGEMUSEUM

📍P4 📍Dijver 12 🚌Markt 🕐9:30am–5pm Tue–Sun (last entry: 4:30pm) 🚫1 Jan, 25 Dec 🌐bezoekers.brugge.be

This small but mighty museum chronicles the breadth of Belgian art, but its impressive collection of Flemish Primitive art is the reason for its world renown. Acclaimed works by Hieronymous Bosch and Bruges-born Jan van Eyck are particular highlights.

Bruges' premier fine arts museum, the Groeninge holds a fabulous collection of early Flemish and Dutch Masters. This small museum displays its collection in rotation, along with various temporary exhibitions. The works on display are by artists such as Jan van Eyck (d 1441) and Hieronymous Bosch (1450–94), famous for the strange creatures of his moral allegories. Hugo van der Goes is well represented too, as is Gerard David (d 1523). These early works are displayed on the ground floor of the museum, along with a collection of later Belgian painters, most notably Paul Delvaux (1897–1994) and René Magritte (1898–1967).

Originally built between 1929 and 1930 on land belonging to the former Eekhout Abbey, the Groeninge was expanded in 1994 to a design by architect Joseph Viérin. Today, it is divided between two buildings. The main portion of the museum is on one level, with a series of rooms displaying the early Flemish Masters as well as works from the 17th to 20th centuries.

↑ *The Reconciliation of Jacob and Esau* by Jan van den Hoecke

↑ Entrance of the renowned Groeningemuseum

 TOP 3 ARTWORKS IN THE MUSEUM

Virgin and Child with Canon (1436)
Jan van Eyck's detailed oil painting on oak is noted for its realism. It shows van Eyck's patron, the canon, being presented to St Donatian by St George.

The Moreel Triptych (1484)
This triptych, by German-born artist Hans Memling, was designed to adorn the altar inside the Sint-Jakobskerk *(p134)* in Bruges. It depicts the prominent Bruges family Moreel, and is said to be the first ever group portrait.

Last Judgement (early 16th century)
Painted on three oak panels, this detail from Hieronymous Bosch's famous triptych shows scenes of cruelty.

2

GRUUTHUSEMUSEUM

📍P4 **🏠Dijver 17** **📞(05) 044 8743** **🚌Markt**

Journey through the fascinating history of this canal-laced city at this beloved museum. Housed within a spectacular old building, the Gruuthusemuseum hosts over 600 historical exhibits, including intricate tapestries, medieval toys and opulent pieces of furniture.

The Gruuthusemuseum occupies a large medieval mansion close to the Dijver Canal. In the 15th century it was inhabited by the merchant (or Lord of the Gruuthuse) who had the exclusive right to levy a tax on the "Gruut", an imported mixture of herbs added to barley during the beer-brewing process. The mansion's labyrinthine rooms, with their ancient chimneypieces and wooden beams, remain intact and hold a priceless collection of fine and applied arts. Inside the museum, there are tapestries, woodcarvings, furniture and even a medical section devoted to cures of everyday ailments. The kitchen and original 1472 chapel transport visitors back to medieval times.

> **Inside the museum, there are tapestries, woodcarvings, furniture and even a medical section devoted to cures of everyday ailments.**

Exterior of the medieval Gruuthuse-museum and *(inset)* a 17th-century wool tapestry designed by Cornelis Schut ↓

GREAT VIEW
From the Balcony

Head to the historic balcony of the Gruuthusemuseum for stunning views of Bonifaciusbrug (one of Bruges's most picturesque bridges) and the lovely Onze-Lieve-Vrouwekerk.

EXPERIENCE MORE

③
Heilig Bloed Basiliek

📍 P3　🏛 Burg 15
📞 (050) 33 6792, 33 3767　🕐 9:30am–noon & 2–5pm daily

Bruges is home to an abundance of beautifully preserved medieval buildings, the oldest being the Heilig Bloed Basiliek (the Basilica of the Holy Blood), which opened in 1157. This intricately constructed building holds one of the most sacred reliquaries in Europe. The basilica is divided into two distinct sections, the lower part being the evocative St Basil's chapel with its plain stone-pillared entrance and arches. The upper chapel was rebuilt in the 19th century after the French destroyed it in the 1790s. Here, brightly coloured decorations surround a silver tabernacle of 1611 which houses a sacred phial, supposed to contain a few drops of blood and water washed from the body of Christ by Joseph of Arimathea. The phial was brought here from Jerusalem in 1150, and is still the object of great veneration. The church also has a fascinating museum of paintings, vestments and other artifacts.

④
The Markt

📍 N3

A market has been held in Bruges' main square since the 10th century. It is an impressive open space lined with 17th-century houses and overlooked by the Belfort on one side. The oldest façade on the square (dating from the 15th century) belongs to the Huis Bouchoute, which

↑ Colourful 17th-century houses in the Markt, Bruges' town square

was the home of the English king Charles II during part of his exile in 1656–7. In the middle is a statue of Pieter de Coninck and Jan Breydel, two 14th-century guildsmen who led a rebellion against the French in 1302. Known as the *Bruges Matin*, they led Flemish soldiers to attack the French at dawn on 18 May 1302, killing almost all of them. This bloody uprising paved the way for a form of independence for the Low Countries' major towns. Rights such as the freedom to trade were subsequently enshrined in the towns' charters until the 15th century.

Today the Markt remains a hub of activity. Photographers come here to take pictures of the iconic surrounding buildings, tourists linger in the lovely pavement cafés and horse-drawn carriages (which take visitors on tours of the city) depart from the square.

TOP 4 LOCATIONS FROM THE FILM *IN BRUGES*

The Belfort

This iconic tower is seen throughout Martin McDonagh's tragi-comedy, most famously in the film's bloody climax sequence.

The Markt

The film's leading duo, Ken (Brendan Gleeson) and Ray (Colin Farrell), enjoy a couple of pints in this lovely market square *(p123)*.

Rozenhoedkaai

While sightseeing, Ken and Ray wander past this beautiful quay. It's one of the best views in the city *(p132)*.

Relais Bourgondisch Cruyce

Fans can stay in the same charming boutique hotel *(p127)* Ken and Ray stay in during the film.

5 The Belfort

📍 P3 **🏛 Markt** **🕐 9:30am–6pm daily (last entry 5pm)**

The Markt *(p123)* is dominated by this octagonal bell tower, rising 83 m (272 ft) above the square. Built between the 13th and 15th centuries, it was used to store the town's charter, and is a constant reminder of the city's past as a centre of trade. Inside, a winding staircase leads up to the roof, which has delightful views across Bruges.

On the way up the 366 stairs, there are plenty of points to stop off at. First, is the former treasury, where the city's public funds were once held along with stamps and seals. Then there's the Belfort's most unique feature, the carillon: a mighty musical instrument composed of 47 bells, played by a hand keyboard, which dates from the 1500s and continues to provide public performances.

The carved façade of the Stadhuis was completed in 1376, but the niche statues are modern effigies of the counts and countesses of Flanders.

6 Stadhuis

📍 P3 **🏛 Burg 12** **📞 (050) 44 8711** **🕐 9:30am–5pm daily** **🚫 1 Jan, 25 Dec**

The carved façade of the Stadhuis was completed in 1376, but the niche statues are modern effigies of the counts and countesses of Flanders. These were added in the 1960s to replace those destroyed by the French army over a century earlier. The building is still used as a town hall. It is also a popular venue for weddings. Inside, a staircase leads up from the foyer to the Gothic

↓ The impressive Belfort towering over Bruges

↑ The lavishly decorated Gothic Hall of the 14th-century Stadhuis

Hall, which is open to visitors year round. This magnificent parliamentary chamber was built around 1400. The ceiling has some lavish woodcarvings including 16 beautiful *corbels* (brackets). A series of paintings around the hall was completed in 1895, each portraying a key event in the city's history.

Next to the Stadhuis is the Brugse Vrije museum, which houses a massive wood, marble and alabaster chimney designed by painter Lanceloot Blondeel. It is one of the best sculptural works of 16th-century Flanders.

7

Historium Brugge

P3 **Markt 1** **(050) 27 0311** **10am–6pm daily**

This inventive encounter with the city's past uses music, film and a range of special effects to give visitors a vivid sense of the sights, sounds and even smells of 15th-century Bruges.

There are seven rooms here, each themed according to a different aspect of the city's history. One explores the quays of Bruges, hubs of trade and commerce, while another takes you inside the studio of master artist Jan van Eyck. Others explore the medieval stock exchange, bathhouse and Flanders' guilds.

8

Concertgebouw

N4 **'t Zand** **concert gebouw.be**

Built as part of the celebrations for Bruges' European City of Culture, this concert hall features a 28-m (92-ft) tower with great views.

Angular and polygonal, the modern building has caused controversy for being at odds with Bruges' famously historic architecture, although the colour and organic nature of its terracotta tiles soften the contrast somewhat. Inside, the main auditorium hosts hundreds of shows every year, ranging from modern dance to orchestral performances.

9

The Vismarkt

P3 **Braambergstraat** **8am–1pm Tue–Sat**

From the Burg, an attractive arched path called the Alley of the Blind Donkey (Blinde Ezelstraat) leads to the open-air fish market with its elegant 19th-century colonnades. Fish is still sold here early each morning and business is brisk.

The fish business has not been ever-present here, however – in the 18th century, the smell of the produce became so overpowering that the trade was banned. It was reinstated when architect Jean-Robert Calloigne designed the building which still dominates the square today.

> **BRUGES AND MYTHOLOGY**
>
> Bruges' long history has seen it develop a rich corpus of mythology and folklore. The Basilica of the Holy Blood *(p123)* houses a relic said to contain the blood of Christ, while Minnewater Lake *(p130)* is named for two star-crossed lovers, Minna and Stromberg – it's said that to cross the bridge here is to guarantee a life in love.

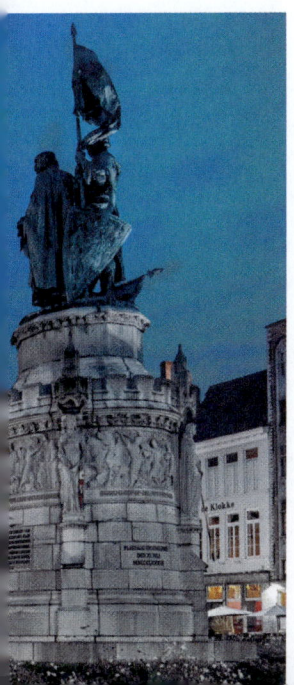

FIDÈLE THE DOG

Belgium's most famous dog, Fidèle (2003–2016), was a yellow Labrador who could be seen lazing on a windowsill of the Côté Canal hotel, where he lived. Fidèle loved this spot near the Burg, and he could so reliably be found there that boats on the Groenerei canal, below his window, would stop so their passengers could take his photo.

10
The Burg

P3

This pleasant cobbled square a few metres from the Markt was once the political and religious focus of Bruges. It is also the site of the original fort around which the city grew. Some of the most imposing civic buildings are located here. The beautiful sandstone Stadhuis (p124) or town hall has a façade dating from 1376 and is adorned with turrets and statues. In contrast, the Proostdij or Provost's House was

built of grey stone in 1662 in the Baroque style and features an ornate entrance.

Other historic buildings lining the square include the Basilica of the Holy Blood (p123) and a Neo-Classical property dating from 1727 which was once the manor of the Franc of Bruges, a former castellan of Flanders. Head to the basement of the Crowne Plaza hotel for a glimpse at the foundations of St Donatian's cathedral, which was destroyed in 1799.

11
Onze-Lieve-Vrouwekerk

N4 **Mariastraat**
(050) 34 5314
9:30am–5pm Mon-Sat, 1:30–5pm Sun & holy days **During services; areas including the southern aisle may be closed for ongoing renovations**

The Church of Our Lady took over 200 years to build, starting in 1220. The interior, with its white walls, stark columns and black-and-white tiled floor, has a medieval simplicity, while the side chapels and pulpit are lavishly decorated.

One of the church's artistic highlights is Michelangelo's sculpture *Madonna and Child* (1504–5), at the end of the southern aisle. This marble statue was imported by a Flemish merchant, and was the only one of the artist's works to leave Italy during his lifetime. In the choir there are fine paintings by Pieter Pourbus

←
Michelangelo's *Madonna and Child*, Onze-Lieve-Vrouwekerk

including a *Last Supper* (1562), and the finely carved mausoleums of the Burgundian prince Charles the Bold and his daughter Mary.

12
Sint-Janshospitaal

N4 **Mariastraat 38**
9:30am–5pm Tue-Sun
1 Jan, 25 Nov

This site has been occupied since the 12th century by the Sint-Janshospitaal, which closed as a working hospital only in 1976. During Bruges's prosperous Burgundian era in the 15th century, the great painter Hans Memling (c 1430–94) created a number of exquisite paintings, commissioned specially for the hospital chapel in about 1479. The remarkable museum here today therefore has two aspects. First, there are the evocative medieval hospital wards with antique beds, medical instruments, paintings and

Sint-Jans-hospitaal's Hans Memling collection and *(inset)* the building's entrance

documentation, as well as an old *apotheek* (pharmacy). Then, in the open-plan site of the old chapel, there is a small but supreme collection of Memling's paintings, including the St Ursula Shrine, a reliquary painted with scenes from the legend of St Ursula.

13

Sint-Salvatorskathedraal

N4 **Steenstraat 1**
(050) 33 61 88 **Daily**
1 Jan, 25 Dec

Built as a parish church from the 12th to the 15th centuries, this large, yellow-brick building became Bruges' cathedral in 1834 when the French army destroyed the existing one. Sint-Salvatorskathedraal has the distinction of being the oldest parish church in Bruges. The interior is enormous and quite plain except for a handsome set of Brussels tapestries hanging in the choir, and an elegant 1682 organ adorned with angels.

The church's rood loft (a gallery on top of the rood screen of a church), which houses an organ, is of special note. There are also medieval tombs and a superb collection of Flemish paintings dating back to the 14th–18th centuries. Also worth a visit is the treasure-chamber, which showcases paintings by Dieric Bouts, Hugo van der Goes and other Flemish Masters.

STAY

Casa Romantico
There's a rural charm to this high-end city-centre hotel, with wood-panelled walls and vintage furniture. A swimming pool, sauna and jacuzzi are on hand to help you relax.

P4 **Eekhoutstraat 37** **casa-romantico.be**

Hôtel Notre Dame
A good-value budget option near the church of the same name, Notre Dame offers quaint rooms and a hearty continental breakfast.

N4 **Mariastraat 3** **hotelnotredame.be**

Relais Bourgondisch Cruyce
This luxury hotel is set in a historic half-timbered canalside property. There's a cosy bar and tearoom.

P3 **Wollestraat 41** **relaisbourgondisch cruyce.be**

Hotel Groeninghe
A lovely B&B-style property, Hotel Groeninghe occupies an old house dating back to 1858. Rooms are simple but comfortably and traditionally appointed, overlooking a quiet street and a pretty plant-strewn garden.

N4 **Korte Vuldersstraat 29** **hotelgroeninghe.be**

DRINK

Bauhaus

Housed in a tall medieval building, this atmospheric bar stocks nearly 50 Belgian beers. Guided tastings are held every day at 10pm.

📍Q2 🏠Langestraat 135 🌐bauhaus.be

Retsins Lucifernum

This Gothic-themed bar has a great cocktail menu and regular live music.

📍P3 🏠Twijnstraat 6 🌐lucifernum.be

Barazar

Set inside the Hotel Flanders, this popular spot serves a wide variety of Belgian beers (including wheat and no-alcohol varieties) and cocktails.

📍Q3 🏠Langestraat 40 🌐hotelflanders. com/barazar

De Kelk

If it's live music you're after, head to this Art Deco-styled bar, where craft beers from Belgium and beyond are served to a soundtrack of live pop, rock, blues and more.

📍Q3 🏠Langestraat 69 🌐dekelk.be

Café Rose Red

A cosy café-bar inside Hotel Cordoeanier, Rose Red is known for Trappist beers – made traditionally by monks from one of Belgium's six Trappist monasteries.

📍P3 🏠Cordoeaniersstraat 16 🌐rosered.be

←
A row of whitewashed cottages in the pretty Kantcentrum area

14

Volkskundemuseum

📍Q2 🏠Balstraat 43 📞(050) 44 8764 🕐9:30am–5pm Tue–Sun, Easter & Whit Mon

The Volkskundemuseum is one of the best folk museums in Flanders. It occupies a terrace of brick almshouses behind a neighbourhood café called the "Zwarte Kat" (Black Cat), which serves as the entrance. Each of the almshouses is dedicated to a different aspect of Flemish life, with workshops displaying old tools. Various crafts, such as a cobbler's and a blacksmith's, are represented here.

15

Kantcentrum

📍Q2 🏠Balstraat 16 📞(050) 33 0072 🕐9:30am–5pm Mon–Sat (Apr–Sep: daily)

The lacemaking tradition in Bruges dates back to the 16th century, when the bobbin method was invented. The area of whitewashed cottages to the east of Potterierei Street is one of several old neighbourhoods where the city's lace workers plied their craft. Mostly, the women worked at home, receiving their raw materials from a supplier who also bought the finished product.

Today, lacemaking skills are kept alive at the Kantcentrum, the Lace Centre on Balstraat, where locals fashion lace in a variety of styles, both modern and traditional. It is a busy place, and visitors can see the lacemaking demonstrations held from Monday to Saturday afternoons in summer. Some of the finished pieces are sold in the Kantcentrum shop at very reasonable prices.

→

One of the last four windmills that still stand along the canal

> **The historic English Convent was where many English Catholics sought asylum following the execution of Charles I in 1649.**

16 English Convent

Q2 **Carmersstraat 85** **(050) 33 2424** **2-3:30pm & 4:30-5:30pm Mon-Thu & Sat; Mass 8:30am Sun**

The historic English Convent was where many English Catholics sought asylum following the execution of Charles I in 1649, and during Oliver Cromwell's subsequent rule as Lord Protector. The convent buildings are not open to the public, but the nuns provide a well-informed tour of their beautiful church, built in the Baroque style in the 1620s. The interior of the convent has a delightful sense of space, its elegant proportions enhanced by its cupola, but the highlight is the altar, a grand affair made of around 20 types of marble.

17 The Kruispoort and the Windmills

Q2

Medieval Bruges was heavily fortified. It was encircled by a city wall which was itself protected by a moat and strengthened by a series of massive gates. Most of the wall was knocked down in the 19th century, but the moat has survived and so has one of the gates, the Kruispoort, a monumental structure dating from 1402 that guards the eastern approach to the city. The earthen bank stretching north of the Kruispoort marks the line of the old city wall, which was once dotted with some 20 windmills. Today, only four remain overlooking the canal. The first, the Bonne Chieremolen, was brought here from a Flanders village in 1911, but the second – Sint-Janshuismolen – is original to the city. The northernmost mill of the four is De Nieuwe Papegai, an old oil mill that was relocated here in 1970.

18 Beluik der Gefusilleerden

Q2

Bruges was occupied by the German Army during both World Wars. This bullet-marked wall is located just south of the Kruispoort and commemorates a dozen men executed by a German firing squad in 1916. Eleven of them were Belgian, shot for resisting German rule. The twelfth was Captain Fryatt, a British merchant navy officer, whose arrest and execution here caused almost as much outrage around Europe as the death of Edith Cavell in Brussels a year earlier.

Did You Know?
Beluik der Gefusilleerden roughly translates to "wall of those who were shot dead".

↑ A charming medieval castle set on the banks of Minnewater

 19

Minnewater

 P5

Just south of the Begijnhof, Minnewater is a peaceful park with a canalized lake. There were already swans here in 1448 when Maximilian of Austria ordered they be kept in memory of his councillor, Pieter Lanchals, who was beheaded by the Bruges citizens.

Once this was a bustling harbour which connected to the canal network and the sea. It is now a popular spot for walkers and picnickers who may view the pretty 15th-century lock gate and house and the 1398 tower (Poedertoren). There is an adjoining park which holds music concerts in summer.

One story suggests that Minnewater takes its name from *minnes* (sprites) said to inhabit the lake. Another has it that it was named for Minna, a local woman who died beside the lake after being denied the chance to marry her true love. Despite this sad ending, the lake is associated with romance.

 20

Begijnhof

 N5 **Wijngaardplein 1**
(050) 33 00 11 **Daily**

Béguines were members of a lay sisterhood active between the 13th and 16th centuries. They lived and dressed as nuns but did not take vows and were therefore able to return to the secular world at will. The *begijnhof* or béguinage is the walled complex in a town that housed the beguines. In Bruges, this is an area of quiet tree-lined canals faced by white, gabled houses, with a pleasant lawn at its centre. Visitors and locals enjoy strolling here and may visit the small, simple church which was built in 1602. The nuns who live in the houses are no longer béguines, but Benedictine sisters who moved here in the 1930s. One of the houses is open to visitors.

 21

Museum Onze-Lieve-Vrouw-ter-Potterie

P1 **Potterierei 79**
(050) 44 8711 **9:30am–12:30pm & 1:30–5pm Tue–Sun, Easter & Whit Mon**

Located by the canal in one of the quietest parts of Bruges, the Museum Onze-Lieve-Vrouw-ter-Potterie (Our Lady of Pottery) occupies part of a hospital that was founded in 1276 to care for elderly women. There is a 14th- and 15th-century cloister, and many of the sick rooms house a collection of paintings, the best of which are some 17th- and 18th-century portraits of aristocrats. The hospital church is in excellent condition, too; it is a warm place with stained-glass windows and Baroque altarpieces.

TOP 3

BEACHES NEAR BRUGES

Oostduinkerke Strand
Koksijde; 40 km (25 miles) from Bruges
A stretch of white sand.

Strand van Blankenberge
Blankenberge; 14 km (8 miles) from Bruges
One of Belgium's most famous beaches.

Strand Oostende
Ostend; 20 km (12 miles) from Bruges
Splendid esplanade, pier and soft sand.

EAT

Zet'joe
This Belgian-French place offers dishes like Zeebrugge shrimp with bouillon of potatoes.

📍P3 🏠Langestraat 11 🌐zetjoe.be

€€€

ONE Minnewater
Overlooking romantic Minnewater Park, this cosy brick-walled spot serves Flemish classics.

📍P5 🏠Arsenaalstraat 55 🌐one-minne water.be

€€€

'T Gezelleke
A pub-style restaurant set around a fireplace, 'T Gezelleke offers favourites like Flemish stew.

📍P2 🏠Carmersstraat 15 🌐tgezelleke.be

€€€

WuaKmole
Head to this lively joint for Latin street-food classics like empanadas, *tequeños*, ceviche and more – not to mention top-notch margaritas.

📍Q2 🏠Langestraat 93 🌐wuakmole.com

€€€

22

Schuttersgilde Sint-Sebastiaan

📍Q2 🏠Carmersstraat 174 📞(050) 33 16 26 🕐May-Sep: 10am-noon Tue-Thu, 2-5pm Sat; Oct-Apr: 2-5pm Tue-Thu & Sat

The Archers' guild (the Schuttersgilde) was one of the most powerful of the militia guilds, and their 16th- and 17th-century red-brick guild-house now houses a museum.

The commercial life of medieval Bruges was dominated by the guilds, each of which represented the interests of a particular group of skilled workmen. The guilds guarded their privileges jealously and, among many rules and customs, marriage between children whose fathers were in different guilds was greatly frowned upon. The guild claimed the name St Sebastian after an early Christian martyr, whom the Roman Emperor Diocletian had executed by his archers. The bowmen followed the emperor's orders – medieval painters often show a severely injured Sebastian – but miraculously, Sebastian's wounds healed before he was killed by club-wielding assassins. The guildhouse is famous for its collection of paintings, gold and silver trinkets and guild emblems.

23

Jeruzalemkerk

📍Q2 🏠Peperstraat 🕐Mon-Sat

The Jeruzalemkerk is Bruges' most unusual church. The present building dates from the 15th century. It was built on the site of a 13th-century chapel commissioned by a family of wealthy Italian merchants, the Adornes, whose black marble tomb can be seen inside. Based on the design of the church of the Holy Sepulchre in Jerusalem, the Jeruzalemkerk has a tower with two tiers of wooden lanterns topped by a tin orb. Inside, the lower level contains a macabre altarpiece, carved with skulls and demons. Behind the altar is a vaulted chapel; leading from this is a tunnel guarded by an iron grate. Along the tunnel, a lifelike model of *Christ in the Tomb* can be seen at close quarters.

> **Based on the design of the church of the Holy Sepulchre in Jerusalem, the Jeruzalemkerk has a tower with two tiers of wooden lanterns topped by a tin orb.**

A SHORT WALK
BRUGES

Distance 1.6 km (1 miles) **Time** 21 minutes
Nearest station Stationsplein

With good reason, Bruges is one of the most popular tourist destinations in Belgium. An unspoiled medieval town, Bruges' winding streets pass by picturesque canals lined with fine buildings. The centre of the city is amazingly well preserved. The city's trade was badly affected when the River Zwin silted up at the end of the 15th century and Bruges was never heavily industrialized, retaining most of its medieval buildings as a result. As a further bonus, it also escaped major damage in both World Wars.

Today, the streets are well maintained: there are no billboards or high rises, and traffic is heavily regulated. All the major attractions are located within the circle of boulevards that marks the line of the old medieval walls.

0 metres 100
0 yards 100
N

*Gabled houses line the historic **Markt** (p123) at the heart of Bruges. A market is held every Wednesday in the square.*

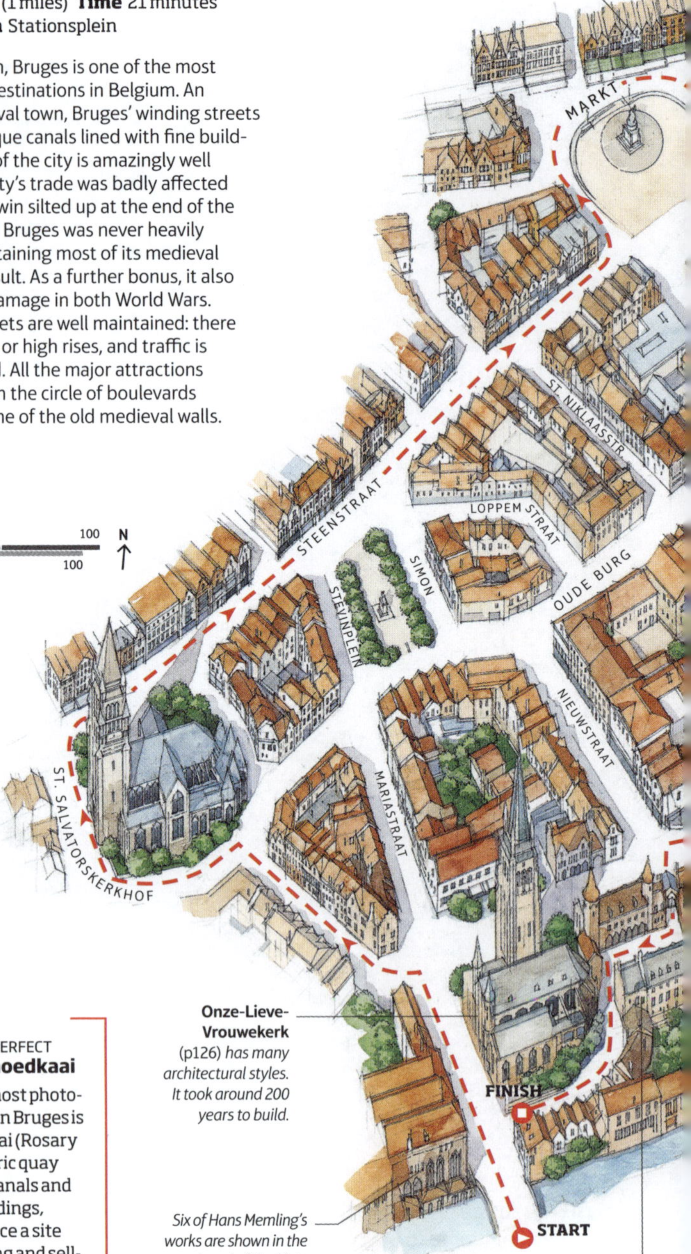

MARKT
ST NIKLAASSTR
LOPPEM STRAAT
STEENSTRAAT
SIMON
STEVINPLEIN
OUDE BURG
NIEUWSTRAAT
ST. SALVATORSKERKHOF
MARIASTRAAT

PICTURE PERFECT
Rozenhoedkaai

Perhaps the most photographed spot in Bruges is Rozenhoedkaai (Rosary Quay), a historic quay overlooking canals and medieval buildings, which was once a site used for buying and selling Catholic rosaries.

Onze-Lieve-Vrouwekerk
(p126) has many architectural styles. It took around 200 years to build.

FINISH

*Six of Hans Memling's works are shown in the chapel of the **Sint-Janshospitaal** (p126), a city hospital until 1976.*

START

Gruuthusemuseum
(p122)

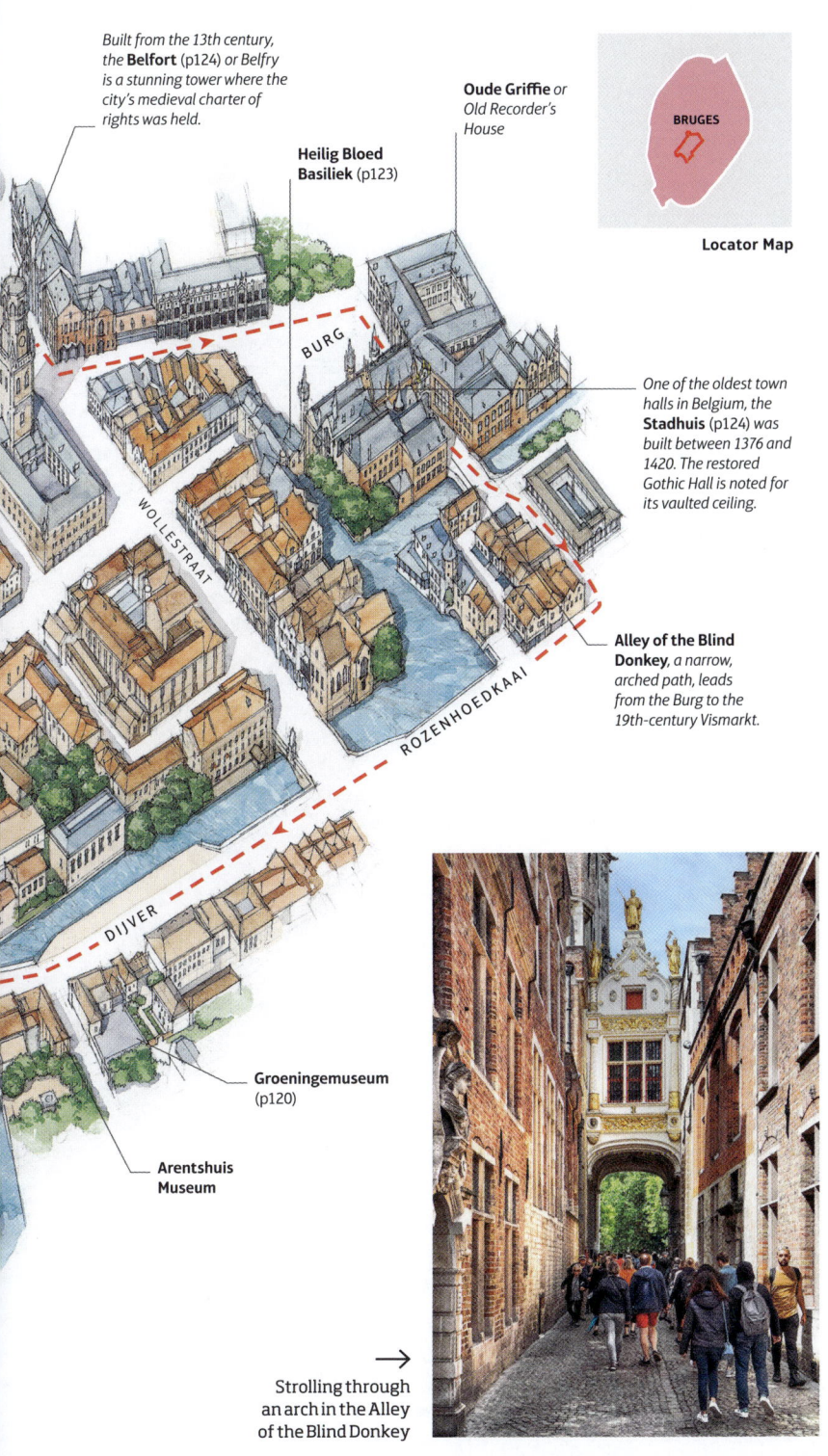

Built from the 13th century, the **Belfort** (p124) or Belfry is a stunning tower where the city's medieval charter of rights was held.

Heilig Bloed Basiliek (p123)

Oude Griffie or Old Recorder's House

BURG

Locator Map

BRUGES

One of the oldest town halls in Belgium, the **Stadhuis** (p124) was built between 1376 and 1420. The restored Gothic Hall is noted for its vaulted ceiling.

WOLLESTRAAT

ROZENHOEDKAAI

Alley of the Blind Donkey, a narrow, arched path, leads from the Burg to the 19th-century Vismarkt.

DIJVER

Groeningemuseum (p120)

Arentshuis Museum

→ Strolling through an arch in the Alley of the Blind Donkey

A LONG WALK
AROUND HISTORIC BRUGES

Distance 3.5 km (2 miles) **Stopping-off points**
There are a multitude of cafés and restaurants around the Markt, but very few beyond Vlamingstraat.

Almost all the most famous sights of Bruges are in the centre and to the southwest of the centre. But the commercial and residential heart in Bruges' medieval period was to the north of the Markt. This is where a cosmopolitan collection of European merchants had their grand national "lodges", which oversaw the trade that passed into the city along a network of canals. Only small traces of this former glory remain, hidden among a collection of waterways, bridges and residential streets of exceptional tranquillity and charm.

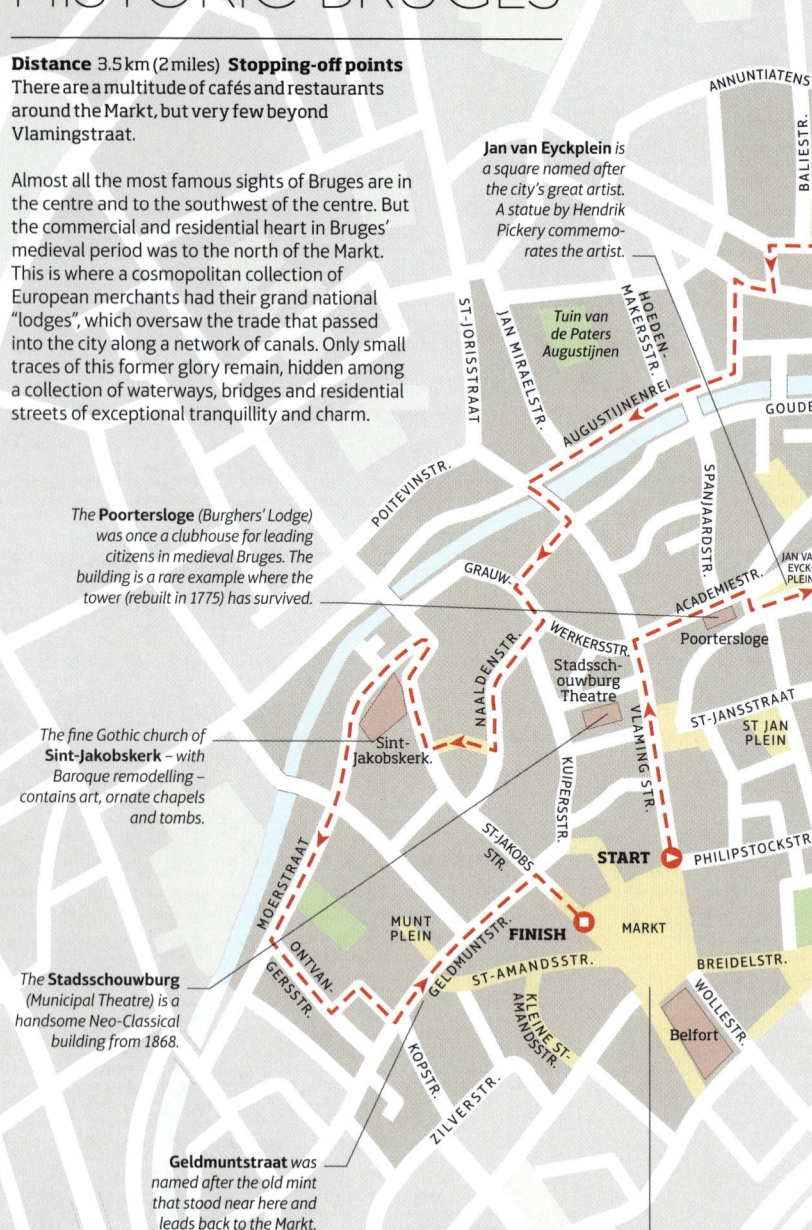

Jan van Eyckplein is a square named after the city's great artist. A statue by Hendrik Pickery commemorates the artist.

The **Poortersloge** *(Burghers' Lodge) was once a clubhouse for leading citizens in medieval Bruges. The building is a rare example where the tower (rebuilt in 1775) has survived.*

The fine Gothic church of **Sint-Jakobskerk** *– with Baroque remodelling – contains art, ornate chapels and tombs.*

The **Stadsschouwburg** *(Municipal Theatre) is a handsome Neo-Classical building from 1868.*

Geldmuntstraat *was named after the old mint that stood near here and leads back to the Markt.*

Like most of the old trading cities of Flanders, Bruges clusters around its old market square, the **Markt** *(p123), which is the perfect place to begin your walk.*

An attractive church, **Sint-Gilliskerk** *dates from the 13th–15th centuries.*

A row of almshouses here make up the **Volkskundemuseum** *(p128). The objects on display paint a vivid picture of life in old Bruges.*

Locator Map

Around Historic Bruges

BRUGES

SNAGGAARDSTRAAT

Sint-Gilliskerk

LANGEREI

POTTERIEREI

E. ZORGHESTR.

RIJKEPIJNDERS STR.

ROPEERDSTR.

Tuin van het Engels Klooster

English Convent

CARMERS STR.

The fascinating **Kantcentrum** *(p128).*

GOUDEN-HANDSTR.

-HANDREI

GENTHOF

Volkskundemuseum

BALSTR.

Kantcentrum

Jeruzalemkerk

ST-ANNAREI

Café Vlissinghe

SPIEGELREI

SPINOLAREI

VERVERSDIJK

Sint-Annakerk

PEPERSTRAAT

RODESTRAAT

The **Sint-Annakerk** *is a pretty parish church from 1497.*

MOLENMEERS

VERBRANDNIEUWLAND

RIDDERS-STR.

BOOMGAARD STR.

| 0 metres | 200 |
| 0 yards | 200 |

N

Café Vlissinghe *is reputedly Bruges' oldest tavern, dating back to 1515.*

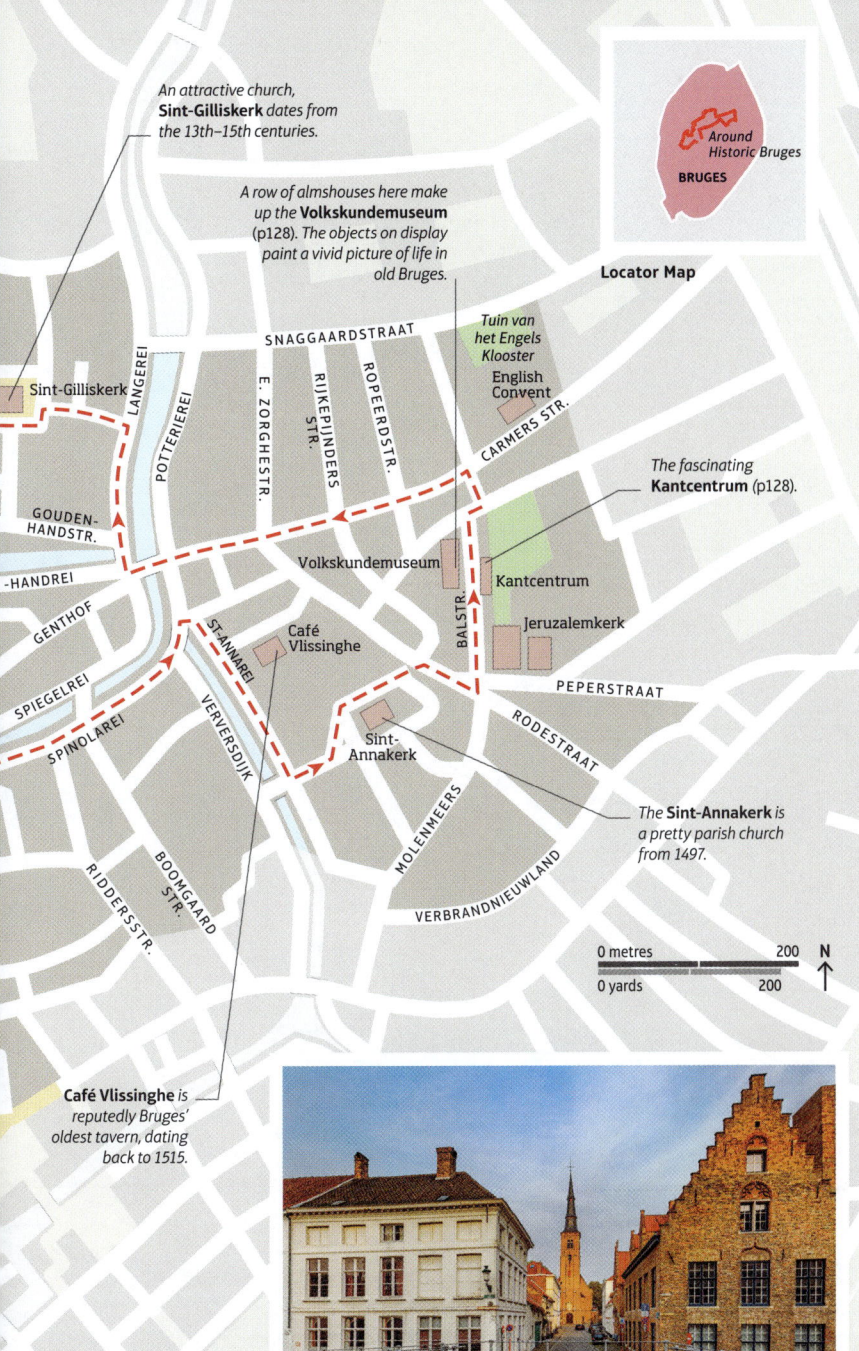

→ A cobbled street leading up to the historic church of Sint-Annakerk

ANTWERP

Antwerp has been inhabited for millennia: the Romans first settled here around 150 CE, followed by the Franks, who established the 9th-century castle which later became Het Steen. But it wasn't until the decline of Bruges in the 15th century that Antwerp rose to prominence. When the Zwin inlet silted up and cut Bruges off from the sea, the city's powerful trading houses moved to Antwerp. Some of the grand guildhalls in the Grote Markt date from this period, as does the Onze-Lieve-Vrouwekathedraal (Cathedral of Our Lady). Antwerp grew wealthy thanks to the goods that flowed through its port – sugar, diamonds, textiles, priceless artworks – and it soon became the richest city in Europe. At this time, wealthy merchants patronized the arts, and painters like Peter Paul Rubens pioneered the Flemish Baroque style. Rubens bought his grand residence, the Rubenshuis, in 1610, developing it into a striking palazzo. Creativity continued to flourish into the 20th century when the city became famous as the home of fashion luminaries the Antwerp Six – its fashion scene is still prominent today and the city is often marketed as Belgium's capital of cool. Antwerp also continues to play an important role in the 21st-century Flemish Movement.

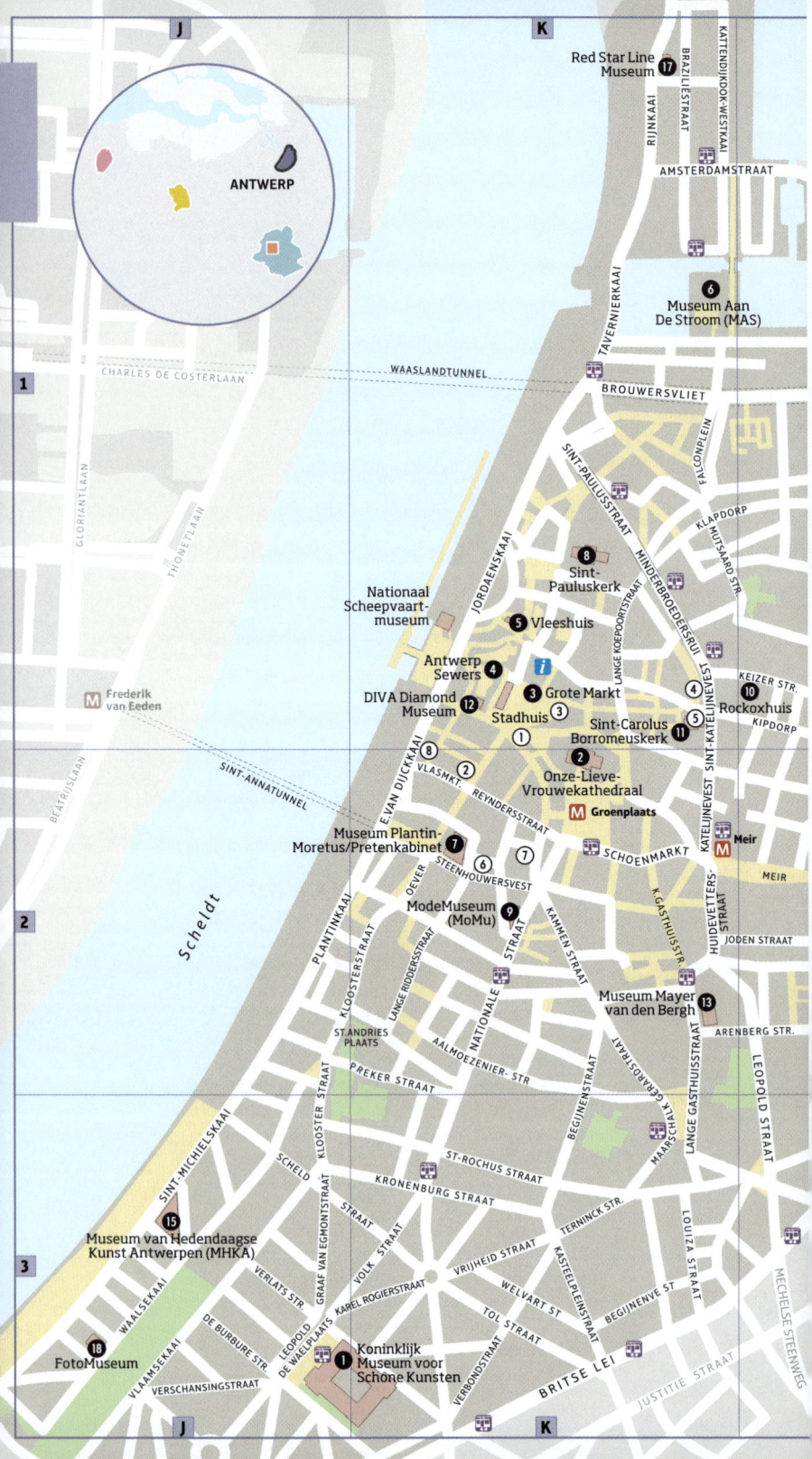

ANTWERP

Red Star Line Museum 17

Museum Aan De Stroom (MAS) 6

CHARLES DE COSTERLAAN

WAASLANDTUNNEL

BROUWERSVLIET

Nationaal Scheepvaart-museum

Sint-Paulsuskerk 8

Vleeshuis 5

Frederik van Eeden

Antwerp Sewers 4

DIVA Diamond Museum 12

Grote Markt 3

Stadhuis 1

SINT-ANNATUNNEL

Scheldt

Museum Plantin-Moretus/Pretenkabinet 7

ModeMuseum (MoMu) 9

St. Andries Plaats

Rockoxhuis 10

Sint-Carolus Borromeuskerk 11

Onze-Lieve-Vrouwekathedraal

Groenplaats

Schoenmarkt

Meir

Museum Mayer van den Bergh 13

Arenberg Str.

St-Rochus Straat

Museum van Hedendaagse Kunst Antwerpen (MHKA) 15

Kronenburg Straat

Vrijheid Straat

Welvart St

Britse Lei

FotoMuseum 18

Koninklijk Museum voor Schöne Kunsten 1

ANTWERP

Must See

❶ Koninklijk Museum voor Schone Kunsten

Experience More

❷ Onze-Lieve-Vrouwekathedraal
❸ Grote Markt
❹ Antwerp Sewers
❺ Vleeshuis
❻ Museum Aan De Stroom (MAS)
❼ Museum Plantin-Moretus/ Pretenkabinet
❽ Sint-Pauluskerk
❾ ModeMuseum (MoMu)
❿ Rockoxhuis
⓫ Sint-Carolus Borromeuskerk
⓬ DIVA Diamond Museum
⓭ Museum Mayer van den Bergh
⓮ Sint-Jacobskerk
⓯ Museum van Hedendaagse Kunst Antwerpen (M HKA)
⓰ Rubenshuis
⓱ Red Star Line Museum
⓲ FotoMuseum

Eat

① Fish A'Go Go
② Falafel Tof
③ Meat Factory
④ Shuk
⑤ Satay

Drink

⑥ Marigold
⑦ Billie's
⑧ Den Hopsack

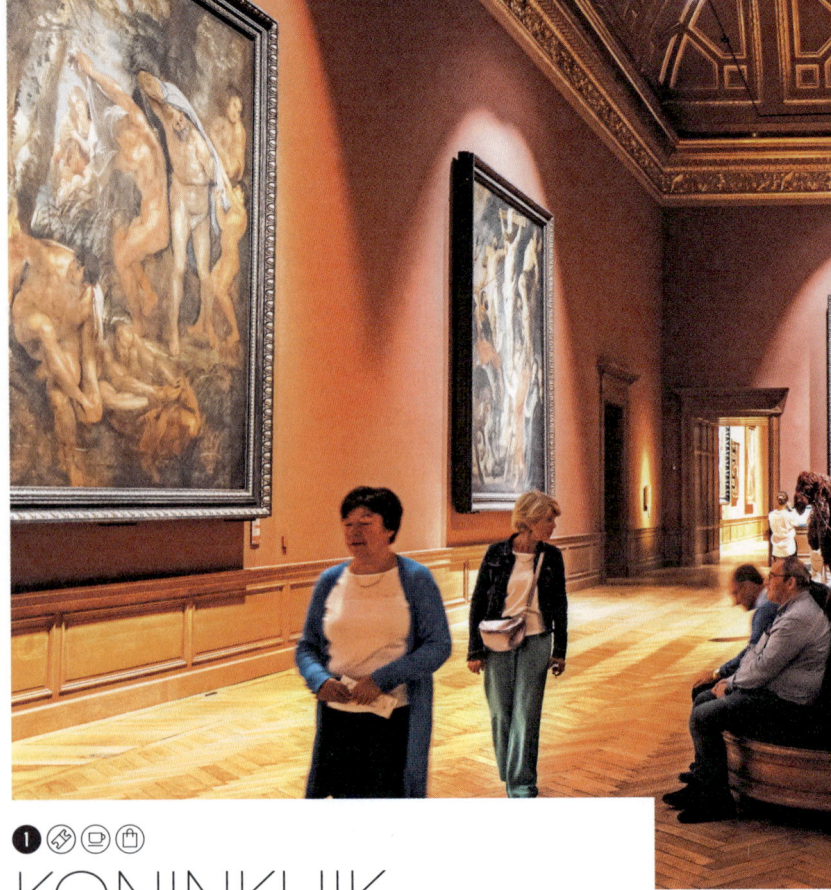

KONINKLIJK MUSEUM VOOR SCHONE KUNSTEN

☉ J3 ⌂ Leopold de Waelplaats 1–9 🚌🚊 4, 8, 12, 24
🕐 10am–5pm daily (to 6pm Sat & Sun) 🅦 kmska.be/en

Set in a massive late 19th-century Neo-Classical building, the Koninklijk Museum voor Schone Kunsten (KMSK) exhibits Antwerp's largest and most impressive fine art collection.

This museum's permanent collection features both ancient and modern works spanning seven centuries of art. The earlier collection contains medieval Flemish painting and continues through the 19th century, with the "Antwerp Trio" of Rubens, van Dyck and Jordaens well represented. Modern exhibits include the work of Belgian artists Magritte, Ensor and Delvaux, as well as a major collection of work by Rik Wouters. Tissot and Van Gogh are among the international artists on show. The museum also has a world-renowned research institution that conducts studies on the details of the artworks and makes its findings accessible to all art lovers.

Did You Know?

Many artworks here were looted from churches during the French occupations of the 18th century.

Admiring the staggering paintings in the KMSK's acclaimed collection

1. The museum features a staircase gallery of paintings on the second floor.

2. *Saint Barbara* by Jan van Eyck is a small illustration on an oak panel dating from 1437. It depicts the saint imprisoned in the tower where she converted to Christianity.

3. The Neo-Classical façade of the museum has massive granite columns.

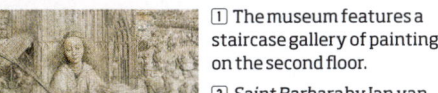

> 💬 INSIDER TIP
> **KMSKA LATE**
>
> On Thursday evening, the museum's after-hours programme, KMSKA LATE, gives you a chance to take a stroll around the galleries at dusk and enjoy a cocktail.

Brabo Fountain set in the centre of Grote Markt, surrounded by guildhouses ↑

EXPERIENCE MORE

2

Onze-Lieve-Vrouwekathedraal

🅚K2 🏠Groenplaats 21 or Handschoenmarkt ⏰10am-5pm Mon-Fri, 10am-3pm Sat, 1-4pm Sun 🌐dekathedraal.be

This magnificent structure rises above the winding streets of the medieval city centre. Inside, the impression of light and space owes much to its seven-aisled nave and vaulted ceiling. The collection of paintings and sculptures includes three works by Rubens, of which two are triptychs – *The Raising of the Cross* (1610) and *The Descent from the Cross* (1612).

The cathedral's mighty belfry stands at 123 m (404 ft), making it the tallest in the Benelux countries. Napoleon,

no less, was very enamoured of the tower, comparing its delicate construction to the Mechlin lace for which Flanders was famous at the time. Only the cathedral's smaller tower can be climbed, however.

3

Grote Markt

🅚K1 ℹ️Tourist office: (03) 232 0103

Antwerp's central square, or Grote Markt, is flanked by the ornately gabled Stadhuis (town hall), which was completed in 1564 by the architect and sculptor Cornelis Floris. The square's north side has a series of guildhouses, each of which is decorated with gilded figures. The tallest of these is the House of the Crossbowmen

at number seven, on top of which is a statue of St George and the dragon. The Brabo fountain, set at the centre of Grote Markt, is one of Antwerp's noted landmarks.

The square is at the heart of Antwerp not only physically – you'll find yourself passing through it repeatedly as you walk around the city – but in a civic and cultural sense, too. It is also a regular venue for flea markets and food traders. Most of all, it's a great place to sit outside one of the several café-bars and watch the city go by.

4

Antwerp Sewers

🅚K1 🏠Ruihuis, Suikerrui 21 ⏰10am-5pm Tue-Fri, 10am-6pm Sat & Sun; tours at 11am, 1pm, 3pm 🌐en.ruien.be

The Antwerp sewers, or *ruien*, form the subterranean belly of the city and reveal a part of its history. Various tours explain

> The Onze-Lieve-Vrouwekathedraal's mighty belfry stands at 123 m (404 ft), making it the tallest in the Benelux countries.

how these were a vast above-ground network of canals from the 13th to 19th centuries, making Antwerp comparable to Bruges or Amsterdam. By the 19th century, however, the waterways were proving to be conduits for waste and disease, and they were finally covered in the 1870s. It's possible to take a 15-minute boat ride through the tunnels or, for the more adventurous, there's a 90-minute walk with an interactive tablet. Visitors can also join a two-hour guided walk, during which you can ask the guide questions. There's also an exhibition on the history of the *ruien*. Protective suits and boots are provided (women are advised not to wear skirts).

5

Vleeshuis

📍 K1 🏛 Vleeshouwers-straat 38-40 📞 (03) 292 6100 🕐 10am-5pm Thu-Sun, Easter Mon 🚫 1 & 2 Jan, 1 May, Ascension, 1 & 2 Nov, 25 & 26 Dec

There has been a Vleeshuis (Meat Hall) on this site since 1250, but the existing hall was completed in 1504 to a design by architect Herman de Waghemakere. The structure features slender towers with five hexagonal turrets and rising gables, all built in alternate strips of stone and brick – giving the building a streaky-bacon-like appearance.

The fine Gothic interior has been renovated to create a museum called "Sounds of the City", presenting 600 years of Antwerp's musical life. Exhibits take you back to the ballrooms and concert halls of Flanders, and indeed up its belfries – audiovisual displays demonstrate the carillon, a vast instrument made up of 23 or more church bells, as well as the less cumbersome harpsichords, trumpets, pianos and accordions which sound-tracked life in centuries past. There are also exhibits on how some of these instruments are made, and beautiful sheet music manuscripts are on display, too.

6

Museum Aan De Stroom (MAS)

📍 K1 🏛 Hanzesteden-plaats 🕐 10am-5pm Tue-Fri and during winter, 10am-6pm Sat & Sun 🚫 1 Jan, 1 May, Ascension, 1 Nov, 25 Dec 🌐 mas.be

Located in the old docks area just north of the historical centre is Antwerp's most innovative project, the Museum Aan De Stroom (MAS), meaning "Museum on the River". This museum combines the best of the collections from the former Maritime and Folklore Museums along with some of the Vleeshuis's collection. A broad range of objects on display covers everything from paintings and silverware to woodcarvings, archaeological finds, folk art, maritime artifacts and model ships. The pieces span the prehistoric era through to the present day. The museum also has a cultural events space, which will display highlights from the Koninklijk Museum voor Schone Kunsten *(p142)*.

An exhibit from the Pre-Columbian America collection at MAS →

Fish A'Go Go
This cosy shack offers comforting seafood dishes such as shrimp croquettes, mussels in white wine and garlic, and razor clams.

📍 K1 🏛 Handschoen-markt 1 🌐 fishagogo.be

€€€

Falafel Tof
Some of the best sandwiches and wraps in the city are on offer at Falafel Tof.

📍 K2 🏛 Hoogstraat 32 📞 (03) 3291 6660

€€€

Meat Factory
Not a subtle name, but this spot is highly acclaimed for its burgers and steaks. It also serves fantastic desserts.

📍 K1 🏛 Grote Markt 28 📞 (03) 3336 7445

€€€

Shuk
Widely popular, this relaxed place offers a menu inspired by Middle Eastern street food.

📍 K1 🏛 Minderbroeder-srui 64 🌐 shuk.be

€€€

Satay
Alongside the eponymous satay, this Southeast Asian restaurant serves chicken *gado gado* (Indonesian salad), Thai noodle bowls, teriyaki beef and more.

📍 K1 🌐 Wijngaard-brug 8 🌐 satay.be

€€€

DRINK

Marigold
This exquisitely stylish bar has a mid-century vibe and a menu of classic cocktails to match.

◉K2 ⌂Vrijdagmarkt 18
🌐marigold.bar

Billie's
Find a range of Belgian beers at this brick-walled pub. It has a good selection of Trappist, wheat, blonde and dark brews.

◉K2 ⌂Kammenstraat 12 🌐billiesbier.be

Den Hopsack
Savour a refreshing beer while watching live performances, ranging from jazz to rock and blues, offered three nights a week at this vibrant venue.

◉K2 ⌂Grote Pieter Potstraat 24
🌐denhopsack.be

↑ Museum Plantin-Moretus overlooking a pretty courtyard

❼ Museum Plantin-Moretus/ Pretenkabinet

◉K2 ⌂Vrijdagmarkt 22–23
🕙10am–5pm Tue–Sun & Easter Mon 🔒1 Jan, 1 May, Ascension, 1 Nov, 25 Dec
🌐museumplantin moretus.be

Set in a 16th-century house of printer Christophe Plantin, this museum has been listed as a UNESCO World Heritage Site. The house's ancient rooms and narrow corridors resemble the interiors painted by Flemish and Dutch Masters. The museum focuses on the early years of printing, when

Plantin and others began to produce books that were different from the earlier, illuminated manuscripts.

Antwerp was a centre for printing in the 15th and 16th centuries, and Plantin was its most successful printer. Today, his workshop displays several historic printing presses, as well as woodcuts and copper plates. Plantin's library can also be seen. One of the gems here is an edition of the Gutenberg Bible – the first book to be printed using moveable type, a technique invented by Johannes Gutenberg in 1455.

❽ Sint-Pauluskerk

◉K1 ⌂Sint-Paulusstraat 22 or Veemarkt 14 🕙Apr–Oct: 10am–5pm Tue–Sun; tours: 3pm Sun & public hols 🌐stpaulus antwerpen.be

Completed in the early 17th century, this church is known for its combination of Gothic and Baroque features. The exterior dates from 1571, and has an elaborate Baroque gateway. The interior is noted for its intricately carved choir stalls. It also displays a series of paintings depicting the Fifteen Mysteries of the Rosary, one of which, *The Scourging of the Pillar*, is an exquisite canvas by Rubens. There are also paintings by van Dyck.

❾ ModeMuseum (MoMu)

◉K2 ⌂Nationalestraat 28
🕙10am–6pm Tue–Sun (to 9pm first Sun of the month)
🌐momu.be

As the influential fashion designers called the "Antwerp Six" rose to fame in the 1980s, the city entered the sphere of international haute-couture, and still has a glowing reputation for nurturing new talent. This fashion museum provides the historical context to Antwerp's rise. The changing exhibitions feature fashion items and accessories, shown in innovative ways.

→ Nave and altar of the Sint-Carolus Borromeus-kerk and *(inset)* its stunning façade

Rockoxhuis

📍L1 🏠Keizerstraat 12
🕐10am–5pm Tue–Sun
📅1 & 2 Jan, Ascension,
1 & 2 Nov, 25 & 26 Dec
🌐rockoxhuis.be

Mayor of Antwerp Nicolaas Rockox (1560–1640) was a humanist, philanthropist, and a friend and patron of Rubens. These attributes are reflected in his beautifully renovated home – a series of rooms set around a formal courtyard garden. The rooms contain a superb collection of contemporary furniture and miscellaneous artifacts. The paintings and drawings include work by Rubens, Jordaens and van Dyck, as well as work by Frans Snyders (1579–1657).

Sint-Carolus Borromeuskerk

📍K1 🏠Hendrik Conscienceplein 🕐10am–12:30pm & 2–5pm Mon–Sat
🌐mkantwerpen.be

This Jesuit church is known for its elegant Baroque façade, which forms one flank of a charming 17th-century square. Rubens played a part in the design of both the exterior and interior when the church was built in 1615–21, and supplied 39 ceiling paintings, but sadly these were lost in a fire in 1718. The surviving parts of the interior indicate how lavish it once was.

___

DIVA Diamond Museum

📍K1 🏠Suikerrui 17
🕐10am–6pm Mon, Tue & Thu–Sun 🌐divaantwerp.be

Set in its original home near the River Schledt, this modern space opened to the public in 2022 after extensive renovations. The museum traces the fascinating story of how Antwerp came to be the centre of the world diamond industry when jeweller Lodewyk van Bercken invented the *scaif* – a polishing wheel infused with olive oil and diamond dust – in the 15th century, which helped to cut stones in symmetrical shapes. It also details how diamonds are mined, polished and traded, and their subsequent uses in couture, art and industry, with the help of historical artifacts such as industrial machinery and delicate items of jewellery. A major highlight is the history of Flemish gold and silversmithery. The museum also explains the Kimberley Process, a UN-backed certification scheme which eliminates the trade of conflict diamonds.

THE DIAMOND TRADE

Despite the modest post-war architecture of Antwerp's diamond district, it stands as the global epicentre of the world diamond trade. Exclusive diamond exchanges facilitate multimillion deals daily, which remain closed to the public. Predominantly governed by the Jain community, who migrated from India in the late 20th century, the trade also includes a significant Orthodox Jewish minority, who were once the primary influencers in this industry.

13

Museum Mayer van den Bergh

K2 Lange Gasthuisstraat 19 10am-5pm Tue-Sun, Easter Mon 1 & 2 Jan, 1 May, Ascension, 1 Nov, 24 & 25 Dec museum mayervandenbergh.be

Fritz Mayer van den Bergh (1858–1901) was the scion of a wealthy trading family, but instead of following in his father's footsteps, he chose to devote himself to collecting art and curios. This museum was established by his mother 43 years after his death to display his collections. Among the many treasures are tapestries, furniture, ivories, stained glass, medieval and Renaissance sculptures and a number of excellent paintings, including *Dulle Griet* (Mad Meg), a powerful image of a chaotic world by Pieter Brueghel the Elder.

Other Brueghel highlights include *Twelve Proverbs on Wooden Plates* (1558), which astutely showcases the painter's sense of humour and feel for the vernacular with a series of 12 small paintings, each representing a different popular proverb of the time. There is also a poignant statue by Heinrich von Konstanz of John the Apostle resting his head on Jesus's shoulder.

←
Infanticide in Bethlehem at the Museum Mayer van den Bergh

14

Sint-Jacobskerk

L2 Lange Nieuwstraat 73-75, Eikenstraat Apr-Oct: 2-5pm daily; Nov-Mar: 9am-noon Mon-Sat

Noted as Rubens' burial place – his tomb is in his family's chapel behind the high altar – this sandstone church was built from 1491 to 1656. Sint-Jacobskerk's rich interior contains the tombs of several other notable Antwerp families, as well as a collection of 17th-century art, including sculptures by Hendrik Verbruggen, and paintings by van Dyck, Otto Venius (Rubens' first master) and Jacob Jordaens.

15

Museum van Hedendaagse Kunst Antwerpen (M HKA)

J3 Leuvenstraat 32 11am-6pm Tue-Sun (to 9pm Thu) 1 Jan, 1 May, Ascension & 25 Dec muhka.be

This museum is what you might expect from a city famed for its sense of style and design. A huge, sculptural building that was once a 1920s dockside grain silo and warehouse has been transformed into a series of unusual spaces to display international contemporary art from 1970 through to the present. This includes works by many of the artists who have helped to place Belgium at the forefront of the art scene, such as Panamarenko, Luc Tuymans, Jan Fabre and Wim Delvoye.

Particular highlights of the collection include Panamarenko's sketches of helicopters and jet suits, and Luc Tuymans' series of moving, often unnerving, portraits. Recent special exhibitions have focused on, among others, Marcel van Maele (1931–2009), a Belgian outsider artist who spent 30 years of his life hitchhiking across the world.

16

Rubenshuis

L2 Wapper 9-11 7, 8, 9, 11, 12 For refurbishment until 2027 rubenshuis.be

Rubenshuis, on Wapper Square, was Pieter Paul Rubens' home and studio for the last 29 years of his life, from 1611 to 1640. The city bought the premises just before World War II, but by then the house was little more than a ruin, and what can be seen today is the result of careful restoration. It is divided into two

A detailed exhibit on emigration to America, Red Star Line Museum

18

FotoMuseum

J3 Waalsekaai 47
10am–6pm Tue–Sun
25 & 26 Dec, 1 & 2 Jan
fomu.be

Antwerp's excellent museum of photography, displaying a wide range of historical artifacts and images, has undergone a complete makeover, and embraced the moving image as well by incorporating the Antwerp Film Museum (which offers scheduled film viewings). Exhibits rotate every year or so, but often highlight the work of up-and-coming Belgian photographers such as Emilio Azevedo, whose work explores the historical and cultural roots of ecological crises; concurrent exhibits are often held which focus on the work of a single, more established artist, such as Ghanaian photographer James Barnor.

sections. To the left of the entrance are the narrow rooms of the artist's living quarters, equipped with period furniture. Behind this part of the house is the kunstkamer, or art gallery, where Rubens exhibited both his own and other artists' work, and entertained his friends and wealthy patrons, such as the Archdukes Albert and Isabella. To the right of the entrance lies the main studio, a spacious salon where Rubens worked on and displayed his paintings. A signposted route guides visitors through the house.

late 19th century up to 1934. These included some of the most prominent artists and scientists of the 20th century – Irving Berlin and Albert Einstein, to name just two. The exhibits put individual stories at the centre of things, and outline the often rough and demeaning conditions which passengers were subjected to on the journey.

17

Red Star Line Museum

K1 Montevideostraat 3
10am–5pm Tue–Sun 1
Jan, 1 May, Ascension Day,
1 Nov, 25 Dec redstar
line.be

Located in the old Red Star Line terminal in the port area of the city, this fascinating museum tells the story of Antwerp's historic shipping company, and the over two million people it took to a new life in North America from the

PORT OF ANTWERP

The Port of Antwerp was the source of the city's wealth in its Flanders heyday, with diamonds, spices and priceless artworks passing through. It remains important today, and is visually striking, with its echoing hangars, towering cranes and shipping containers. The port area is home to some great museums like Red Star Line and MAS, and is also features stunning pieces of architecture such as the Havenhuis (Port Authority Building), designed by Zaha Hadid.

A SHORT WALK
AROUND GROTE MARKT

EXPERIENCE Antwerp

Distance 2 km (1.2 miles) **Time** 25 minutes
Nearest station Groenplaats

Fanning out from the east bank of the River Scheldt, Antwerp has long been one of the leading trading cities of northern Europe. Today, the city's industries lie away from its medieval core, whose narrow streets and fine buildings cluster around the cathedral and Grote Markt. Packed with evidence of Antwerp's rich history, this is a delightful area to wander. Most sites of interest are within easy walking distance of Grote Markt, whose surrounding streets house museums, shops and exuberant cafés and bars.

To Koninklijk Museum voor Schone Kunsten

STEENPLEIN

JORDAENSKAAI

KUIPERSSTRAAT

SUIKERRUI

OUDE KOORNMARKT

*Flanking Grote Markt is the elegant 16th-century **Stadhuis**, designed by Cornelis Floris (1514–75).*

*The statue on the **Brabo Fountain** depicts the fearless soldier Silvius Brabo. Said to be the nephew of Julius Caesar, Brabo is shown throwing the hand of the mythical giant, Antigonius, into the River Scheldt.*

0 metres   50
0 yards   50
N ↑

← The Stadhuis, dominating the centre of Grote Markt

START ▶

Occupied by the Butcher's Guild for three centuries, the **Vleeshuis** features striking layers of brick and stone that look like alternating strips of fat and lean meat.

Locator Map

Around Grote Markt

ANTWERP

Sint-Pauluskerk was built in 1571. Inside this church, there is a noted collection of paintings, including one especially fine work by Rubens.

To Centraal Station

ZIRKSTRAAT

VERSMIDSTRAAT

→ The historic Groenplaats lined with food stalls

Antwerp's prosperous trade links in the 16th century are reflected in **Grote Markt's** series of guildhalls on the north side of the square.

Onze-Lieve-Vrouwekathedraal is the largest Gothic cathedral in Belgium. It occupies a 1-ha (2.5-acre) site in Antwerp's centre.

To Rubenshuis

The **Groenplaats** or Green Square is a pleasant open space with trees. Lined with cafés, bars and restaurants, it is a popular spot with both locals and visitors for a peaceful stroll or meal.

Did You Know?

The reconstruction of Grote Markt's Renaissance façades was based on Flemish paintings.

FINISH

A LONG WALK
AROUND ANTWERP

Distance 3.5 km (2 miles) **Stopping-off points** For a coffee, stop at the Grand Café Horta, or head straight to the spectacular RAS/Zuiderterras restaurant **Nearest station** Centraal Station

Antwerp handles 80 per cent of the world's entire trade in rough diamonds. This walk starts at an architectural jewel in the otherwise rather modest diamond district, the Centraal railway station, and heads west to the Meir, Antwerp's main shopping thoroughfare, before visiting the haunts of Rubens and his contemporaries at the Rubenshuis, Sint-Jacobskerk and the Rockoxhuis. It then passes through medieval Antwerp to reach the broad sweep of the River Scheldt.

Follow the route west to reach Hendrik Conscienceplein. Overlooking the square is the fine Baroque façade of the **Sint-Carolus Borromeuskerk** *(p145).*

Just beyond the cathedral is **Grote Markt** *(p142), Antwerp's spectacular main square, which is home to the town hall, along with many restaurants and taverns.*

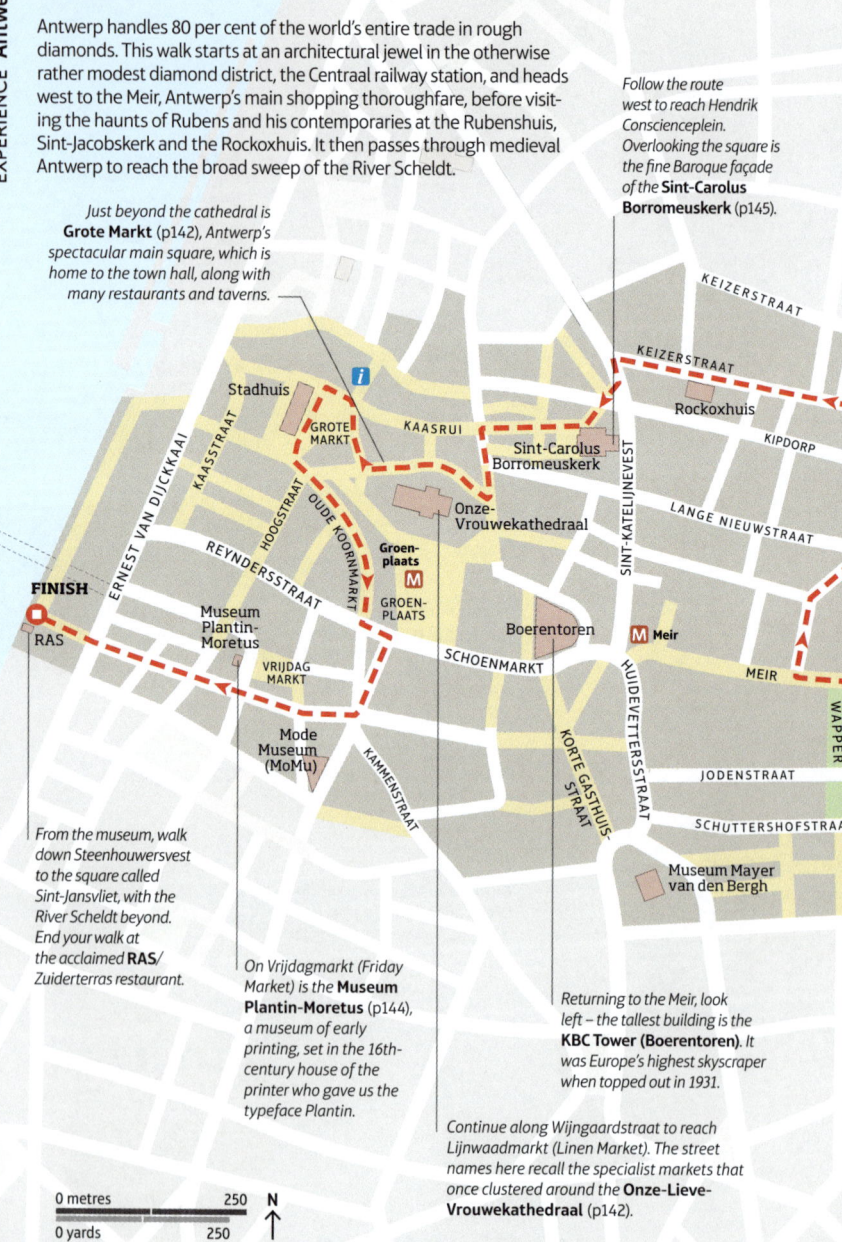

From the museum, walk down Steenhouwersvest to the square called Sint-Jansvliet, with the River Scheldt beyond. End your walk at the acclaimed **RAS**/*Zuiderterras restaurant.*

On Vrijdagmarkt (Friday Market) is the **Museum Plantin-Moretus** *(p144), a museum of early printing, set in the 16th-century house of the printer who gave us the typeface Plantin.*

Returning to the Meir, look left – the tallest building is the **KBC Tower (Boerentoren)**. *It was Europe's highest skyscraper when topped out in 1931.*

Continue along Wijngaardstraat to reach Lijnwaadmarkt (Linen Market). The street names here recall the specialist markets that once clustered around the **Onze-Lieve-Vrouwekathedraal** *(p142).*

ANTWERP

Around
Antwerp

Locator Map

By walking up Lange Klarenstraat, you can reach **Sint-Jacobskerk** *(p146), which is the burial place of Rubens.*

↑ Stunning Neo-Classical façade of Antwerp's Centraal Station

KEIZERSTRAAT

ST JACOBSTR.

SINT-JACOBSMARKT

Sint-Jacobskerk

LANGE NIEUWSTRAAT

ITALIËLEI

OSY STRAAT

VAN ARTEVELDESTRAAT

FRANKLIN ROOSEVELT PLAATS

Astrid Ⓜ

GEMEENTESTRAAT

MEIR

De Vlaamse Opera

ANNEESSENS STR.

STATIE STRAAT

KONINGIN ASTRIDPLEIN

LEYSSTR.

Ⓜ **Opera**

DE KEYSERLEI

START

Diamantmuseum

Rubenshuis

KIPDORPVEST

FRANKRIJKLEI

QUELLINSTRAAT

APPELMANSSTRAAT

Diamant Ⓜ

VESTINGSTRAAT

PELIKAANSTRAAT

Centraal Station

OMMEGANCKSTRAAT

Zoo

HOPLAND

APPELMANSSTRAAT

MEI STRAAT

THEATERPLEIN

PLOEGSTRAAT

Next, walk west along the pedestrianized high street (the Meir) until you reach Wapper Square on your left. On the left-hand side of the street is the **Rubenshuis** *(p146) while the stylish Grand Café Horta is at the end of the Wapper.*

Get a feel for Antwerp's diamond district by walking down Pelikaanstraat and **Vestingstraat**.

Begin in **Centraal Station**, *a palatial Neo-Classical building completed in 1905 that is worth visiting in its own right.*

GHENT

There is physical evidence of Ghent having been inhabited since the Stone Age, but there is little written history until 650 CE, when French bishop Amandus established two abbeys here dedicated to St Bavo and St Peter. From these humble origins the city developed into a prominent city-state, its defences bolstered by the 1180 construction of Het Gravensteen – home of the Counts of Flanders – and its wealth made through the cloth trade. By the time the mighty Belfort was built in 1380, Ghent was one of the largest cities in Europe. Later, in the 16th and 17th centuries, Ghent's fortunes declined, largely due to the wreckage of the Eighty Years' War, which was fought between rebel armies (who used Ghent as a prominent base) and the Spanish government of the Netherlands. In the 18th century, Ghent's textile industry rose to prominence once again after entrepreneur Lieven Bauwens (later the mayor of Ghent) travelled to Britain as a spy and smuggled back a spinning mule and steam engine; as a result, Ghent became, arguably, mainland Europe's first industrialized city. The city continued to grow and prosper and today, many of its former trade hubs and well-preserved buildings have been revitalized as popular tourist spots.

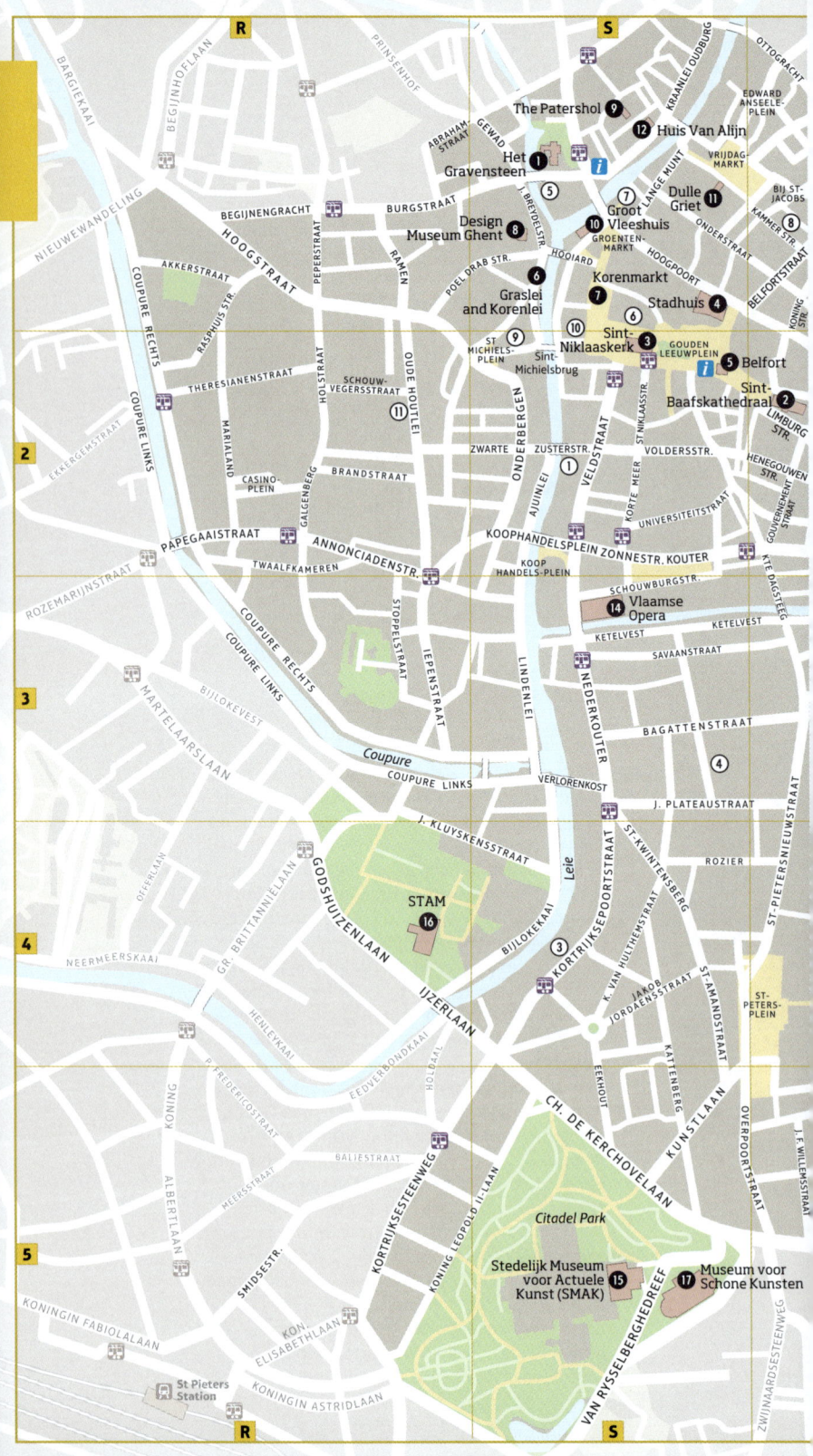

R

S

The Patershol **9**

12 Huis Van Alijn

Het
Gravensteen **1**

5

7 Dulle
Griet **11**

Groot
Vleeshuis

Design
Museum Ghent **8**

10
GROENTEN-
MARKT

6

Korenmarkt

7

Graslei
and Korenlei

Stadhuis **4**

6

ST
MICHIELS-
PLEIN

9

10

Sint-
Niklaaskerk

3

Gouden
Leeuwplein

Sint-
Michielsbrug

5 Belfort

1

2 Sint-
Baafskathedraal

14 Vlaamse
Opera

4

STAM

16

3

Citadel Park

Stedelijk Museum
voor Actuele
Kunst (SMAK) **15**

17 Museum voor
Schone Kunsten

St Pieters
Station

R

S

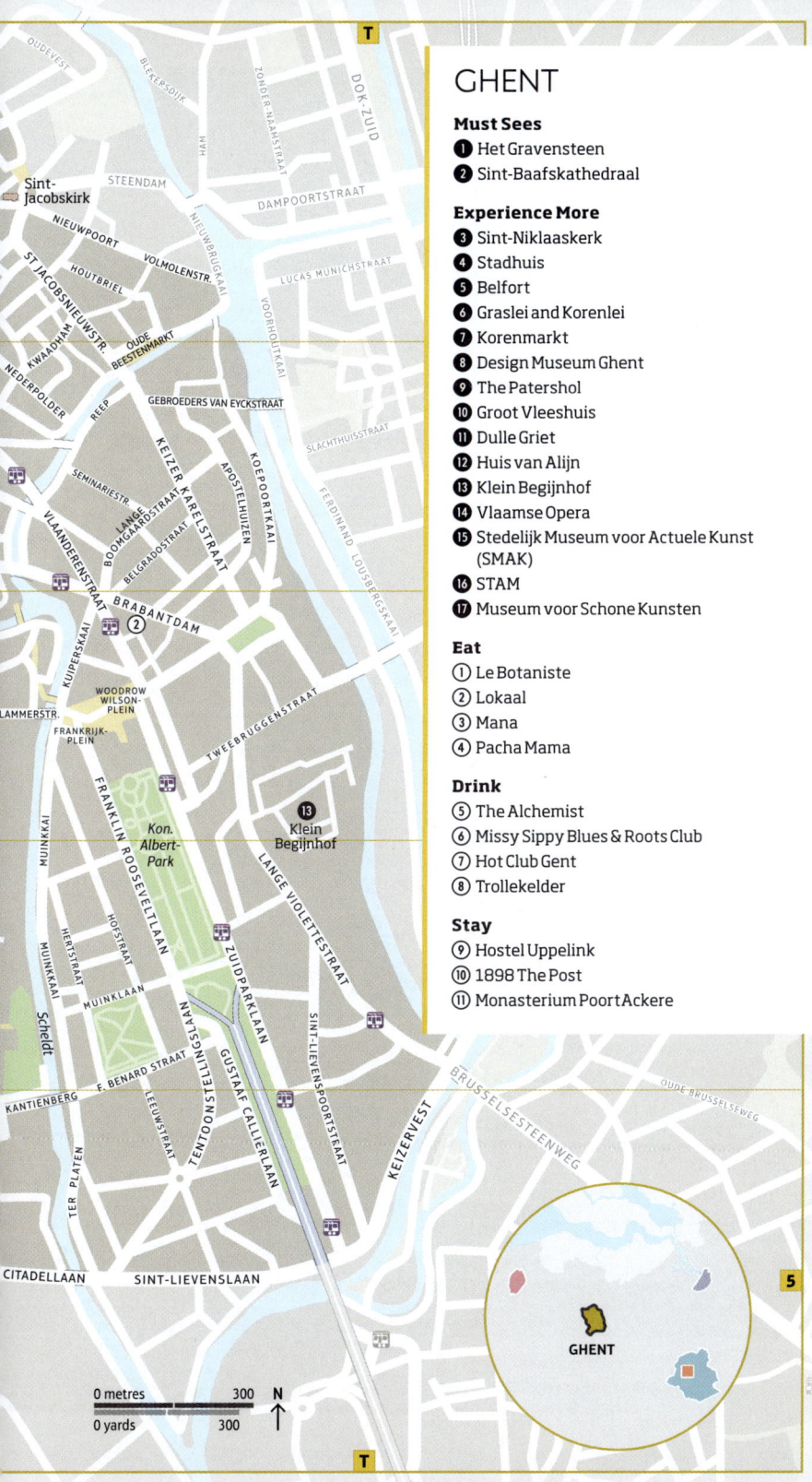

GHENT

Must Sees
❶ Het Gravensteen
❷ Sint-Baafskathedraal

Experience More
❸ Sint-Niklaaskerk
❹ Stadhuis
❺ Belfort
❻ Graslei and Korenlei
❼ Korenmarkt
❽ Design Museum Ghent
❾ The Patershol
❿ Groot Vleeshuis
⓫ Dulle Griet
⓬ Huis van Alijn
⓭ Klein Begijnhof
⓮ Vlaamse Opera
⓯ Stedelijk Museum voor Actuele Kunst (SMAK)
⓰ STAM
⓱ Museum voor Schone Kunsten

Eat
① Le Botaniste
② Lokaal
③ Mana
④ Pacha Mama

Drink
⑤ The Alchemist
⑥ Missy Sippy Blues & Roots Club
⑦ Hot Club Gent
⑧ Trollekelder

Stay
⑨ Hostel Uppelink
⑩ 1898 The Post
⑪ Monasterium Poort Ackere

Paddling past the massive stone fortress of Het Gravensteen ↑

1

HET GRAVENSTEEN

📍 S1 🏛 Sint-Veerleplein 🕐 Apr–Oct: 10am–6pm daily; Nov–Mar: 9am–5pm daily 🚫 1 Jan, 24, 25 & 31 Dec 🌐 visitgent.be

Discover the more gruesome side of Ghent's history at this imposing medieval fortress. Occupied for hundreds of years, Het Gravensteen tells the tales of this area's turbulent political past, as well as unveiling the terrifying methods of torture used here.

Once the seat of the counts of Flanders, the imposing stone walls of Het Gravensteen (or the Castle of the Counts) eloquently recall the unsettled and violent context of Ghent's early medieval past. Parts of the castle date back to the late 1100s, but most sections are later additions. Up until the 14th century, the castle was Ghent's main military stronghold, and from then until the late 1700s, it was used as the city's prison. Later, it became a cotton mill.

From the gatehouse, a long and heavily fortified tunnel leads up to the courtyard, which is overseen by two large buildings, the count's medieval residence and the earlier keep. Arrows guide visitors round the interior of both buildings. Inside, atmospheric halls, narrow passageways and stone towers await, while the upper rooms host a spine-chilling collection of medieval torture instruments.

One of the highlights of the castle is the amusing audio guide, recorded by Belgian comedian Wouter Deprez and included in the entrance ticket. Visual guides of the recording in Flemish or international sign language are also available for those with hearing impairments.

→

The spacious, multi-arched interior of the historic castle

 HIDDEN GEM
Taquen's Mural

Visible only from one of the towers of Het Gravensteen is a mural by Spanish artist Taquen. Commissioned in 2020, the mural celebrates artist Jan van Eyck, and is a re-creation of his self-portrait, *Man in a Red Turban*.

SINT-BAAFSKATHEDRAAL

📍 T2 🏠 Sint-Baafsplein 🕐 Cathedral: 8:30am–6:30pm Mon–Sat, 1–5:30pm Sun; van Eyck painting: 10am–5pm Mon–Sat, 1–5:30pm Sun 🚫 1 Jan 🌐 sintbaafskathedraal.be

With its staggering 89-m- (292-ft-) tall bell tower, Sint-Baafskathedraal (St Bavo's Cathedral) looms over the city centre. This cathedral is famous for its Gothic architecture and the treasure trove of artwork it houses.

In the 7th century, St Bavo (or Bavon) became Ghent's patron saint, after he abandoned his life of wealth to become a missionary in France and Flanders and then a hermit. He was buried here in 653 CE. Built in several stages, Sint-Baafskathedraal has features representing every phase of Gothic style, from the early chancel through to the later cavernous nave, the cathedral's architectural highlight. It is home to one of Europe's most remarkable paintings, Jan van Eyck's polyptych *The Adoration of the Mystic Lamb* (1432).

GREAT VIEW
Climb the Tower

Some of the finest views over Ghent can be seen by climbing the bell tower of Sint-Baafskathedraal. However, the tower is only open to the public during the ten-day Ghent Festivities in July.

THE ADORATION OF THE MYSTIC LAMB

In a sidechapel of Sint-Baafskathedraal is one of the greatest cultural treasures of northern Europe. *The Adoration of the Mystic Lamb* (1432) is a monumental, multi-panelled painting by Jan van Eyck, and his lesser-known brother, Hubrecht. What you see today is almost entirely original; only the lower left panel is a modern copy, following its theft in 1934. This is remarkable given the painting's history: it was rescued from Protestant church-wreckers in 1566 and from fire in 1822; parts of it were removed by French soldiers in 1794, and other parts were sold in 1816. Audio guides (included in the price of the entry ticket) explain the significance of the 12 panels.

↑ A series of stained-glass windows in the cathedral

↑ Sint-Baafskathedraal's opulent Gothic altar

↑ St Baafskathedraal's magnificent façade in the city centre

EXPERIENCE MORE

3

Sint-Niklaaskerk

📍 S2 🏠 Cataloniëstraat 3
🕐 10am–4pm daily
🌐 sintniklaaskerk.be

This merchants' church, built in the 13th–15th centuries, was dedicated to their patron saint, St Nicholas, Bishop of Myra (and Santa Claus). The church is a fine example of the distinctive and austere style called Scheldt Gothic. The interior was once packed full of guild shrines and chapels, until Protestant church-wreckers destroyed them in 1566; today it is remarkable for its pure architectural forms, with soaring columns brightly lit by high windows. The interior is punctuated by an extravagant Baroque altar screen, a clarion call to the Counter-Reformation, unusual for such latter-day alterations.

4

Stadhuis

📍 S1 🏠 Botermarkt 1
🕐 Tours: 2:30pm onwards from the tourist office (Sint-Veerleplein 5)

The Stadhuis façade displays two architectural styles. Overlooking Hoogstraat, the older half dates from the early 16th century, its tracery in the elaborate Flamboyant Gothic style. The simpler, newer part, which flanks the Botermarkt, is a characteristic example of post-Reformation architecture. The statues in the niches on the façade were added in the 1890s. Among this group of figures is the original architect, Rombout Keldermans, who is shown studying his plans.

The building is still the city's administrative centre. Guided tours pass through a series of rooms, including the Pacification Hall. This was once the

Guildhouses on the Graslei and Korenlei embankments ↑

Court of Justice and the site of the signing of the Pacification of Ghent (a treaty between Catholics and Protestants against Habsburg rule) in 1576.

5

Belfort

📍 S2 🏠 Sint-Baafsplein 3
📞 (09) 233 3954 🕐 10am–6pm daily; tours: 3:30pm
🗓 1 Jan, 25, 26 & 31 Dec

Ghent's belfry, a prominent landmark rising 91 m (299 ft) to the gilded-copper dragon on the tip of its spire, is situated between the cathedral and the town hall. A lift to its parapet at 65 m (213 ft) offers

←

The Scheldt-Gothic architecture of Sint-Niklaaskerk, and *(inset)* one of its stained-glass windows

magnificent views over the city. Originally built in 1313, the Belfort was restored in the 19th and 20th centuries. Its bells today include a 54-bell carillon. It plays tunes to accompany the clock chimes every 15 minutes, and for keyboard concerts every Sunday around noon and evenings on the first Friday of the month. Below the Belfort is the *Lakenhalle* (Cloth Hall), a fine Flemish-Gothic building from 1425, where the city's cloth trade was carried out. The building is also attached to what was once a small prison.

6
Graslei and Korenlei
 S1

These two embankments face each other across the Tusschen Brugghen, once Ghent's main medieval harbour. The Graslei, on the eastern side, possesses a fine set of guildhouses. Among them, at No. 14, is the sandstone façade of the Guildhouse of the Free Boatmen, which is decorated with detailed nautical scenes. The Corn Measurers' guildhouse next door is adorned by bunches of fruit and cartouches. The earliest building here is the 12th-century Spijker (Staple House) at No. 10. This simple Romanesque structure stored

the city's grain supply for hundreds of years until a fire destroyed its interior.

The gabled buildings of the Korenlei, facing the Graslei across the water, date from later centuries, but gracefully complement the Graslei. The views from Sint-Michielsbrug, the bridge at the southern end, are among the most beautiful in Ghent.

7
Korenmarkt
S1 Cataloniëstraat
Daily

This square in Ghent's old town, beside the impressive Sint-Niklaaskerk, feels like the heart of the city. There's always something going on here, and its bevy of open-sided cafés and bars bustle with life whenever the weather allows. The road which the church backs onto is called Klein Turkije (Little Turkey). Apparently a corruption of the Dutch phrase *"ter keie gaan"* ("to hit rock bottom"), the name is a reference to the road's past life as a venue for post-bankruptcy public auctions. It's a much happier affair now with a line of buzzing pubs and bars. On the opposite side is Donkersteeg (Dark Alley), which is home to vibrant fashion boutiques.

EAT

Le Botaniste
Wholesome vegan restaurant with a plant-based décor and a menu to match. Dishes include Mexican *chili con carne,* peanut curry and veggie tagines.

S2 Hoornstraat 13
lebotaniste.eu

Lokaal
Local produce is celebrated in the small but ever-changing menu of this café-restaurant. Try their sweet potato lasagne and apple crumble with pumpkin miso.

T3 Brabantdam 100
lokaal.gent

Mana
This restaurant is all about what's fresh and seasonal, and offers just one main meal a day, with a soup and dessert.

S4
Kortrijksepoortstraat 220 mana.gent

Pacha Mama
Rich veggie curries and stews are a mainstay at this laid-back spot, with daily menus.

S3 Jan-Baptist Guinardstraat 9
(09) 330 3335

DRINK

The Alchemist

Enjoy an extensive menu of gins, beers and cocktails at this atmospheric pub, featuring shabby-chic décor and a lively and friendly ambience.

📍 S1
🏠 Rekelingestraat 3

Missy Sippy Blues & Roots Club

Head here to have a drink while enjoying one of the best sound-tracks in town. Live blues, rock, and jazz music performances take place on at least four nights every week.

📍 S1 🏠 Klein Turkije 16
🌐 missy-sippy.be

Hot Club Gent

This dark and ethereal jazz bar was founded to preserve and promote jazz music. It hosts several live music performances each week. There's also a wide selection of both classic cocktails and Belgian beers.

📍 S1
🏠 Schuddevisstraatje 2
🌐 hotclub.gent

Trollekelder

This cavernous place – its name translates to "Troll Cellar" – has a whopping 300 beers on offer, including some of the latest creations from local micro-breweries. A new local brewery and beer are in the spotlight each month.

📍 T1 🏠 Walter de Buckplein 4
🌐 trollekelder.be

8

Design Museum Ghent

📍 S1 🏠 Jan Breydelstraat 5
📞 (09) 267 9999 🕐 Until 2025 🌐 designmuseum gent.be

This decorative arts museum has a large collection of works contained within an elegant 18th-century townhouse. The displays are arranged in two sections, beginning at the front with a series of lavishly furnished period rooms that feature textiles, furniture and artifacts from the 17th to the 19th centuries.

At the back, a modern extension to the building focuses on modern design from Art Nouveau to contemporary works, and includes furniture by Victor Horta (*p103*), Marcel Breuer and Ludwig Mies van der Rohe.

9

The Patershol

📍 S1

North of the Kraanlei and behind the Huis van Alijn folk museum are the quaint

cobbled lanes and low brick houses of the Patershol, a district that developed in the 17th century to house the city's weavers and Carmelite Friars (Paters). This once down-at-heel area underwent extensive refurbishment in the 1980s and is now one of the trendiest parts of town, with upmarket restaurants, cafés and shops.

10

Groot Vleeshuis

📍 S1 🏠 Groentenmarkt 7
📞 (09) 223 23 24 🕐 10am-6pm Tue–Sun

The "Great Meat Hall" was built in 1407–19, and its long, low interior space still reflects

Enjoying an afternoon out at the Patershol's chic cafés ↑

its basic, original purpose as a covered butchers' market, complete with ancient beams and wonky flooring. Into this simple space, a large, modern glass box has been ingeniously inserted to serve as a centre to promote East Flemish food: on the one side, a small restaurant serves good-value Flemish dishes; on the other is a delicatessen.

↑ Re-creation of a 20th-century grocery store at the Huis van Alijn folk museum

 11

Dulle Griet

📍 S1 🏠 Groot Kanonplein (off Vrijdagmarkt)

This giant iron cannon, sitting on the embankment of the River Leie, is very popular in the folklore of Ghent. Cast in about 1450, 5 m (16 ft, 5 in) long and weighing 16 tonnes (16 tons), it could fire heavy stone cannonballs the size of a beachball.

It was brought to Ghent in 1578, during a period of conflict with Spain. Dulle Griet translates to "Mad Meg", a legendary Flemish medieval character who embodied mad, violent frenzy and disorder. The cannon is painted in its original red, reflecting its other nickname "Groten Rooden Duyvele" (meaning "Great Red Devil").

HIDDEN GEM
Dr Guislain Museum

A ten-minute drive from the Patershol is Belgium's oldest asylum (1837), now a museum. It was revolutionary for Dr Joseph Guislain's humane and progressive treatments.

  12

Huis van Alijn

📍 S1 🏠 Kraanlei 65 🕐 11am–5:30pm Tue–Sat, 10am–5:30pm Sun 🚫 1 Jan, 25 Dec 🌐 huis vanalijn.be

This is one of Belgium's best folk museums, evocatively showcasing daily life in the past through a huge collection of fascinating artifacts – including dolls and other toys, games, clothes, furniture, kitchenware, funerary mementoes, as well as complete shops and crafters' workshops.

There is also a puppet theatre, which presents plays (in Dutch) throughout the year. The museum is set in a sequence of rooms in a pretty group of whitewashed almshouses, "The House of Alijn", surrounding a grassy courtyard. Although mainly built in the 16th century, the almshouses were originally founded in 1363 as a children's hospital. Interestingly, this was done not out of philanthropy, but as an act of penance by the Rijm family for the murder of two members of the rival Alijn family.

Relaxing by Ghent's scenic River Leie

Bright red houses dating from the 17th century in Klein Begijnhof

15

Stedelijk Museum voor Actuele Kunst (SMAK)

9 S5 **A** Jan Hoetplein 1 **O** 10am–6pm Tue–Sun **W** smak.be

SMAK is one of Europe's most dynamic modern art galleries, a leading force in the art world that has helped to bring the spotlight on the Belgian art scene. Despite its stratospheric reputation, the museum has only existed since 1999. It was founded by prominent Belgian art impresario Jan Hoet, with the intention of creating a world-class space which would showcase the finest contemporary art, from 1945 onwards, from Belgium and beyond. After Hoet's retirement, operations were overtaken by a collective of artists headed by legendary Belgian painter Luc Tuymans. The airy and attractive building dates from 1949 but was remodelled in the 1990s.

The museum's extensive permanent collection includes over 3,000 works from across major art movements including Cobra, pop art, minimal art, conceptual art and *Arte Povera*. It features works by artists such as Bacon, Beuys, Broodthaers, Long, Muñoz, Nauman, Panamarenko, Tuymans and Warhol, along with works by local artists. Temporary exhibitions showcase international artists at the cutting edge of contemporary art. The museum complex also houses a café and a bookshop.

13

Klein Begijnhof

9 T3 **A** Lange Violettestraat 205 **O** 6:30am–10pm daily

The Klein Begijnhof (Small Béguinage) is the prettiest of Ghent's three béguinages (*p87*). It was founded as a community of single women in 1235. It has been occupied ever since, but the residents today are no longer béguines. Rows of step-gabled, whitewashed houses – most dating from the 17th century – enclose a small park and Baroque church, creating a tranquil refuge. The church is beautiful, although not always open – knock on the door and the warden may be willing to give you a tour.

14

Vlaamse Opera

9 S3 **A** Schouwburgstraat 3 **O** For performances; guided tours: third Sat of the month **W** opera ballet.be

This classic opera house was built in 1837–40; it has been restored to reclaim its reputation as one of the most spectacular theatres in Europe, with an auditorium and adjoining salons encrusted with gilding, chandeliers and sculptures. The resident company is the much-respected Vlaamse Opera (Flemish Opera), which formed when the opera companies of Ghent and Antwerp merged. Most performances are followed by interviews with the production team and the cast; after-parties are also held free of charge in the main hall.

GHENT'S MUSIC SCENE

Ghent has a lively music scene, bolstered by its vibrant student population. Many local artists have had international success, including electronic outfit Soulwax (and their alter-ego, 2manydjs), indie rockers Evil Superstars and monster guitar-riffers Raketkanon. Among the city's famous classical composers are Renaissance masters Alexander Agricola and Jacob Obrecht.

Browsing artworks in the "Story of Ghent" exhibition at STAM

> STAM provides an introduction to the city's rich history and cultural heritage, tracing its evolution to the present day.

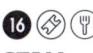

16 STAM

R4 **Bijlokesite, Godshuizenlaan 2** **9am–5pm Mon, Tue, Thu & Fri, 10am–6pm Sat & Sun** **1 Jan, 24, 25 & 31 Dec** **stamgent.be**

Located on a site that brings together a 14th-century Gothic abbey, a 17th-century monastery and splendid 21st-century architecture, STAM is Ghent's city museum. It provides an introduction to the city's rich history and cultural heritage, tracing its evolution to the present day.

The permanent "Story of Ghent" exhibition provides a detailed insight into the city's history, with themed rooms re-creating Flemish mansions and noble castles, and a vast aerial photograph of the city. There are also gorgeous wire-framed models depicting iconic buildings like Het Gravensteen. Don't miss the towers of Ghent built with LEGO. A children's trail with interactive, multisensory exhibits has also been created.

17 Museum voor Schone Kunsten

S5 **Fernand Scribedreef, Citadelpark 3** **10am–6pm Tue–Sun (to 10pm on select days, check website)** **mskgent.be**

Ghent's largest collection of fine art is housed in this Neo-Classical building. Medieval paintings include the *Bearing of the Cross* by Hieronymus Bosch (1450–1516), and works by Rubens, Anthony van Dyck (1599–1641) and Jacob Jordaens (1593–1678). Modern works displayed include *Perspective II: Manet's Balcony* (1950) by René Magritte.

From 2023 until 2026, sections of the world-famous *Adoration of the Mystic Lamb* by the van Eyck brothers *(p158)* are being restored in a studio behind glass – a rare opportunity to observe this craft.

Occasionally, "late" evenings are held, when the museum stays open until 10pm; you can walk among the dimly lit exhibits while enjoying a drink to live classical music. Visitors also heading to Antwerp's Royal Museum of Fine Arts and the Groeninge Museum in Bruges should invest in the Flemish Art Collection combo ticket.

STAY

Hostel Uppelink

An upmarket hostel with both private and shared dorms, and a bar. City tours and kayaking are on offer.

S2 **Sint-Michielsplein 21** **hosteluppelink.com**

1898 The Post

A stylish hotel with luxurious rooms and a popular cocktail bar, The Cobbler.

S1 **Graslei 16** **1898thepost.com**

Monasterium PoortAckere

Housed in a medieval monastery, this hotel has lovely period features and a garden.

R2 **Oude Houtlei 56** **monasterium.be**

Sijne Excellentie op desen ...
waer uyt een ieder met
van t'governement van

A SHORT WALK

GHENT

Distance 1.5km (1 mile) **Time** 20 minutes
Nearest station Gent Gravensteen

As a tourist destination, the Flemish city of Ghent has long been overshadowed by its neighbour, Bruges. In part this reflects their divergent histories. The success of the cloth trade during the Middle Ages was followed by a period of stagnation for Bruges, while Ghent became a major industrial centre in the 18th and 19th centuries. The resulting pollution coated the city's antique buildings in layers of grime from its many factories. In the 1980s, Ghent initiated a restoration programme. The city's medieval buildings were cleaned, industrial sites were tidied up and the canals were cleared. Today, it is the intricately carved stonework of its churches and antique buildings, as well as the city's excellent museums and stern, forbidding castle, that give the centre its character.

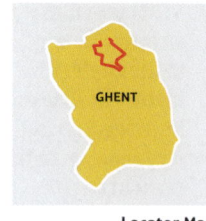

Locator Map

*Ghent's centre is dominated by the thick stone walls of **Het Gravensteen** (p156).*

START

*The **Design Museum Ghent** (p162) is housed in an 18th-century mansion and covers art and design from the 1600s to the present. Its exhibits include many charming period rooms.*

*One of Ghent's most picturesque streets, the **Graslei** (p161), situated on the city's medieval harbour, overlooks the River Leie.*

***Korenmarkt** (p161) was once the city's corn market. Today, it is lined with numerous popular cafés.*

Exploring bustling Korenmart, lined with cafés and stores

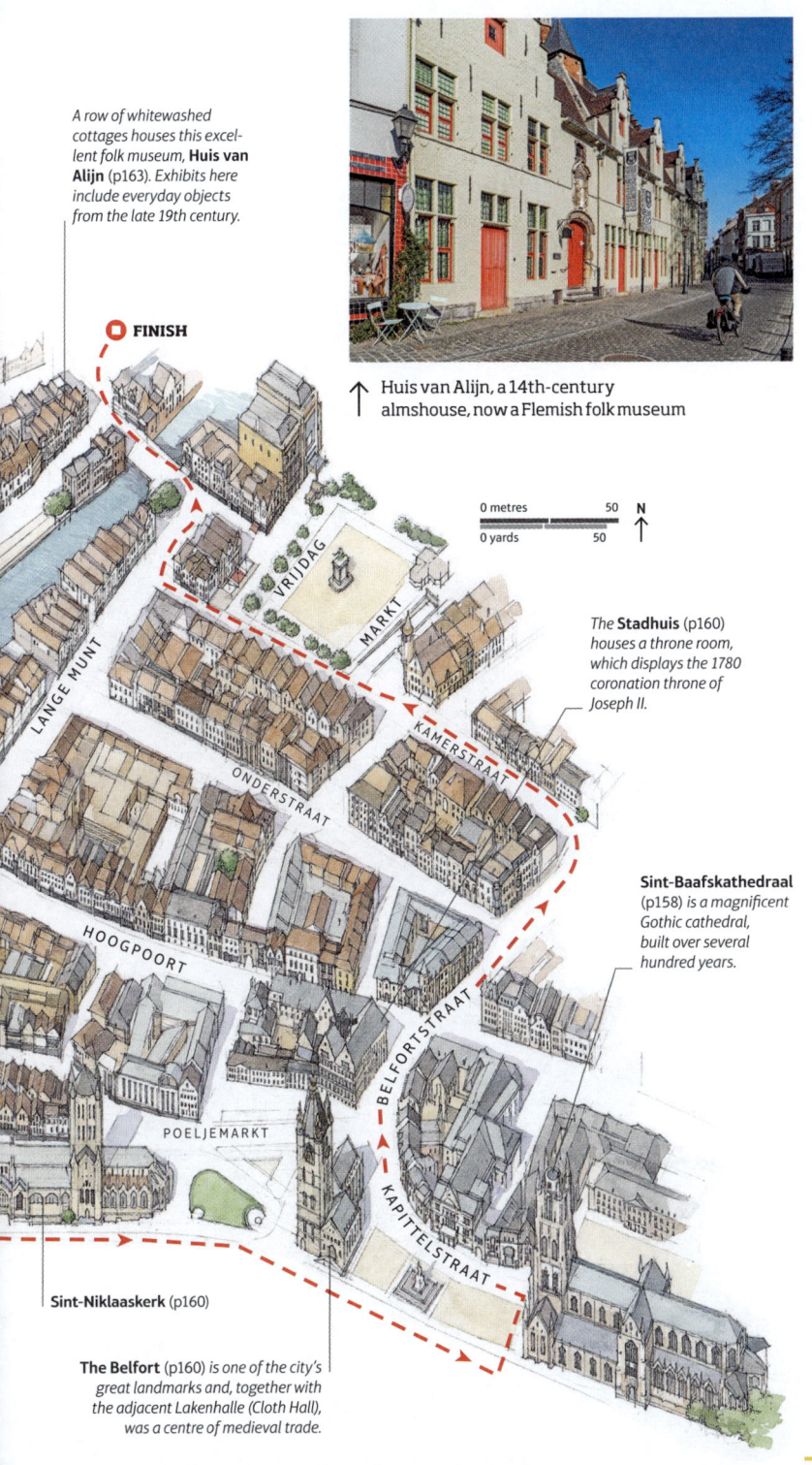

*A row of whitewashed cottages houses this excellent folk museum, **Huis van Alijn** (p163). Exhibits here include everyday objects from the late 19th century.*

FINISH

↑ Huis van Alijn, a 14th-century almshouse, now a Flemish folk museum

VRIJDAG MARKT

0 metres 50
0 yards 50

N ↑

*The **Stadhuis** (p160) houses a throne room, which displays the 1780 coronation throne of Joseph II.*

LANGE MUNT

ONDERSTRAAT

KAMERSTRAAT

Sint-Baafskathedraal (p158) *is a magnificent Gothic cathedral, built over several hundred years.*

HOOGPOORT

BELFORTSTRAAT

POELJEMARKT

KAPITTELSTRAAT

Sint-Niklaaskerk (p160)

The Belfort (p160) *is one of the city's great landmarks and, together with the adjacent Lakenhalle (Cloth Hall), was a centre of medieval trade.*

DAYS OUT

While Belgium's four major cities are packed with attractions, just outside lie an array of elegant towns, tranquil countryside and sites rich in military history. Around 10 miles (16 km) east of Brussels is its medieval equal, Leuven. Although Brussels was chosen as the capital of the Brabant region in the 13th century, Leuven's status is evident in its stately Gothic Stadhuis (Town Hall) and churches. Smaller in scale but just as charming are the towns of Mechelen and Dendermonde, both home to impressive squares and buildings.

Much of this area has been shaped by war. South of Brussels is the town of Waterloo, which is first mentioned in historical records in 1102 as a small hamlet on the edge of the Sonian Forest, though it didn't begin to develop until the 17th century. Since then it has become synonymous with military history as the site of Napoleon's famous defeat at the hands of the Duke of Wellington in 1815. Today, an iconic bronze lion and fantastic museum tell the story of the fall of one of history's great military leaders. The countryside near Ypres, meanwhile, witnessed unprecedented bloodshed during World War I, and the city itself was almost completely destroyed in the fighting, only to be rebuilt brick by brick in an amazing feat of engineering. Numerous museums and cemeteries in the surrounding area bring this devastating period of history to life.

Hull

North Sea

Middelburg

N255

N62

Terneuzen

Zeebrugge
Knokke-Heist
Blankenberge
N49
Maldegem
Eeklo
Zelzate
Wachtebeke
N49

Oostende
Bruges
Zomergem
N9
Evergem

De Panne
Nieuwpoort
Gistel
Eernegem
Beernem
E40
Aalter
Ghent
Merelbeke

Koksijde
E40
Torhout
Ruiselede
De Pinte
A10

Veurne
Diksmuide
Lichtervelde
Deinze
E17
Gavere
Herzele

WEST-VLAANDEREN
N8
N35
N32
E403
Roeselare
OOST-VLAANDEREN
N46
Brakel
N8

Langemark
Izegem
N49
Waregem
Oudenaarde
Geraardsbergen

Poperinge
9 YPRES
A19
Harelbeke
N60

Kemmel
Menen
Kortrijk
N36
Avelgem
Ronse
Frasnes-lez-Buissenal

Ploegsteert
N50
Mouscron
Celles
E429

A25
Dottignies
N48

La Gorgue
Lille
Tournai
ATH 8
Attre
N56

A21
Rumes
Antoing
Leuze
N7

Bléharies
Péruwelz
E42
HAINAUT

A2
Valenciennes
N51

Somain

Douchy-les-Mines
Jenlain

FRANCE

DAYS OUT

Must Sees
1 Leuven
2 Waterloo

Experience More
3 Dendermonde
4 Pajottenland
5 Mechelen
6 Lier
7 Halle
8 Ath
9 Ypres

0 kilometres 20
0 miles 20

N

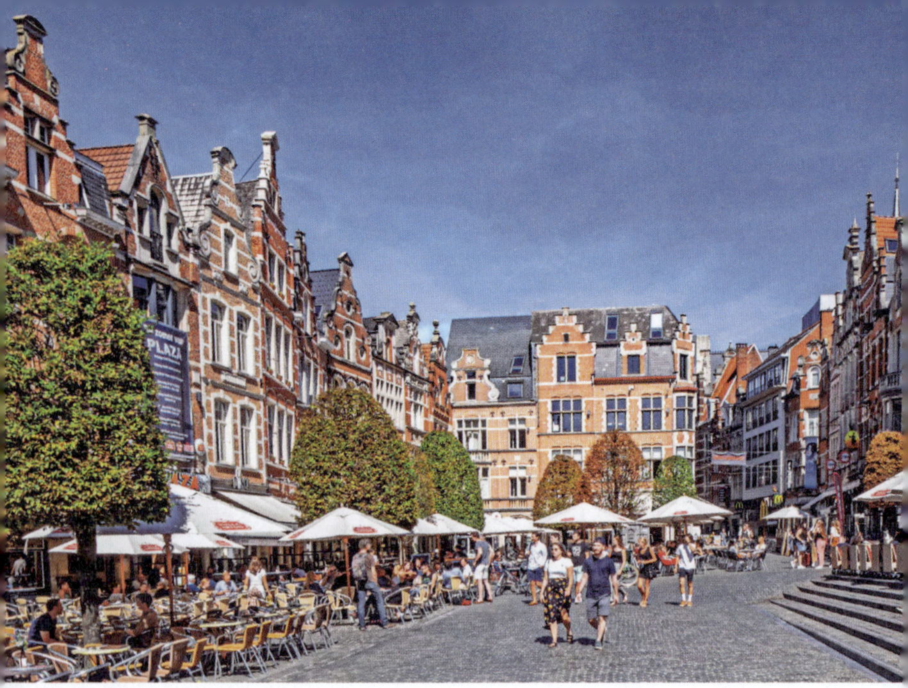

1

LEUVEN

Naamsestraat 1, (016) 20 3020 Bondgenotenlaan
Grote Markt 9

Near Brussels, the historic Flemish city of Leuven traces its origins to a camp constructed here by Julius Caesar. In medieval times, the city became a centre of the cloth trade, but it was as a seat of learning that it achieved international prominence. In 1425, Pope Martin V and Count John of Brabant founded Leuven's university, and by the mid-1500s it was one of Europe's most prestigious academic institutions, the home of such famous scholars as Erasmus and Mercator. Even today, the university exercises a dominant influence over the city and gives it a vibrant atmosphere.

AN ACADEMIC HISTORY

Founded in 1425, KU Leuven is one of the oldest universities in Europe (and the oldest in the Low Countries). It has witnessed numerous academic achievements over the years: Erasmus founded a centre for humanism here in 1517, Professor Georges Lemaître conceived of his famous Big Bang Theory in 1931 and the university's Rega Institute developed an antiviral agent against dengue in 2021. In 2025, the university celebrates 600 years of learning.

1

Oude Markt

This cobblestoned square is flanked by an ensemble of high-gabled buildings. Some of these date from the 18th century; others are newer. At ground level, these buildings have the largest concentration of bars and cafés in town, and as such attract the city's university students.

2

Stadhuis

Grote Markt (016) 20 3020 Daily

Built between 1439 and 1463 from the profits of the cloth trade, Leuven's Stadhuis, or town hall, was designed to demonstrate the wealth of the city's merchants. This distinctive, tall building is renowned for its lavishly carved and decorated façade. A line of narrow windows rises up over three floors beneath a steeply pitched roof adorned with dormer windows and pencil-thin turrets. It is, however, in the fine quality of its

↑ Beautiful high-gabled brick buildings and cafés in Oude Markt

stonework that the building excels, with delicately carved tracery and detailed medieval figures beneath 300 niche bases. There are grotesques of every description as well as representations of folktales and biblical stories, all carved in exuberant late-Gothic style. Within the niche alcoves is a series of 19th-century statues depicting local dignitaries and politicians. Guided tours of the interior are available, and include tours of three lavishly decorated reception rooms.

③

Fochplein

Adjacent to the Grote Markt is the Fochplein, a narrow square containing some of Leuven's most popular shops, selling everything from fashion to food. In the middle is the Fons Sapienza, a modern fountain that shows a student pouring water through his empty head – a pithy view of the city's student population.

④

M-Museum Leuven

🏠 Leopold Vanderkelen-straat 28 ⏰ 11am-6pm Fri–Tue, 11am-10pm Thu 🌐 mleuven.be

The former Museum Vander Kelen-Mertens has been revamped as "M" and provides a dynamic space for high-profile art exhibitions. It also gives credence to Leuven's claim as a major city of the arts. The original collection still remains in the 17th–18th-century mansion, which was owned by the Vander Kelen-Mertens family until it was donated to the city in 1918. The rooms were refurbished in a variety of styles, ranging from a Renaissance salon to a Rococo dining room, each with the appropriate antique furniture, silverware and ceramics. Much of the art on permanent display is by the early Flemish Masters, including the work of Quentin Metsys (1465–1530), who was born in Leuven and introduced Italian style to northern European art.

DRINK

Bar Rustic
A trendy spot, the Rustic has a wooden bar stocking a vast selection of beers from Leuven and beyond.

🏠 Oude Markt 50
📞 0483 59 44 88

De Metafoor
Set on a quiet street, this cosy bar offers a range of board games for visitors.

🏠 Oude Markt 50
📞 0483 59 44 88

Sinatra
Named after Frank Sinatra, this cocktail bar's menu features classic cocktails - and Belgian beers, of course.

🏠 Mechelsestraat 67
🌐 sinatraleuven.be

> **HIDDEN GEM**
> ### Kruidtuin Garden
>
> Belgium's oldest botanical garden, dating back to 1738, is nestled in the campus of the University of Leuven. It is known for its impressive weeping willows and peaceful ponds.

are intercepted by an impressive 1499 rood screen and a Baroque wooden pulpit. The church also houses the Museum Schatkamer van Sint-Pieter (Treasury), which has three paintings by Dirk Bouts (1415–75). Born in the Netherlands, Bouts spent most of his working life in Leuven, becoming its official artist.

and christened it "Stella", which means star. It offers a variety of interactive guided tours on weekends from May to October. These last for 90 minutes and are offered in Dutch and English. All tours take place in the brewing hall, covering local beer-making history and the secrets of the brewing process, with the option to finish with a beer in the bar.

⑤

Sint-Pieterskerk and Museum Schatkamer van Sint-Pieter

🏠 Grote Markt 📞 (016) 29 5133 🕐 10am–4:30pm Mon, Tue, Thu–Sat; 11am–4:30pm Sun 🗓 1 & 2 Jan, 15 Aug, 25 & 26 Dec

Across the square from the Stadhuis rises Sint-Pieterskerk, a massive church built over a period of 200 years from the 1420s. Inside this beautiful church, the sweeping lines of the nave

⑥

Stella Artois Brewery

🏠 Vuurkruisenlaan 🕐 Sat & Sun; tours and tasting: May–Oct: 1pm & 3pm Sat & Sun (Jul & Aug: also 11am)

With brewing being an important part of Leuven's history since the 16th century, a visit to Belgium's beer capital would not be complete without a brewery tour. The iconic Stella Artois Brewery launched its first Christmas beer in 1926

⑦

Sint-Michielskerk

🏠 Naamsestraat 🕐 Apr–Oct: 1:30–4:30pm Tue–Sun

One of Leuven's most impressive churches, Sint-Michielskerk was built for the Jesuits in the middle of the 17th century. The church was badly damaged during World War II, with only its façade surviving. The

↑ The atmospheric Groot Begijnhof, a UNESCO World Heritage Site

monumental Baroque building has since been carefully restored.

The church's majestic exterior is made of white sandstone and ironstone.

> **One of Leuven's most impressive churches, Sint-Michielskerk was built for the Jesuits in the 17th century.**

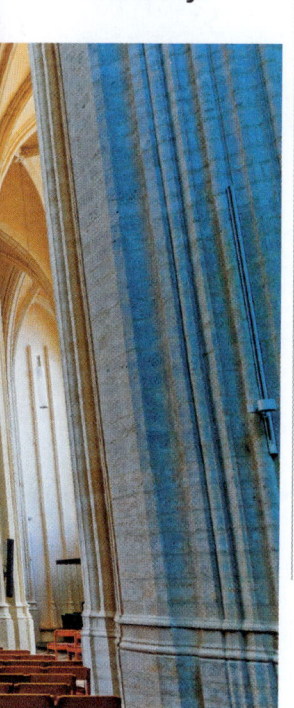

The graceful façade with its flowing lines is an excellent illustration of the ornate Baroque style. It features Ionic columns, pilasters and friezes, and bears resemblance to an altar. The stunning 1660 carved woodwork around the altar and choir are also well worth seeing.

---

⑧
Groot Begijnhof

🏠 Schapenstraat
🕐 Daily, for street access only

Founded around 1230, the Groot Begijnhof, now a UNESCO World Heritage Site, was once one of the largest béguinages in Belgium, home to several hundred béguines (*p87*). In the 17th century, during its heyday, nearly 360 béguines lived here.

The complex of 72 charming red-brick cottages (dating mostly from the 17th century) is set around the grassy squares and cobbled streets near the River Dijle. Leuven University bought the complex in 1961 and converted the cottages into student accommodation.

←

The gorgeous nave of the 15th-century Sint-Pieterskerk

EAT

Taste
Delicately presented gourmet cuisine is the order of the day here. Try the spider crab with langoustine and parsley sauce and pigeon with fresh ginger.

🏠 Naamsestraat 62
🌐 leuventaste.be

€€€

Den Angelus
Conveniently placed near the train station, this good-value spot showcases produce from a local farm with dishes like beef and beer stew, and cuckoo with mushrooms.

🏠 Bondgenotenlaan 102
🌐 den-angelus.be

€€€

Raffat
A vibrant Pakistani restaurant, Raffat has a menu inspired by hearty home cooking: delicious Lahori barbecue chicken, lamb kebabs and masala mac-and-cheese are all on offer.

🏠 Naamsestraat 45
🌐 raffat.be

€€€

Thai House
An affordable restaurant serving traditional Thai street food, Thai House is known for its pad thai, yellow curry and veggie spring rolls. Wash down your meal with an ice-cold Chang.

🏠 Tiensestraat 54
🌐 thaihouse.be

€€€

WATERLOO

🚉 Waterloo

The Battle of Waterloo was fought on 18 June 1815. It pitted Napoleon and his French army against the Duke of Wellington, who was in command of troops mostly drawn from Britain, Germany and the Netherlands. The two armies met outside the hamlet of Waterloo, to the south of Brussels, and the result was decisive. The battle began at 11:30am and just nine hours later the French were in full retreat. Today, the battlefield is one of the biggest and best preserved European historical and cultural sites.

TOP
3

FILMS ABOUT NAPOLEON

Désirée (1954)
Marlon Brando won acclaim for portraying Napoleon in this romantic historical drama.

Waterloo (1970)
This epic war film stars Rod Steiger as Napoleon and Christopher Plummer as the Duke of Wellington.

Napoleon (2023)
Joaquin Phoenix plays Napoleon in this historical epic from legendary director Ridley Scott.

①

Musée Wellington

🏛 Chaussée de Bruxelles 147 🕐 Apr–Sep: 9:30am–6pm daily; Oct–Mar: 10am–5pm daily 🚫 1 Jan, 25 Dec 🌐 museewellington.be

The Waterloo Inn, where the Duke of Wellington spent the night before the battle, has been turned into a museum, its rooms packed with curios alongside plans and models of the actual battle. One of the more unusual exhibits is the artificial leg of Lord Uxbridge, one of Wellington's commanders. His leg was blown off during the battle and buried in Waterloo. After his death, the leg was sent to join the rest of him in England and, as recompense, his relatives sent his artificial one back to Waterloo. The museum also has a dedicated room for temporary exhibitions and special events.

②

Église St-Joseph

🏛 Chaussée de Bruxelles
📞 (02) 352 0910

Across the road from the Musée Wellington is the church of St-Joseph, which was originally built as a royal chapel at the end of the 17th century. Its dainty cupola predates the battle, after which it was extended, with the newer portions containing dozens of memorial plaques and flagstones dedicated to British soldiers who died at Waterloo. Several of these plaques were paid for by contributions from ordinary soldiers in honour of their officers.

③

Butte du Lion

🏛 315 Route du Lion, Ring Ouest exit 25, 5 km (3 miles) S of Waterloo 📞 (02) 385 1912 🕐 Daily

Dating from 1826, the Butte du Lion is a 45-m- (148-ft-) high earthen mound built on the spot where the future King of the Netherlands, the Prince of Orange, was

Map labels: Église St-Joseph ②, Musée Wellington ①, Waterloo, Domaine d'Argenteuil, Caraute, Chenois, Champ de Mai, Le Roussart, La Grange des Champs, Le Ménil, Braine-l'Alleud, Butte du Lion, Mémorial 1815 ④ ③, Panorama de la Bataille ⑤, Butte du Lion 45 m (148 ft), Plancenoit, Napoleon's Last Headquarters ⑥ 3.5 km (2 miles)

0 kilometres 1.5
0 miles 1.5
N

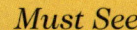

The 19th-century Butte du Lion, topped by a magnificent cast-iron lion ↑

wounded during the battle. Steps lead to the top, which is guarded by a huge cast-iron lion, and from here, there is a great view over the battlefield. A plan of the battle is displayed at the top and for a small charge, added to the ticket for the Mémorial 1815, you can hire a virtual-reality headset that allows you to "see" how the troops were deployed across the landscape.

---

④

Mémorial 1815

📍 Route du Lion, Braine l'Alleud, N5, 5 km (3 miles) S of Waterloo ⏰ Apr–Sep: 9:30am–6:30pm daily; Oct–Mar: 10am–6pm daily 🌐 waterloo1815.bc

This interactive display with its blood-curdling soundtrack immerses visitors in the events of the battle of Waterloo. The admission price includes entry to the Butte du Lion and Panorama de la Bataille, which are on the same site, and also to nearby Hougoumont Farm, where some of the most ferocious fighting took place, re-imagined here in another dramatic multimedia exhibit.

⑤

Panorama de la Bataille

📍 252–254 Route du Lion, Braine-L'Alleud, N5, 5 km (3 miles) S of Waterloo 📞 (02) 385 1912 ⏰ Apr–Sep: 9:30am–6:30pm daily; Oct–Mar: 10am–6pm daily

This is perhaps the most fascinating of the several attractions beneath the Butte du Lion. This circular painting of the Battle of Waterloo by artist Louis Demoulin was erected in 1912. It is 110 m (360 ft) long and stretches right round a circular, purpose-built gallery. This is one of the few late 19th-century panoramic, circular paintings that remain intact.

⑥

Napoleon's Last Headquarters

📍 66 Chaussée de Bruxelles, Vieux-Genappe, N5, 7 km (4.5 miles) S of Waterloo 📞 (02) 384 2424 ⏰ Daily 🚫 1 Jan, 25 Dec

Napoleon spent the eve of the battle in a farmhouse, Le Caillou. That farmhouse has been transformed into a museum, often referred to as the Caillou Museum. Among the items on display are a number of artifacts from Napoleon's army, a bronze death mask of the emperor and his army-issue bed. In the garden is an ossuary, which contains bones of some of the soldiers who died during the battle.

WALLONIA

Waterloo sits within Wallonia, the southern region of Belgium which is primarily French-speaking. Walloons, as its residents are known, number around 3.24 million, making up a quarter of Belgium's population, and have a distinct culture – as well as their own language, Walloon (spoken only by around 300,000 in rural regions). Wallonia has a lot of political autonomy; it is even free to pursue a different foreign policy from the rest of Belgium.

EXPERIENCE MORE

3

Dendermonde

 Stadhuis, Grote Markt; www.visit dendermonde.be

This quiet, industrial town is 20 km (12 miles) southeast of Ghent. Its strategic position, at the confluence of the Scheldt and Dender rivers, has drawn a string of invaders, including the Germans in 1914. But Dendermonde is perhaps best-known as the site of the Steed Bayard, a carnival held every ten years at the end of May.

Today, the main town square is framed by the towers of the Vleeshuis or Meat Hall. The 14th-century Town Hall is also worth visiting, as is the Onze-Lieve-Vrouwekerk (Church of Our Lady), which has two lovely paintings by Anthony van Dyck.

4

Pajottenland

 Grote Markt 1, Halle; www.visitflanders.com

The Pajottenland forms part of the Brabant province to the southwest of Brussels, and is bordered by the Dender River.

The gentle rolling hills of the landscape contain many farms, some of which date back to the 17th century.

The village of Onze-Lieve-Vrouw-Lombeek, just 12 km (7 miles) west of Brussels, is named after its stunning 14th-century Gothic church.

A short distance south of the village lies the area's main attraction, the castle and grounds of **Gaasbeek**. The castle was remodelled in the 19th century, but actually dates from the 13th century. It has a moat and a thick curtain wall, strengthened by huge semicircular towers. The castle's interior holds an excellent collection of fine and applied

---

THE STEED BAYARD

Dendermonde's famous carnival of the Steed Bayard takes place every ten years at the end of May – the next one is in 2030. The focus of the festival is a horse, the Steed Bayard itself, represented in the carnival by a giant model. It takes 34 bearers to carry the horse, which weighs 700 kg (1,540 lb) and is 5.8 m (19 ft) high. A pro-cession of locals dressed in medieval costume re-enacts the Steed Bayard legend – a complex tale of chivalry, family loyalty and betrayal. The four Aymon brothers (who were said to be the nephews of Emperor Charlemagne) ride the horse, and it is their behaviour towards the animal which serves to demonstrate their moral worth.

Picnicking in the grounds of Gaasbeek in the Pajottenland, and *(inset)* its imposing castle and towers

arts. Among the treasures are rich tapestries, 15th-century alabaster reliefs, silverware and a 16th-century hunting horn which belonged to the Protestant leader Count Egmont. The Pajottenland is also known for its beers, especially Lambic and gueuze.

Gaasbeek

 Kasteelstraat 40 ◉ Castle: Jul-Oct: 10am-6pm Tue-Sun; grounds: daily ⓦ kasteelvan gasbeek.be

---

5
Mechelen

🗺️🚌 𝒊 Hallestraat 2, Grote Markt; www.visit. mechelen.be

The seat of the Catholic Archbishop of Belgium, Mechelen was the administrative capital of the country under the Burgundian prince, Charles the Bold, in 1473. Today, it is an appealing town whose expansive main square is flanked by pleasant cafés and bars. To the west of the square is the main attraction, **Sint-Romboutskathedraal**, a

huge cathedral that took some 300 years to complete. The building might never have been finished but for a deal with the Vatican: the cathedral was allowed to sell special indulgences (which absolved the purchaser of their sins) to raise funds, on condition that the pope received a percentage. Completed in 1546, the cathedral's tower has Belgium's finest carillon, a set of 49 bells, whose peals ring out at weekends and on public holidays. The church also contains *The Crucifixion* by Anthony van Dyck.

There are also three 16th-century houses by the River Dijle. They are not open to visitors, but their exteriors are delightful. The "House of the Little Devils" is adorned with carved demons. Mechelen is famous for its local beers, and visitors should try the Gouden Carolus, a dark brew said to have been beloved by Emperor Charles V.

Sint-Romboutskathedraal

🚶 🏛️ Sint-Romboutskerkhof ◉ Cathedral: 8:30am-5:30pm daily; tower: 1-6pm Sun-Fri, 10am-6pm Sat (last entry: 4:40pm)

6
Lier

 𝒊 Grote Markt 58; www.visitlier.be

Lier is an attractive town, just 20 km (12 miles) southeast of Antwerp. The town's Grote Markt is a cobbled square with historic buildings such as the 18th-century Stadhuis and the 14th-century Belfort. Nearby is the **Stedelijk Museum Wuyts**, with its collection of paintings by Flemish artists including Jan Steen, Brueghel and Rubens.

East of here, the church of Sint-Gummaruskerk, with its stone pillars and vaulted roof, evokes medieval times, and the carved altarpiece is notable for its intricate biblical scenes. The stained-glass

windows are among the finest in Belgium and were a gift from Emperor Maximilian I in 1516.

One of Lier's highlights is the **Zimmertoren**, a 14th-century watchtower that now houses the clocks of Lodewijk Zimmer (1888–1970), a Lier merchant who wanted to share his love of timepieces.

Stedelijk Museum Wuyts

⊘ 🏛️ Florent van Cauwenberg Straat 14 📞 (03) 800 0396 ◉ 10am-5pm Tue-Sun ◉ Public hols

Zimmertoren

⊘ 🏛️ Zimmerplein 18 📞 (03) 800 0395 ◉ 10am-noon, 1-5pm Tue-Sun

---

EAT

Graspoort
This vibrantly decorated restaurant serves Asian and South American twists on local produce.

🏛️ Begijnenstraat 28, Mechelen ⓦ gras poort.be

€€€

Numerus Clausus
Sample French haute cuisine, including the haddock tenderloin and duck breast, at this lovely spot.

🏛️ Numerus Clausus, Lier ⓦ numerusclausus.be

€€€

La Pizzeria
Dendermonde's best pizzas are on offer here, along with a range of tempting pasta dishes.

🏛️ Brusselsestraat 104, Dendermonde ⓦ lp-pizzeria.be

€€ⓔ

STAY

Villa Servais

A lemon-yellow villa dating from 1847, with rooms themed around prominent former visitors, including pianist Franz Liszt. Sumptuous breakfasts and afternoon teas are served.

🏠 Servaislaan 8, Halle
🌐 villaservais.be

La Petite Histoire

This townhouse has five roomy apartments, named and themed for female artists. "Yoko", for instance, has a Japanese minimalist aesthetic, while "Frida" has bold Mexican-inspired design.

🏠 Rue de Brantignies 23, Ath 🌐 lapetite histoire.be

Ariane Hotel

Hosting a high-end restaurant, lovely garden terrace and stylish rooms, this family-run hotel is the place to stay in Ypres.

🏠 Slachthuisstraat 58, Ypres 🌐 ariane.be

Halle

🏛 🚌 ℹ Stadhuis, Grote Markt; www.visit halle.be

Located on the outskirts of Brussels, in the picturesque province of Brabant, Halle is a peaceful little town. It has been a major religious centre since the 13th century because of the cult of the Black Virgin, an effigy in the

↑ An impressive float at the annual Parade of the Giants in the town of Ath

Onze-Lieve-Vrouwebasiliek, the town's main church. The holy statue's blackness is due to its stained colour, which is said to have occurred through contact with gunpowder during the religious wars of the 17th century.

The Virgin has long been one of Belgium's most venerated icons and each year, on Whit Sunday, the statue is paraded through the town.

Ath

🏛 🚌 ℹ Rue de Pintamont 18; (068) 26 5170

This quiet town is known for its festival – the Ducasse – which occurs every year on the fourth weekend in August. It features the "Parade of the Giants", a procession of decorated giant figures representing characters from local folklore and the Bible.

You can delve further into Ath's history at the Espace Gallo-Romain, a marvellous museum which displays finds from the period during

which the Gauls came under the control of the Roman Empire. The museum takes you through the life of an ordinary fisher in this era, through archaeological finds from nearby Pommerœul in 1975. These include the remains of two 2,000-year-old boats, along with pottery and personal effects. Also in town is the Stone Museum, the restored home of a

→ Menin Gate, which honours the lives lost in the 1915 Battle of Ypres

former quarry master which documents the history of quarrying, masonry and stonework in Belgium and across Europe.

A few kilometres northeast is one of the most popular attractions in the region, the **Château d'Attre**. This beautiful 18th-century palace was built in 1752 by the Count of Gomegnies, chamberlain to the Habsburg Emperor Joseph II.

Château d'Attre

🏠 Attre 🚌 To Attre 🕐 Jul & Aug: 1–6pm Sat & Sun; Apr–Jun, Sep & Oct: 2–6pm Sun 🌐 attre.be

---

Ypres

🚉🚌 ℹ️ **34 Market Square; (057) 23 9220**

During World War I, Ypres, or "Ieper" in Flemish (and familiar to British soldiers as "Wipers"), was a supply depot for the

FLANDERS FIELDS

Flanders saw devastating losses in World War I, largely from the battles for Ypres, which inspired Canadian soldier John MCrae to write his poem, beginning: "In Flanders Fields, the poppies blow / Between the crosses, row on row…" This image of the poppy, which grew over the graves of fallen soldiers, became forever associated with war remembrance.

British army. The Germans shelled Ypres to pieces, but after the war, the city was rebuilt to its earlier design, complete with a replica of its 13th-century Lakenhalle. Part of its interior has been turned into the "In Flanders Fields" Museum, a series of displays that attempt to conjure the full horrors of World War I. There is also the Menin Gate memorial, inscribed with the names of over 50,000 British and Commonwealth troops who died in the area; the gate is undergoing restoration until 2025. Every

evening at 8pm, the "Last Post" is played by the buglers of the Last Post Association as an act of remembrance. It is free for everyone to attend.

There is more to Ypres than its wartime history, however. Beyond the Lakenhalle (whose tower you can climb for an additional fee), the city's cathedral is well worth a visit. Every three years on the second Sunday in May, Ypres hosts the Kattenstoet, a parade of giant cat floats led by locals in colourful cat costumes and accompanied by brass bands and horses.

A DRIVING TOUR
WORLD WAR I
BATTLEFIELDS

Distance 60 km (37 miles) **Stopping-off points** Hotels and restaurants are concentrated in Ypres. Note that the Menin Gate will be undergoing restoration until 2025.

In 1914, the invading German army forced the Belgians to retreat to the far northeast, behind the River IJzer. To impede further German advance, the Belgians opened the sluice gates of the river and flooded the landscape, which formed an effective obstacle as far south as Diksmuide. South of here, the Germans confronted the Allies along a ridge called the Ypres Salient. Between 1915 and 1917, this was the front line, where the stalemate of trench warfare cost over 500,000 lives. Today, the area around the Salient is a pretty landscape dotted with monuments, museums and cemeteries.

The Belgians dug in along the canal of **Diksmuide**. *Some of their trenches have been preserved at* **Dodengang**.

Dressing stations and the **Essex Farm Cemetery** *recall where Canadian medic John McCrae served, and wrote his poem "In Flanders Fields" (p183).*

Woumen

De Blankaart Spaarbekken

De Blankaart

N369

Merkem

Noordschote

Bikschote

Zuidschote

N369

Boezing

← World War I trenches at Dodengang, surrounded by poppies

Elverdinge

N8

John McCrae Site
Essex Farm
Cemetery

Brielen

Vlamertinge

N381

Dikkebus

N375

N331

Underground mining and an explosion beneath German lines in 1917 resulted in the water-filled Lone Tree Crater, which is now called the **Pool of Peace**.

French Memorial and Ossuary

Heuvelland

Pool of Peace

The French fatalities in the battle of 1918 are remembered in a monument on **Kemmel Hill**, *and 5,000 lie nearby in the* **French Ossuary**.

Locator Map

World War I Battlefields

Langemark, *a haunting German military cemetery, has the flat tombstones of some 44,000 soldiers laid out beneath a cloak of trees.*

The **Guynemer Monument** *at Poelkapelle – a sculpture of a stork – celebrates the pioneer of military aviation Georges Guynemer, who was lost, presumed dead, near here in 1917.*

At the **Canadian Forces Memorial** *in Sint-Juliaan, the large bust of The Brooding Soldier honours the 2,000 soldiers who died after the first ever gas attack in 1915.*

Tyne Cot Cemetery *is the largest Commonwealth cemetery in the world, with nearly 12,000 graves.*

Memorial Museum Passchendaele *in Zonnebeke houses World War I artifacts, and includes impressively reconstructed dugouts and trenches.*

The imposing Menin Gate in **Ypres** *(p183) lists the names of 55,000 Commonwealth soldiers.*

Sanctuary Wood Museum *on Hill 62 houses a private military collection, and leads to a wood where original trenches have been preserved.*

A battered, scarred hilltop, the much-disputed **Hill 60** *faced devastating attacks from underground mines.*

The monastic **Irish Peace Tower** *was built in 1998 at Mesen to commemorate the Irish dead, and as a symbol of reconciliation.*

Klerken

Langemark

Guynemer Monument

Poelkapelle

Canadian Forces Memorial

Tyne Cot Cemetery

N313

Zonnebeke

N38

Memorial Museum Passchendaele

A19

Ypres

N37

Beselare

N8

N8

Geluveld

Zillebeke

Hill 62, Sanctuary Wood Museum

Hill 60, Zillebeke

Zandvoorde

Hollebeke

Houthem

Wijtschate

N336

N365

Mesen-Messines

Irish Peace Tower

FINISH

Bruges   Antwerp
Ghent
Brussels

N35

0 kilometres   4

0 miles   4

N

NEED TO KNOW

Exploring Ghent's canals by boat

BEFORE YOU GO

Things change, so plan ahead to make the most of your trip. Be prepared for all eventualities by considering the following points before you travel.

AT A GLANCE

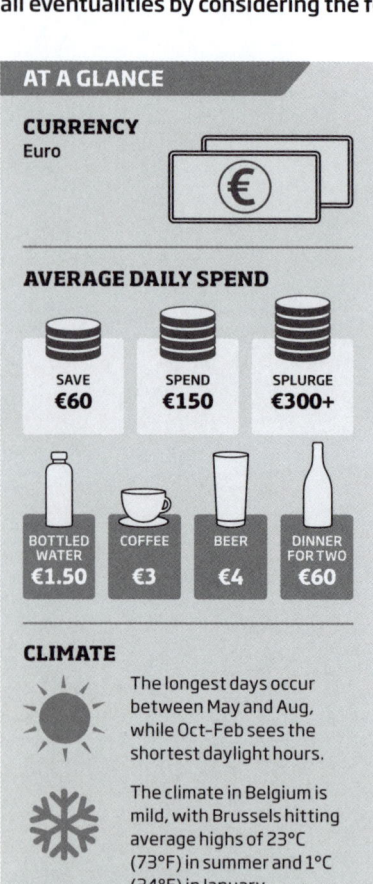

CURRENCY
Euro

AVERAGE DAILY SPEND

SAVE	SPEND	SPLURGE
€60	€150	€300+

BOTTLED WATER	COFFEE	BEER	DINNER FOR TWO
€1.50	€3	€4	€60

CLIMATE

The longest days occur between May and Aug, while Oct-Feb sees the shortest daylight hours.

The climate in Belgium is mild, with Brussels hitting average highs of 23°C (73°F) in summer and 1°C (34°F) in January.

July and December see the most rainfall across Belgium, but showers occur year round.

ELECTRICITY SUPPLY

Power socks are type C and E, fitting two-pronged plugs. Standard voltage is 230v.

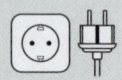

Passports and Visas

For entry requirements, including visas, consult your nearest Belgian embassy or check on the Belgian **Ministry of Foreign Affairs** website. Citizens of the UK, US, Canada, Australia and New Zealand do not need a visa for stays of up to three months but in future must apply in advance for the European Travel Information and Authorization System (**ETIAS**); roll-out has continually been postponed so check the website for details. Visitors from other countries may also require an ETIAS, so check before travelling. EU nationals do not need a visa or an ETIAS.
ETIAS
W etias.com
Ministry of Foreign Affairs
W diplomatie.belgium.be/en

Government Advice

Now more than ever, it is important to consult both your and the Belgian government's advice before travelling. The **UK Foreign, Commonwealth and Development Office (FCDO)**, the **US State Department**, the **Australian Department of Foreign Affairs and Trade** and the Belgian Ministry of Foreign Affairs offer the latest information on security, health and local regulations.
Australian Department of Foreign Affairs and Trade
W smartraveller.gov.au
UK Foreign, Commonwealth and Development Office (FCDO)
W gov.uk/foreign-travel-advice
US State Department
W travel.state.gov

Customs Information

You can find information on laws relating to goods and currency taken in or out of Brussels, Bruges, Antwerp and Ghent on the **Belgian Customs and Excise** website.
Belgian Customs and Excise
W finance.belgium.be/en/customs_excises

Insurance

We recommend taking out a comprehensive insurance policy covering medical care, theft, loss of belongings, cancellations and delays, and reading the small print carefully. UK citizens are eligible for free emergency medical care in Belgium provided they have a valid European Health Insurance Card (EHIC) or UK Global Health Insurance Card (**GHIC**). Australia has a reciprocal healthcare agreement with Belgium and citizens can access essential medical treatment as long as they are registered to Medicare.
GHIC
W ghic.org.uk

Vaccinations

No inoculations are required to visit Belgium. You may wish to be vaccinated against tick-borne encephalitis if you are planning to spend time in forested areas.

Booking Accommodation

Belgium offers a wide range of accommodation, from five-star hotels to campsites. Lodgings tend to fill up quickly in the summer and around the Christmas period, so book in advance.

Money

Belgium's currency is the euro. Major credit and debit cards are accepted by most businesses, while prepaid currency cards and American Express are accepted in some. Contactless payments are common, but it's always a good idea to carry some cash. Cash machines (ATMs) are everywhere. Tipping is appreciated, but not expected beyond the 10–15 per cent service charge, which restaurants usually add on.

Travellers with Specific Requirements

Belgium has made great strides in adapting to travellers with specific requirements, and many hotels and restaurants, particularly in the big cities, include provisions. Major museums including the BELvue and Royal Museums of Fine Arts also have fantastic audio guides and braille displays for visitors with visual impairments.

Access on intercity public transport is good, and the **SNCB** train network offers free assistance at stations for travellers with reduced mobility. That said, the historic nature of many boutique hotels, particularly in places like Ghent and Bruges, makes lift and ramp access impossible. Navigating the cobbled squares and streets of these old cities can also be difficult and boats tend not to have room for wheelchairs.
SNCB
W belgiantrain.be

Language

Belgium's official languages are Dutch, Flemish and German. French is the primary language in the Brussels region (and Wallonia), while Bruges, Antwerp and Ghent are primarily Dutch-speaking. The standard of English is usually excellent.

Opening Hours

Situations can change quickly and unexpectedly. Always check before visiting attractions and hospitality venues for up-to-date opening hours and booking requirements.

Mondays Most museums and tourist attractions and some restaurants are closed for the day.
Sundays Most shops are closed, and public transport services are reduced.
Public holidays Post offices and banks close.

PUBLIC HOLIDAYS	
1 Jan	New Year
21 April (2025)	Easter Monday
1 May	Labour Day
29 May (2025)	Ascension Day
9 Jun (2025)	Whit Monday
21 Jul	Belgian National Day
15 Aug	Assumption Day
1 Nov	All Saints Day
11 Nov	Armistice Day
25 Dec	Christmas Day

GETTING AROUND

Whether you're visiting for a short city break or multi-stop tour of Belgium, discover how best to reach your destination and travel like a pro.

AT A GLANCE

PUBLIC TRANSPORT COSTS

BRUSSELS TO ANTWERP

€10

single journey by train

BRUSSELS TO GHENT

€10.20

single journey by train

GHENT TO BRUGES

€10

single journey by train

SPEED LIMIT

MOTORWAY	DUAL CARRIAGEWAYS
120 km/h (75mph)	**120** km/h (75mph)

SINGLE CARRIAGEWAYS	URBAN AREAS
70 km/h (43mph)	**50** km/h (31mph)

Arriving by Air

Most travellers arriving by air arrive at **Brussels Airport**, although **Bruges-Ostend Airport** and **Antwerp International Airport** also serve some international flights, particularly with TUI. The distances between the places covered in this book are not great enough for domestic flights between them to be an option.
Antwerp International Airport
w antwerp-airport.com
Bruges-Ostend Airport
w ostendbruges-airport.com
Brussels Airport
w brusselsairport.be

Train Travel

International Train Travel

Many international visitors to Belgium arrive by train, thanks to the major **Eurostar** terminal at Brussels-Midi/Zuid. Eurostar typically runs nine direct services per day between London Pancras International and Brussels, taking just under two hours. It's recommended that international travellers arrive at the Eurostar terminal 90 minutes before departure, although security checks and passport control are usually shorter than at international airports. From the Eurostar terminal at Brussels-Midi/Zuid, it is easy to transfer to connecting trains to other cities in Belgium. Select "Any Belgian Station" when booking your ticket to include onward travel to Bruges, Antwerp or Ghent (this is not necessarily cheaper than buying separate tickets).
Eurostar
w eurostar.com

Regional and Local Trains

Belgium's rail network is efficient and well developed. It is overseen by the national rail company **SNCB**, through whose website you can find timetables and book tickets. Distances between Belgium's four main cities mean that train journeys between them are short, rarely lasting longer than an hour – although the number of stops can mean that they take longer than on an intercity bus. (Direct trains,

GETTING TO AND FROM THE AIRPORT

Transport	Journey Time	Fare
Brussels City Bus (STIB 12)	30 mins	€7
Taxi to Brussels	30 mins	€50
Train to Brussels Central	17 mins	€12
Train from Brussels Airport to Ghent	55 mins	€18
Intercity Bus (Airport Express) from Brussels Airport to Antwerp	45 mins	€10
Bus (51, 52, 53) and train from Antwerp Airport to Antwerp	20 mins	€9
Bus (6) and train from Bruges-Ostend Airport to Bruges	1 hr	€8
Taxi from Bruges-Ostend Airport to Bruges	40 mins	€60

RAIL JOURNEY PLANNER

This map is a handy reference for intercity train travel around Belgium. Journey times are for the fastest available service.

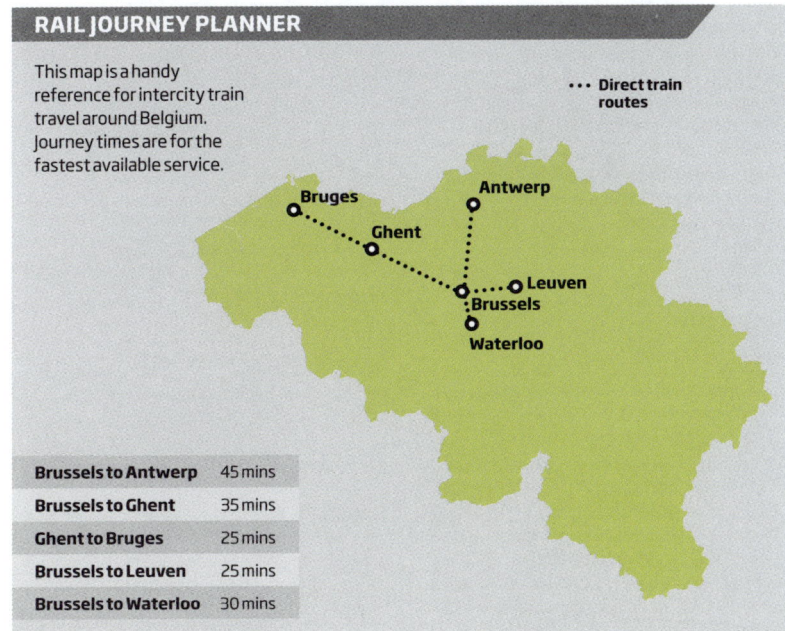

Brussels to Antwerp	45 mins
Brussels to Ghent	35 mins
Ghent to Bruges	25 mins
Brussels to Leuven	25 mins
Brussels to Waterloo	30 mins

by contrast, can be much quicker.) Trains are often very comfortable – many are double-decker, with plenty of space.

Train tickets are significantly more expensive than bus tickets but are still good value. First-class tickets are available, but they do not provide a very different experience other than offering slightly more legroom. You cannot book tickets any longer than a month in advance, and booking in advance does not tend to make them any cheaper. Train tickets can be bought online or at stations, from ticket machines or staffed ticket offices. Websites and machines have the advantage of English-language options, though most attendants at stations speak very good English, too.

SNCB

w belgiantrain.be

Long-Distance Buses

Belgium has an efficient intercity bus network, with many cities connected by **Flixbus**. These buses can sometimes be even quicker than the country's trains, thanks to the short distances involved and the greater number of stops on the train network. However, travellers will tend to have less space to themselves on a bus – with lower prices reflecting this. There does not tend to be any VIP or first-class option on these bus routes, but most of the vehicles are modern and comfortable, with in-seat plug sockets and Wi-Fi as standard.

Flixbus
🇼 global.flixbus.com

Public Transport

Local transport in Belgium is just as developed as it is on the national level, with numerous options for getting around the country's major cities. Brussels is covered by trains, trams, buses and metro, most of which is run by the Brussels Intermunicipal Transport Company (**STIB/MIVB**). Safety and hygiene measures, timetables, ticket information, transport maps and more can be obtained from the STIB/MIVB website. Ghent and Antwerp both have efficient tram and bus networks, while Bruges has a handy bus network. Public transport in all three cities is largely run by **De Lijn**; the De Lijn app (*p194*) features timetables, route maps and tickets to purchase.

De Lijn
🇼 delijn.be
STIB/MIVB
🇼 stib-mivb.be

Tickets

In Brussels, tickets for the train network are available from the SNCB website or at stations. Contactless payments can be used for transport run by STIB/MIVB (including the Brussels Metro, city trams and most buses). Debit or credit cards, smartphones and smartwatches are all accepted as payment. Paper tickets are available to purchase at metro, tram and bus stations, but it is often cheaper to simply tap in for each journey with a contactless debit or credit card.

For trams and buses in Bruges, Antwerp and Ghent, the De Lijn (*p194*) app allows you to purchase tickets more cheaply than from ticket machines or directly from the driver; 10-journey "Lijn cards" are also available at ticket machines, supermarkets and online. Travellers can also pay using contactless payment methods.

On both the STIB/MIVB and De Lijn networks, trams and buses use interchangeable tickets. A single ticket entitles you to the next 60 minutes' transport on any bus or tram.

Train

Brussels is the only city in this guide to have its own local train network, with the city's various stations and the suburban S-Train routes connected by the SNCB national rail network (*p191*).

Metro

Administered by the STIB/MIVB and opened in the 1970s, the Brussels Metro is an efficient light-rail system made up of four lines, which connect in turn to three lines of the Brussels tram network. Metros run every 6 to 10 minutes during peak hours.

Tram

Quick, clean and comfortable, trams are a feature of life in Belgium's major cities. Brussels, Antwerp and Ghent are all connected by their own individual tram networks, with contactless card payment the easiest way to pay.

Bus

All four of Belgium's major cities have efficient bus networks which offer a cost-effective way to get around the city. Buses tend to cover more stops, and as such, are the most effective way of getting to places in between the stops of the tram network, particularly in suburban areas where stations are spaced further apart.

Taxis

All Belgium's cities and larger towns are served by local taxi companies, which offer an efficient and reliable way to get around; larger cities are also served by the Uber on-demand taxi app. Be sure to establish that drivers are using their meters before you set off. Be warned, too, that taxi prices in Brussels are among the highest in Europe. Tipping taxi drivers is appreciated but not expected. Brussels taxis are black and yellow; elsewhere, they come in all colours.

Driving

Driving around Belgium is a pleasant experience, with well-maintained roads and toll-free motorways. However, if you're sticking to the major centres, driving is unnecessary given the extent of public transport links.

Driving to Belgium

It is easy to drive into and out of Belgium from neighbouring European countries, with no need to stop at borders thanks to its status as a member of the Schengen Area. Be mindful, however, of different speed limits, particularly if you're travelling from Germany where there is no upper speed limit on the *autobahn*; in Belgium, the motorway speed limit is 120 km/h (75 mph).

Car Hire

To hire a car in Belgium you must be 21 years old and have held a full driving licence in your home country for at least a year. International driving permits are only required if you're staying for longer than 185 days. Major car hire companies will require a credit card.

There are many car hire companies in the cities and at Brussels Airport, but to ensure you get the best deal possible, book online in advance with a reputable international firm such as **Avis**, **Europcar** and **Hertz**.

Avis
ⓦ avis.be
Europcar
ⓦ europcar.be
Hertz
ⓦ hertz.com

Rules of the Road

Belgium drives on the right side of the road and overtakes on the left. Using a mobile phone while driving is illegal other than as part of a hands-free system, and wearing a seatbelt is a legal requirement. The roads are very well maintained and clearly signposted, although not in English, so it's best to familiarize yourself with the Dutch and French names of the places you're driving to before you set off. Car insurance is mandatory in Belgium and is included as standard in car hire agreements.

Parking

Brussels and Antwerp have plenty of places to park, with metered street parking and some areas designated as Blue Zones. To park in these you need to buy a time-limited parking disc from a newsagent or petrol station. As is the case in medieval cities across Europe, Bruges and Ghent were not designed for the motorcar and can be trickier to park in, with large pedestrianized zones. However, both cities have plenty of car parks outside of the historic core. Wherever you're staying, it's a good idea to ask your hotel if they have parking facilities, as the price of street and car-park parking can easily add up.

Cycling

As befits such a flat country, Belgium is very bicycle-friendly. Brussels has over 220 km (137 miles) of cycling paths, some of which have themes – such as industrial history, hidden gems and green areas. Antwerp is even more bike-friendly, with over 500 km (311 miles) of cycle paths, including ten "cycle highways" which allow you to cross the city quickly. Ghent and Bruges are similarly cyclist-friendly, though the centres are very walkable and small enough that you might not need a bike. Bruges in particular has beautiful cycle lanes in the "green belt" of

forests and wetlands which surround the city. Cycling is also a great way to get between the big cities and to get to other destinations like Leuven and Waterloo.

You can take a bike on the Eurostar, but only on selected trains and by booking in advance. Bicycles are allowed on the Brussels Metro and on selected low-floor trams. Elsewhere, bikes are not allowed on buses or trams but they are allowed on trains by booking an SNCB bike pass when you buy your ticket.

Bicycle Hire

Brussels and Antwerp are home to hundreds of bicycle rental hubs (open 24/7) where you can pay by card and jump on a bike. Fees are charged by the hour. Companies include **Villo!** and **Blue-bike**. It's almost as easy to hire a bike in Ghent and Bruges, though you'll have to go to a staffed booth or bike shops. Ghent Dampoort and Sint-Pieters stations both have bike hire stands, while **Bruges Bike Rental** is a popular option in Bruges.

Blue-bike
ⓦ blue-bike.be
Bruges Bike Rental
ⓦ brugesbikerental.be
Villo!
ⓦ villo.be

Walking

Belgium's city centres are very walkable, with short distances between most of the major sights. In particular, the historic cores of Bruges and Ghent are completely pedestrianized, making them particularly pleasant places to wander. When walking, be mindful not to step in front of trams or in bike lanes.

Boats and Ferries

A canal ride in Bruges or Ghent is not only a convenient way to get around, it is an unmissable part of the experience. In Bruges this is more of a tourist attraction nowadays, with half-hour boat trips running between March and mid-November from five landing jetties across the city – at Huidenvettersplein, Rozenhoedkaai, Wollestraat, Nieuwstraat and Katelijnestraat. Tickets cannot be reserved; just turn up on the day and buy them from the captain.

In Ghent, a hop-on hop-off water tram service still runs, stopping off at Het Gravensteen, Graslei-Korenlei, Museum Site, St Peter's Abbey, St Bavo's Cathedral and Veldstraat – providing a scenic way to get from A to B. Day tickets cost €15, and two-day tickets cost €20; you can buy them from the boat driver, at the jetty or online.

Ghent Water Tramway
ⓦ hoponhopoff.be

PRACTICAL
INFORMATION

A little local know-how goes a long way in Belgium. Here you can find all the essential advice and information you will need during your stay.

AT A GLANCE

EMERGENCY NUMBERS

POLICE	AMBULANCE
101	**100**

FIRE SERVICE	GENERAL EMERGENCY
100	**112**

TIME ZONE
CET/CEST Central European Summer Time (CEST) runs from the end of March to the end of October.

TAP WATER
Unless otherwise stated, tap water in Belgium is safe to drink. Note than it can appear chalky.

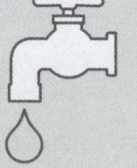

WEBSITES

Visit Brussels
Brussels' official tourism website (visit.brussels).

Visit Flanders
Flanders' official tourism website (www.visitflanders.com).

Floya
Route planner, ticket info and sales app for Brussels's buses and trams.

De Lijn
Route planner, ticket info and sales app for Flanders' buses and trams.

Personal Security

Belgium is generally very safe, but petty crime does take place. Pickpockets work known tourist areas and busy streets. Use your common sense and be alert to your surroundings. If you have anything stolen, report the crime as soon as possible at the nearest police station. Get a copy of the crime report in order to make a claim on your insurance. Contact your embassy or consulate immediately if your passport is stolen or in the event of a serious crime or accident.

Belgium's stance on LGBTQ+ issues is one of the most progressive in Europe, with same-sex same-sex marriages becoming legal in 2003. Belgium's former prime minister Elio Di Rupo is one of very few heads of state to have been openly gay, while deputy prime minister Petra De Sutter is one of the few transgender government ministers. There are annual Pride events in Brussels and Antwerp, and both cities have a thriving LGBTQ+ nightlife scene.

Travellers of colour are unlikely to experience racism in Belgium, which has a very cosmopolitan society – Brussels is said to be the world's second most cosmopolitan city after Dubai, with 62 per cent of its residents either born in a different country or to a migration background (2nd/3rd generation). Any incidents of racism should be reported to the police. The same goes for discrimination based on religion. Freedom of religion is protected by law in Belgium, but incidents of hate crime – particularly rooted in Islamophobia – have risen in recent years, particularly in the Flemish part of the country, where far-right political parties are becoming more popular.

Healthcare

Healthcare in Belgium is of high quality, consistently ranking among the best in Europe and the world. Emergency treatment for citizens of the UK, EU and Switzerland is free of charge if you have an EHIC or GHIC (p189). For other visitors, payment of medical expenses is the patient's responsibility. It is therefore important to arrange comprehensive medical insurance

before you travel. Popular remedies are available over-the-counter at Belgian pharmacies but for more specific drugs and medicines you will need a prescription authorized by a local doctor. Minor health problems can usually be dealt with in a pharmacy, where trained staff can provide professional advice. For more serious injury or illness, head for the emergency department of the nearest hospital.

Smoking, Alcohol and Drugs

Smoking and vaping are banned in indoor public spaces. However, many bars and restaurants have outdoor areas where smoking is permitted. Smoking on the street is also permitted.

Alcohol may not be sold to or bought for anyone under 16 (18 for spirits). Shops along a motorway cannot sell alcohol between 10pm and 7am. The drink-drive limit is strictly enforced – drivers found to have more than 1.2 per ml of alcohol (0.012) in their blood will have to give up their licence for 15 days.

Possession of all recreational drugs, including psychoactive substances formerly known as "legal highs" and now classified as illegal, is a criminal offence.

ID

Visitors to Belgium are required by law to carry ID on their person, such as a passport, national ID card or driving licence. You may be asked for photo ID when buying alcohol.

Responsible Travel

Belgium's historic cities, particularly Bruges and Ghent, are struggling to cope with the huge numbers of tourists who visit every summer. A large part of the problem are day-trippers arriving on coaches; to avoid contributing to overcrowding, slow down and stay for a couple of nights. Belgium is also facing the Europe-wide problem of increasingly hot summers, so be wary of wasting water, take quick showers and reuse towels in hotels, particularly during the summer months. Cycling around city centres and taking public transport between Brussels, Bruges, Antwerp and Ghent is also an easy way to reduce your impact on the environment.

Mobile Phones and Wi-Fi

Free Wi-Fi hotspots are widely available in city centres. Cafés and restaurants will usually give you their Wi-Fi password on the condition that you make a purchase. Do not rely on mobile phones or other devices for navigation or emergency communications in remote areas where mobile reception can be intermittent.

Visitors travelling to Belgium with EU tariffs are able to use their devices without being affected by data roaming charges. Pay-as-you-go SIM cards are available at newsagents and in supermarkets.

Post

Post offices are usually prominently located in city centres and town squares. Stamps can be bought from post offices and newspaper kiosks. Allow four days when sending post to the UK, and up to 15 days for the US or Australia.

Taxes and Refunds

Belgium's VAT rate is 21 per cent. Non-EU residents are entitled to VAT tax refunds, providing they request a tax receipt and regular retail receipt when purchasing goods. Receipts must amount to more than €125. These receipts must be presented to a tax refund office (such as that at Brussels Airport), together with a passport, when leaving the country.

Discount Cards

The **Brussels Card** is a visitor's pass that includes entry to the city's top museums, discounts at participating shops, bars, restaurants and attractions, and (as an optional extra) unlimited free travel on public transport. The **Antwerp City Pass** is very similar, as is the CityCard Ghent, while the **Musea Brugge** card gives access to nine Bruges museums. All can be purchased online. In Ghent, the CityCard Ghent, is available at museums and tourist offices.

Brussels Card
w shop.brusselscard.be
Antwerp City Pass
w antwerpcitypass.be
Musea Brugge
w museabrugge.be

INDEX

IN AN EMERGENCY

Help!	**Help!**	*help*
Stop!	**Stop!**	*stop*
Call a doctor!	**Haal een dokter!**	*haal uhndok-tur*
Call the police!	**Roep de politie!**	*roop duh poe-leet-see*
Call the fire brigade!	**Roep de brandweer!**	*brahnt-vheer*
Where is the nearest telephone?	**Waar ist de dichtsbijzijnde telefoon?**	*vhaar iss duh dikst-baiy-zaiyn duh tay-luh-foan*
Where is the nearest hospital?	**Waar ist het dichtsbijzijnde ziekenhuis**	*vhaar iss het dikst-baiy-zaiyn -duh zee-kuh-hows*

COMMUNICATION ESSENTIALS

Yes	**Ja**	*yaa*
No	**Nee**	*nay*
Please	**Alstublieft**	*ahls-tew-bleeft*
Thank you	**Dank u**	*dhank-ew*
Excuse me	**Pardon**	*pahr-don*
Hello	**Hallo**	*haa-lo*
Goodbye	**Dag**	*dahgh*
Good night	**Goedenacht**	*ghoot-e-naakt*
morning	**Morgen**	*mor-ghugh*
afternoon	**Middag**	*mid-dahgh*
evening	**Avond**	*av-vohnd*
yesterday	**Gisteren**	*ghis-tern*
today	**Vandaag**	*van-daagh*
tomorrow	**Morgen**	*mor-ghugh*
here	**Hier**	*heer*
there	**Daar**	*daar*
What?	**Wat?**	*vhat*
When?	**Wanneer?**	*vhan-eer*
Why?	**Waarom?**	*vhaar-om*
Where?	**Waar?**	*vhaar*
How?	**Hoe?**	*hoo*

USEFUL PHRASES

How are you?	**Hoe gaat het ermee?**	*hoo ghaat het er-may*
Very well, thank you	**Heel goed, dank u**	*hayl ghoot, dhank ew*
How do you do?	**Hoe maakt u het?**	*hoo maakt ew het*
See you soon	**Tot ziens**	*tot zeens*
That's fine	**Prima**	*pree-mah*
Where is/are ...?	**Waar is/zijn ...?**	*vhaar iss/zayn*
How far is it to ...?	**Hoe ver is het naar ...?**	*hoo vehr iss het nar*
How do I get to ...?	**Hoe kom ik naar ...?**	*hoo kom ik nar*
Do you speak English?	**Spreekt u engels?**	*spraykt uw eng-uhls*
I don't understand	**Ik snap het niet**	*ik snahp het neet*
I'm sorry	**Sorry**	*sorry*

SHOPPING

I'm just looking	**Ik kijk alleen even**	*ik kaiyk alleyn ay-vuh*
How much does this cost?	**Hoeveel kost dit?**	*hoo-vayl kost dit*
What time do you open?	**Hoe laat gaat u open?**	*hoo laat ghaat ew opuh*
What time do you close?	**Hoe laat gaat u dicht?**	*hoo laat ghaat ew dikht*
I would like ...	**Ik wil graag ...**	*ik vhil ghraakh*
Do you have ...?	**Heeft u ...?**	*hayft ew*
Do you take credit cards?	**Neemt u credit cards aan?**	*naymt ew credit cards aan?*
Do you take travellers' cheques?	**Neemt u reischeques aan?**	*naymt ew raiys-sheks aan*
This one	**Deze**	*day-zuh*
That one	**Die**	*dee*
expensive	**duur**	*dewr*
cheap	**goedkoop**	*ghoot-koap*
size	**maat**	*maat*
white	**wit**	*vhit*
black	**zwart**	*zvhahrt*
red	**rood**	*roat*
yellow	**geel**	*ghayl*
green	**groen**	*ghroon*
blue	**blauw**	*blah-ew*

TYPES OF SHOP

antiques shop	**antiekwinkel**	*ahn-teek-vhin-kul*
bakery	**bakkerij**	*bah-ker-aiy*
bank	**bank**	*bahnk*
bookshop	**boekwinkel**	*book-vhin-kul*
butcher	**slagerij**	*slaakh-er-aiy*
cake shop	**banketbakkerij**	*bahnk-et-bahk-er-aiy*
chip stop/stand	**frituur/ frietkot**	*free-to-er/ freet-cot*
chemist/ drugstore	**apotheek**	*ah-poe-taiyk*
delicatessen	**delicatessen**	*daylee-kah-tes-suh*
department store	**warenhuis**	*vhaah-uh-houws*
fishmonger	**viswinkel**	*viss-vhin-kul*
greengrocer	**groenteboer**	*ghroon-tuh-boor*
hairdresser	**kapper**	*kah-per*
market	**markt**	*mahrkt*
newsagent	**krantenwinkel**	*krahn-tuh-vhin-kul*
post office	**postkantoor**	*pohst-kahn-tor*
supermarket	**supermarkt**	*sew-per-mahrkt*
tobacconist	**sigarenwinkel**	*see-ghaa-ruh-vhin-kul*
travel agent	**reisburo**	*raiys-bew-roa*

SIGHTSEEING

art gallery	**gallerie**	*ghaller-ee*
bus station	**busstation**	*buhs-stah-shown*
bus ticket	**kaartje**	*kaar-tyuh*
cathedral	**kathedraal**	*kah-tuh-draal*
church	**kerk**	*kehrk*
closed on public holidays	**op feestdagen gesloten**	*op fayst-daa-ghuh ghuh-slow-tuh*
day return	**dagretour**	*dahgh-ruh-tour*
garden	**tuin**	*touwn*
library	**bibliotheek**	*bee-bee-yo-tayk*
museum	**museum**	*mew-zay-um*
railway station	**station**	*stah-shown*
return ticket	**retourtje**	*ruh-tour-tyuh*
single journey	**enkeltje**	*eng-kuhl-tyuh*
tourist information	**dienst voor toerisme**	*deenst vor tor-ism*
town hall	**stadhuis**	*staht-houws*
train	**trein**	*traiyn*

STAYING IN A HOTEL

double room with double bed	**een twees persoons-kamer met een twee persoonsbed**	*uhn tvhays per-soans-ka-mer met uhn tvhay per-soans beht*
single room	**eenpersoons-kamer**	*ayn-per-soans kaa-mer*
twin room	**een kamer met een lits-jumeaux**	*uhn kaa-mer met uhn lee-zjoo-moh*
room with a bath/shower	**kaamer met bad/ douche**	*kaa-mer met baht/doosh*
Do you have a vacant room?	**Zijn er nog kamers vrij?**	*zaiyn er nokh kaa-mers vray*
I have a reservation	**Ik heb gereserveerd**	*ik hehp ghuh-ray-sehr-veert*

EATING OUT

Have you got a table?	**Is er een tafel vrij?**	*iss ehr uhn tah-fuhl vraiy*
I would like to reserve a table	**Ik wil een tafel reserveren**	*ik vhil uhn tah-fel ray sehr-veer- uh*
The bill, please	**De rekening, alstublieft**	*duh ray-kuh-ning ahls-tew-bleeft*
I am a vegetarian	**Ik ben vegetariër**	*ik ben fay-ghuh-taahr-ee-er*
waitress/waiter	**serveerster/ ober**	*sehr-veer-ster/oh-ber*
menu	**de kaart**	*duh kaahrt*
wine list	**de wijnkaart**	*duh vhaiyn-kart*
glass	**het glass**	*het ghlahss*
bottle	**de fles**	*duh fless*
knife	**het mes**	*het mess*
fork	**de vork**	*duh fork*
spoon	**de lepel**	*duh lay-pul*
breakfast	**het ontbijt**	*het ont-baiyt*
lunch	**de lunch**	*duh lernsh*
dinner	**het diner**	*het dee-nay*
main course	**het hoofdgerecht**	*het hoaft-ghuh-rekht*
starter, first course	**het voorgerecht**	*het vhor-ghuh-rekht*
dessert	**het nagerecht**	*het naa-ghuh-rekht*
dish of the day	**het dagschotel**	*het dahg-skhoa-tel*
bar	**het cafe**	*het kaa-fay*
café	**het eetcafe**	*het ayt-kaa-fay*
rare	**rare**	*"rare"*
medium	**medium**	*"medium"*
well done	**doorbakken**	*door-bah-kuh*

MENU DECODER

aardappels	aard-uppuhls	potatoes
asperges	as-puhj	asparagus
bier	beeh	beer
chocola	sho-koh-laa	chocolate
eend	aynt	duck
forel	foh-ruhl	trout
frietjes	free-tyuhs	chips/fries
fruit/vruchten	vroot/vrooh-tuh	fruit
garnaal	gar-nall	prawn
groenten	ghroon-tuh	vegetables
haring	haa-ring	herring
hertenvlees	hair-ten-flayss	venison
kip	kip	chicken
knoflook	knoff-loak	garlic
koffie	coffee	coffee
kreeft	krayft	lobster
lamsvlees	lahms-flayss	lamb
lotte/zeeduivel	lot/seafuhdul	monkfish
mineraalwater	meener-aahl-vhaater	mineral water
mossel	moss-uhl	mussel
oester	ouhs-tuh	oyster
pannekoek	pah-nuh-kook	pancake
rundvlees	ruhnt-flayss	beef
snijbonen	snee-buh-nun	string beans
spruitjes	spruhr-tyuhs	Brussels sprouts
thee	tay	tea
tonijn	tuhn-een	tuna
truffel	truh-fuhl	truffle
varkensvlees	vahr-kuhns-flayss	pork
verse jus	vehr-suh zjhew	fresh orange juice
vis	fiss	fish
vlees	flayss	meat
wafel	vaff-uhl	waffle
water	vhaa-ter	water
wijn	vhaiyn	wine
witloof	vit-lurf	Belgian endive/chicory
zalm	sahlm	salmon
zeebars	see-buhr	seabass
zeebrasem	zee-brah-sum	sea bream

NUMBERS

1	een	ayn
2	twee	tvhay
3	drie	dree
4	vier	feer
5	vijf	faiyf
6	zes	zess
7	zeven	zay-vuh
8	acht	ahkht
9	negen	nay-guh
10	tien	teen
11	elf	elf
12	twaalf	tvhaalf
13	dertien	dehr-teen
14	veertien	feer-teen
15	vijftien	faiyf-teen
16	zestien	zess-teen
17	zeventien	zayvuh-teen
18	achtien	ahkh-teen
19	negentien	nay-ghuh-tien
20	twintig	tvhin-tukh
21	eenentwintig	aynuh-tvhin-tukh
30	dertig	dehr-tukh
40	veertig	feer-tukh
50	vijftig	faiyf-tukh
60	zestig	zess-tukh
70	zeventig	zay-vuh-tukh
80	tachtig	tahkh-tukh
90	negentig	nayguh-tukh
100	honderd	hohn-durt
1000	duizend	douw-zuhnt
1,000,000	miljoen	mill-yoon

TIME

one minute	een minuut	uhn meen-ewt
one hour	een uur	uhn ewr
half an hour	een half uur	een hahlf uhr
half past one	half twee	hahlf twee
a day	een dag	uhn dahgh
a week	een week	uhn vhayk
a month	een maand	uhn maant
a year	een jaar	uhn jaar
Monday	maandag	maan-dahgh
Tuesday	dinsdag	dins-dahgh
Wednesday	woensdag	vhoons-dahgh
Thursday	donderdag	donder-dahgh
Friday	vrijdag	vraiy-dahgh
Saturday	zaterdag	zaater-dahgh
Sunday	zondag	zon-dahgh ln an

PHRASE BOOK: FRENCH

EMERGENCY

Help!	Au secours!	oh sekoor
Stop!	Arrêtez!	aret-ay
Call a doctor	Appelez un medecin	apuh-lay uñ medsañ
Call the police	Appelez la police	apuh-lay lah pol-ees
Call the fire brigade	Appelez les pompiers	apuh-lay leh poñ-peeyay
Where is the nearest telephone?	Où est le téléphone le plus proche	oo ay lah tehlehfon luh ploo prosh

COMMUNICATION ESSENTIALS

Yes/No	Oui/Non	wee/noñ
Please	S'il vous plaît	seel voo play
Thank you	Merci	mer-see
Excuse me	Excusez-moi	exkoo-zay mwah
Hello	Bonjour	boñzhoor
Goodbye	Au revoir	oh ruh-vwar
Good evening	Bon soir	boñ-swar
morning	Le matin	matañ
afternoon	L'apres-midi	l'apreh-meedee
evening	Le soir	swah
yesterday	Hier	eeyehr
today	Aujourd'hui	oh-zhoor-dwee
tomorrow	Demain	duhmañ
here	Ici	ee-see
there	Là bas	lah bah
What?	Quel/quelle?	kel, kel
When?	Quand?	koñ
Why?	Pourquoi?	poor-kwah
Where?	Où?	oo

USEFUL PHRASES

How do you do?	Comment allez vous?	kom-moñ talay voo
Very well, thank you	Très bien, merci	treh byañ, mer-see
How are you?	Comment ça va?	kom-moñ sah vah
See you soon	À bientôt	ah byañ-toh
That's fine	Ça va bien	sah vah byañ
Where is/are ...?	Où est/sont ...?	ooh ay/soñ
Which way to ...?	Quelle est la direction pour ...?	kel ay lah deer-ek-syoñ poor
Do you speak English?	Parlez-vous anglais?	par-lay voo oñg-lay?
I don't understand	Je ne comprends pas	zhuh nuh kom-proñ pah
I'm sorry	Excusez-moi	exkoo-zay mwah

SHOPPING

How much?	C'est combien?	say kom-byañ
I would like ...	Je voudrais	zhuh voo-dray
Do you have ...?	Est-ce que vous avez ...?	es-kuh voo zavay
Do you take credit cards?	Est-ce que vous acceptez les cartes de crédit?	es-kuh voo zaksept-ay leh kart duh kreh-dee
What time do you open/ close?	À quelle heure vous êtes ouvert/ fermé?	ah kel urr voo zet oo-ver/ fermay
this one	celui-ci	suhl-wee see
that one	celui-là	suhl-wee lah
expensive	cher	shehr
cheap	pas cher, bon marché	pah shehr, boñ mar-shay
size (clothing)	la taille	tye
white	blanc	bloñ
black	noir	nwahr
red	rouge	roozh
yellow	jaune	zhownh
green	vert	vehr
blue	bleu	bluh

TYPES OF SHOP

bakery	la boulangerie	booloñ-zhuree
bank	la banque	boñk
bookshop	la librairie	lee-brehree

butcher	la boucherie	boo-shehree
cake shop	la pâtisserie	patee-sree
chemist	la pharmacie	farmah-see
chip shop/stand	la friterie	free-tuh-ree
chocolate shop	le chocolatier	shok-oh-lah-tyeh
delicatessen	la charcuterie	shah-koo-tuh-ree
department store	le grand magasin	groñ maga-zañ
fishmonger	la poissonerie	pwasson-ree
greengrocer	le marchand de légumes	mar-shoñ duh lay-goom
hairdresser	le coiffeur	kwafuhr
market	le marché	marsh ay
newsagent	le magasin de journaux/tabac	maga-zañ duh zhoor-no/ta-bak
post office	le bureau de poste	boo-roh duh pohst
shop	le magasin	maga-zañ
supermarket	le supermarché	soo-pehr-marshay
travel agency	l'agence de voyage	azhons duh vwayazh

SIGHTSEEING

art gallery	la galérie d'art	galer-ree dart
bus station	la gare routière	gahr roo-tee-yehr
cathedral	la cathédrale	katay-dral
church	l'église	aygleez
closed on public	fermeture	fehrmeh-tur
	jour ferié	zhoor fehree-ay
garden	le jardin	zhah-dañ
library	la bibliothèque	beebleeo-tek
museum	le musée	moo-zay
railway station	la gare (SNCB)	gahr (es-en-say-bay)
tourist office	les informations	uñ-for-mah-syoñ
town hall	l'hôtel de ville	ohtel duh vil
train	le train	trañ

STAYING IN A HOTEL

Do you have a vacant room?	est-ce que vous avez une chambre?	es-kuh voo zavay oon shambr
double room	la chambre à deux personnes	shambr ah duh per-son
with double bed	avec un grand lit	ah-vek uñ groñ lee
twin room	la chambre à deux lits	shambr ah duhlee
single room	la chambre à une personne	shambr ah oon pehr-son
room with a bath	la chambre avec salle de bain	shambr ah-vek sal duh bañ
shower	une douche	doosh
I have a reservation	J'ai fait une reservation	zhay fay oon ray-zehrva-syoñ

EATING OUT

Have you got a table?	Avez vous une table libre?	avay-voo oon tahbl leebr
I would like to reserve a table	Je voudrais réserver une table	zhuh voo-dray rayzehr-vay oon tahbl
The bill, please	L'addition, s'il vous plait	l'adee-syoñ, seel voo play
I am a vegetarian	Je suis végétarien	zhuh swee vezhay-tehryañ
waiter/ waitress	Monsieur/ Mademoiselle	muh-syur/ mad-uh-mwah-zel
menu	le menu	men-oo
wine list	la carte des vins	lah kart-deh vañ
glass	verre	vehr
bottle	la bouteille	boo-tay
knife	le couteau	koo-toh
fork	la fourchette	for-shet
spoon	la cuillère	kwee-yehr
breakfast	le petit déjeuner	puh-tee day-zhuh-nay
lunch	le déjeuner	day-zhuh-nay
dinner	le dîner	dee-nay
main course	le grand plat	groñ plah
starter	l'hors d'oeuvre	or duhvr
dessert	le dessert	deh-zehrt
dish of the day	le plat du jour	plah doo joor
bar	le bar	bah
café	le café	ka-fay
rare	saignant	say-nyoñ
medium	à point	ah pwañ
well done	bien cuit	byañ kwee

MENU DECODER

agneau	*ahnyoh*	lamb
ail	*eye*	garlic
bière	*byahr*	beer
boeuf	*buhf*	beef
café	*kah-fay*	coffee
café au lait	*kah-fay oh lay*	white coffee
caffe latte	*kah-fay lat-uh*	milky coffee
canard	*kanar*	duck
chicon	*shee-koñ*	Belgian endive
chocolat chaud	*shok-oh-lah shoh*	hot chocolate
choux de Bruxelles	*shoo duh broocksell*	Brussels sprouts
coquille Saint-Jacques	*kok-eel sañ jak*	scallop
crêpe	*crayp*	pancake
crevette	*kreh-vet*	prawn
eau	*oh*	water
epinard	*aypeenar*	spinach
frites	*freet*	chips/fries
fruits	*frwee*	fruit
gauffre	*gohfr*	waffle
haricots verts	*arrykoh vehr*	green beans
homard	*oh-ma*	lobster
huitre	*weetr*	oyster
jus d'orange	*zhoo doh-ronj*	orange juice
légumes	*lay-goom*	vegetables
limonade	*lee-moh-nad*	lemonade
lotte	*lot*	monkfish
moule	*mool*	mussel
poisson	*pwah-ssoñ*	fish
pommes de terre	*pom-duh tehr*	potatoes
porc	*por*	pork
poulet	*poo-lay*	chicken
saumon	*soh-moñ*	salmon
thé	*tay*	tea
thon	*toñ*	tuna
truffe	*troof*	truffle
truite	*trweet*	trout
veau	*voh*	veal
viande	*vee-yand*	meat
vin	*vañ*	wine
vin maison	*vañ may-soñ*	house wine

NUMBERS

0	**zéro**	*zeh-roh*
1	**un, une**	*uñ, oon*
2	**deux**	*duh*
3	**trois**	*trwah*
4	**quatre**	*katr*
5	**cinq**	*sañk*
6	**six**	*sees*
7	**sept**	*set*
8	**huit**	*weet*
9	**neuf**	*nurf*
10	**dix**	*dees*
11	**onze**	*oñz*
12	**douze**	*dooz*
13	**treize**	*trehz*
14	**quatorze**	*katorz*
15	**quinze**	*kañz*
16	**seize**	*sehz*
17	**dix-sept**	*dees-set*
18	**dix-huit**	*dees-zweet*
19	**dix-neuf**	*dees-znurf*
20	**vingt**	*vañ*
21	**vingt-et-un**	*vañ ay uhn*
30	**trente**	*tront*
40	**quarante**	*karoñt*
50	**cinquante**	*sañkoñt*
60	**soixante**	*swahsoñt*
70	**septante**	*setoñt*
80	**quatre-vingt**	*katr-vañ*
90	**quatre-vingt-dix/nonante**	*katr vañ dees/nonañ*
100	**cent**	*soñ*
1000	**mille**	*meel*
1,000,000	**million**	*miyoñ*

TIME

What is the time?	**Quelle heure est-il?**	*kel uhr eh-til*
one minute	**une minute**	*oon mee-noot*
one hour	**une heure**	*oon uhr*
half an hour	**une demi-heure**	*oon duh-mee uhr*
half past one	**une heure et demi**	*oon uhr ay duh-mee*
a day	**un jour**	*zhuhr*
a week	**une semaine**	*suh-men*
a month	**un mois**	*mwah*
a year	**une année**	*annay*
Monday	**lundi**	*luñ-dee*
Tuesday	**mardi**	*mahr-dee*
Wednesday	**mercredi**	*mehrkruh-dee*
Thursday	**jeudi**	*zhuh-dee*
Friday	**vendredi**	*voñdruh-dee*
Saturday	**samedi**	*sam-dee*
Sunday	**dimanche**	*dee-moñsh*

ACKNOWLEDGMENTS

DK would like to thank the following for their contribution to the previous editions: Zoë Hewetson, Zoë Ross, Sarah Wolff, Timothy Wright, Julia Zyrianova, Antony Mason, Emma Jones, Leigh Phillips

The publisher would like to thank the following for their kind permission to reproduce their photographs:

Key: a-above; b-below/bottom; c-centre; f-far; l-left; r-right; t-top

Alamy Stock Photo: Erik AJV 184clb, Album 50br, Arterra Picture Library / Clement Philippe 22bl, 24clb, 26–27ca, 42–43t, 49bl, 51br, 111b, 115tr, 143, 162–163b, 163tr, 166, 169tr, Arterra Picture Library / Collection Philippe Clement 121cl, Arterra Picture Library / De Meester Johan 113, ARTGEN 52tl, Aurelian Images 160br, Belga News Agency 53bl, Belga News Agency / Benoit Doppagne 46cra, Belga News Agency / David Pintens 47clb, Belga News Agency / Hatim Kaghat 38–39b, 47cl, Belga News Agency / James Arthur Gekiere 46crb, 53cra, Belga News Agency / Jonas Roosens 141clb, Belga News Agency / Kurt Desplenter 46cl, Belga News Agency / Laurie Dieffembacq 32br, 40–41t, Belga News Agency / Nicolas Maeterlinck 47cr, Belga News Agency / Thierry Roge 83t, Gordon Bell 109tr, Berngardt 146bl, Stuart Black 8cla, blickwinkel / W. Pattyn 45crb, Ed Buzia 151tr, Ed Buziak 86–87b, 112, Pocholo Calapre 108–109b, Blanca Saenz de Castillo 10–11b, Cavan Images / CI2 125tl, Louis Champion 158br, Chronicle 52–53t, Tim Clark 182t, Gustavo Enrique Cortez 20clb, Ian Dagnall 124–125b, 127ca, Carl DeAbreu 50cb, Stephen Dorey 20br, elroce 174–175t, Eraza Collection 51clb, Greg Balfour Evans 44–45b, Peter van Evert 43ca, eye35 stock 93br, Falkensteinfoto 49tl, Jose Pedro Fernandes 123cl, Findlay 39tr, Kirk Fisher 160–161t, Florian Lica Photography 129, G.P.Essex 46cla, Renato Granieri 24cl, Shim Harno 49cla, David Coleman | Have Camera Will Travel 83b, 87t, Blanchot Philippe / Hemis.fr 76, Leclercq Olivier / Hemis.fr 144tr, 148bl, Maisant Ludovic / Hemis.fr 10ca, Soberka Richard / Hemis.fr 13cr, Chris Howes / Wild Places Photography 26cla, IanDagnall Computing 158bl, Image Professionals GmbH / LOOK-foto 122–123b, imageBROKER / J. De Meester 180t, imageBROKER / Sonja Jordan 12cl, Imago / Xinhua / Wu Wei 180b, Imago / Zheng Huansong 13br, 37t, 46cr, 47tr, 61clb, 104–105t, incamerastock 48crb, isogood 158cr, Michael Jacobs 22cr, Jimlop collection 49crb, Dennis K. Johnson 43br, Jon Arnold Images Ltd / Walter Bibikow 61br, Christopher Kane 6-7, John Kellerman 72bl, Werner Lerooy 79t, Serhii Liakhevych 105br, Life on white 45cl, Mike Louagie 28–29tx, mauritius images GmbH / Steve Vidler 51tr, Colin Mitchell 65tr, Niday Picture Library 53tr, Nathaniel Noir 24t, 31cl, Old Images 48t, Gonzalez Oscar 22t, PA Images / John Walton 110clb, Bombaert Patrick 65cr, PjrWindows 90cr, PWB Images 77b, Srdjan Rakonjac 160bl, M Ramírez

17bl, 22cl, 116–117, 144br, 176–177b, Lana Rastro 20t, 77t, 89, Sergi Reboredo 40bl, robertharding / Godong 29c, Marcin Rogozinski 63clb, 133br, Boaz Rottem 10clb, Maurice Savage 34–35b, Neil Setchfield 38tl, Eckhard Supp 33cl, Jochen Tack 12–13bc, 54–55, theatrepix 41b, Mauro Toccaceli 68-69, 69cl, 91, 92cl, Dmitry Tonkopi 145b, travelpix 34-35t, Underwood Archives, Inc 53cb, Marc Wauman 4, 75tl, Chun Ju Wu 168bl, Zheng Huansong / Xinhua 46clb, Zoonar / Nikolai Sorokin 181cla

Archives du Musée Horta, Saint-Gilles, Bruxelles: Paul Louis 47tl, 102cra, 102cl, 102b

AWL Images: Davide Camesasca 47crb, Jason Langley 29br, Stefano Politi Markovina 82, Carlos Sanchez Pereyra 27tr, Maurizio Rellini 18, 19t, 24br, 136–137, 152–153, 186–187

Belgian Comics Art Museum: Daniel Fouss 66–67b, 67tl

Bridgeman Images: © Art in Flanders 50tl, © Look and Learn 48bc, Sebastien Vrancx 50-51t

Café Vlissinghe: Jan D Hondt 33t

Courtesy of Zaha Hadid Architects: Hufton / Crow 147b

Dreamstime.com: Arkadi Bojarinov 24t, Marc Bruxelle 95t, Marcello Celli 39br, Svetlana Day 149cr, Dudlajzov 63tr, 114bl, Bonandbon Dw 179, Ekaterinabelova 88, F11photo 60–61t, 79b, Santiago Rodríguez Fontoba 65tc, Isselee 94b, J Vd 183tr, Rodrigo De Souza Mendes Junqueira 12t, Klodien 62cla, 63br, Sergii Koval 11br, Werner Lerooy 28bl, 80tl, Monticelllo 177tl, Michael Mulkens 39cl, 121bl, Nataliya Nazarova 130–131, Olrat 71t, 90t, 100bl, Onlyfabrizio 70bl, Sean Pavone 2-3, Arnaud Piérard 17t, 96, Rhombur 114-115b, Romannerud 52crb, Ekaterina Shevyakova 30–31t, Shoeke27 19bl, 170–171, Tomas1111 73b

Getty Images: Simon Wohlfahrt / AFP 41cl, De Agostini / DEA / A. Dagli Orti 36cra, De Agostini / DEA Picture Library 141cb, Gamma-Rapho / Alain Riviere-Lecoeur 33br, Hulton Archive / Heritage Images 52bc, Moment / mikroman6 49tr, Moment Open / Gabriel Perez 126bl

Getty Images / iStock: Bombaert 16, 56, lucentius 182-183b, TomasSereda 71cra, tunart 8–9, 123tr

Groeninge Museum Brussels: Femke Den Hollander 120

Humus x Hortens: EquinoxLightPhot 31bl

Koninklijk Museum voor Schone Kunsten Antwerpen: 140–141t

Museum Sint-Janshospitaal: Musea Brugge 8clb, 126–127t

© **Royal Museums of Fine Arts of Belgium, Brussels:**
Odile Keromnes 11cr, 110–111t

Red Star Line Museum Antwerp: Frederik Beyens 13t, 42b, 146–147t

Royal Museum of Fine Arts of Belgium, Brussels: 74–75b

Shutterstock.com: Chris Allan 36–37b, Andrei Antipov 35crb, Koray Bektas 156–157, CapturePB 74cr, 78, 84cla, Celli07 157br, Yuriy Chertok 142, Elisabetta Danielli 128, EQRoy 35cl, 66cr, Erik AJV 101t, 141bl, Kirk Fisher 8cl, 164–165, INTERPIXELS 61bl, Luts Iryna 80–81b, Kadagan 135br, KievVictor 85, Werner Lerooy 84t, 106–107, Mistervlad 159, Sean Pavone 11t, SankyPix 44–45t, Luigi Saria 26tl, Thanida Siritan 26–27tc, Wolf-photography 32tl

STAM: Stijn Vanderdeelen 167

Waffle Workshop: 30br

Cover images: *Front and Spine*: **Dreamstime.com**: Emicristea; *Back*: **Alamy Stock Photo**: Florian Lica Photography c; **Dreamstime.com**: Emicristea b, Arnaud Piérard cl; **Shutterstock.com**: INTERPIXELS tr

Front Flap: Alamy Stock Photo: Ed Buzia cra, image BROKER / Sonja Jordan bl, Imago / Zheng Huansong br, PjrWindows cla, robertharding / Godong t, Jochen Tack cb

Pull Out Map: Dreamstime.com: Emicristea

All other images © Dorling Kindersley Limited

Illustrators
Gary Cross, Richard Draper, Eugene Fleury, Paul Guest, Claire Littlejohn, Robbie Polley, Kevin Robinson, John Woodcock

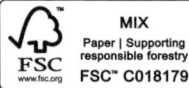
A NOTE FROM DK EYEWITNESS

The rate at which the world is changing is constantly keeping the DK travel team on our toes. While we've worked hard to ensure that this edition of Brussels, Bruges, Antwerp and Ghent is accurate and up-to-date, we know that opening hours alter, standards shift, prices fluctuate, places close and new ones pop up in their stead. So, if you notice we've got something wrong or left something out, we want to hear about it. Please get in touch at travelguides@dk.com

Penguin
Random
House

Main Contributors Clodagh Kinsella, Phil Lee, Dan Stables
Senior Editor Zoë Rutland
Senior Designer Vinita Venugopal, Stuti Tiwari
Project Editor Lucy Sara-Kelly
Editors Nandini Desiraju, Anjasi N.N, Tijana Todorinović
Designer Amisha Gupta
Proofreader Kathryn Glendenning
Indexer Hilary Bird
Senior Picture Researcher Nishwan Rasool
Picture Research Manager Virien Chopra
Picture Researchers Priya Singh, Manpreet Kaur
Publishing Assistant Simona Velikova
Jacket Designers Laura O'Brien, Vinita Venugopal
Jacket Picture Research Claire Guest
Project Cartographer Ashif
Cartography Manager Suresh Kumar
DTP Designers Rohit Rojal
Senior DTP Designers Tanveer Zaidi
Technical Prepress Manager Balwant Singh
Image Retouching Steve Crozier, Jagtar Singh
Production Controller Kariss Ainsworth
Managing Editors Shikha Kulkarni, Beverly Smart, Hollie Teague
Managing Art Editor Gemma Doyle
Senior Managing Art Editor Priyanka Thakur
Art Director Maxine Pedliham
Publishing Director Georgina Dee

First edition 2000

Published in Great Britain by Dorling Kindersley
Limited, 20 Vauxhall Bridge Road,
London SW1V 2SA

The authorised representative in the EEA is
Dorling Kindersley Verlag GmbH. Arnulfstr.
124, 80636 Munich, Germany

Published in the United States by DK Publishing,
1745 Broadway, 20th Floor, New York, NY 10019, USA

Copyright © 2000, 2025 Dorling Kindersley Limited
A Penguin Random House Company

24 25 26 27 10 9 8 7 6 5 4 3 2 1

A CIP catalog record for this book
is available from the British Library.

A catalog record for this book is available
from the Library of Congress.

ISSN: 1542 1554
ISBN: 978 0 2414 6194 5

Printed and bound in China.

www.dk.com